Silent Strength

Other Books by Lloyd John Ogilvie

Enjoying God, Word
Communicator's Commentary, Vol. 5, Acts, Word
Ask Him Anything, Word
Understanding the Hard Sayings of Jesus, Word
A Future and a Hope, Word
Living Without Fear, Word
Making Stress Work for You, Word
God's Best for My Life, Harvest House
You Are Loved and Forgiven, Regal
Conversation with God, Harvest House

Lloyd John Ogilvie

Silent Strength

HARVEST HOUSE PUBLISHERS
Eugene, Oregon 97402

Cover by Terry Dugan Design, Minneapolis, Minnesota.

SILENT STRENGTH

Library of Congress Cataloging-in-Publication Data

Ogilvie, Lloyd John.
Silent strength / Lloyd John Ogilvie.
Hardcover ISBN 0-89081-829-0
Trade Paper ISBN 1-56507-398-3
1. Devotional calendars. I. Title.
BV4811.036 1990 90-35982
242'.2—dc20 CIP

Printed in the United States of America.

97 98 99 00 01 02 03 / BF / 12 11 10 9 8 7 6 5 4 3 2

Introduction

Life "de-powers" us. It saps our energies, depletes our courage, drains our patience. People-pressures get us down; problems stir us up. Often we feel our well has run dry.

We need strength—strength to think clearly, love creatively, endure consistently; strength that fills up our diminished reserves; silent strength that flows from a limitless source, quietly filling us with power.

Christ is our strength. He has been delegated by the Father to care for us, abide in us, and to give us exactly what we need each day to do what He has guided us to accomplish. Our reigning Lord has the authority to forgive us when we fail and pick us up when we stumble. He supervises the release of power so that inflow is more than equal to outgo. Because He knows what's ahead, He prepares us by giving us precisely what the day will demand. Most of all, He promises to be with us and in us, never leaving us or forsaking us.

Silent strength is dependent on a daily time alone with our Lord. This devotional book is to help you maximize this quiet time with the Master. Set aside 15 minutes. Begin by praising the Lord for all He means to you and has done for you. Confess any sins, failures, and mistakes that stand between you and Him. Thank Him for His love and forgiveness. Then spread out your needs before Him. Tell Him you need His strength.

Now it's time to read the passage of Scripture for the day, followed by the daily meditation on how to live in the flow of the Lord's strength. The thought for the day is something to reflect on and live throughout the day.

The final step in this strength-infusing quiet time is dedication. Surrender the day to the Lord. Repeat John Oxenham's words:

> Not for one single day
> Can I discern the way,
>   But this I surely know—
> Who gives the day
> Will show the way
>   So I securely go.

Be sure of this: The Lord shows the way and provides silent strength for each step. When evening comes, you'll be amazed by what He has accomplished through you.

Now a word about the progression of the content of this book. The first month will be spent on the specific theme of the Lord's silent strength. Then we will see how Christ strengthens people in a daily study of the Gospel of John leading up to Easter and beyond into Eastertide. This will be followed by further secrets of strength in Philippians. Then there's a special study of the Beatitudes with some helpful ways to live a Beatitude a day. Pressing on through the summer and fall, we'll claim our freedom in Christ, discover the strength of knowing God's will, and learn how to live out our faith as caring people. The major portion of December will be spent experiencing the true meaning of Christmas.

I have searched the Scriptures to select the most salient passages on how to live by God's supernatural strength. Some verses and passages will be repeated for emphasis or to grasp another aspect of what they reveal to us about strength for a particular struggle.

My prayer is that this book will be used for many years to come. This hope also presented a challenge for arranging devotionals for special days of the Christian year. For example, Easter falls early some years and later in others. I have tried to split the difference. The same is true for Thanksgiving. The fourth Thursday may vary in date in various years. So on those special days, just look for the devotional clearly designated for that time.

I am indebted to June Mears for overseeing the editing and preparation of the manuscript for publication and for Gail Fisher, Barbara Jones, Gloria Kilian, Nancy McDonnell, Veda Manson, Janet Stearns, and Rene Williams for assisting with the typing. And through the busy months of preparation my assistant, Marietta Steward, has been a faithful encourager. I'm grateful for all these dear friends.

My fondest hope for what this book will mean to you is prompted by a frequent expression in letters and conversations with people who have read my previous book of daily devotionals, *God's Best for My Life*, also published by Harvest House. They have exclaimed, "How did you know what I would need today? I read today's Scripture and meditation, and it was as if you knew what I was going through and wrote it just for me!"

Only the Lord can do that. My response is, "Lord, do it again with this book about Your silent strength!"

—Lloyd Ogilive

Silent Strength

The Lord your God in your midst, the Mighty One, will save; He will rejoice over you with gladness, He will quiet you in His love, He will rejoice over you with singing (Zephaniah 3:17).

Silent Strength

Strength is an inside secret. It comes from the Lord's Spirit in the well of our inner being. Because His strength is limitless, our wells need never be empty. His strength is constantly surging up to give us exactly what we need in every moment. His strength gives us supernatural thinking power beyond our IQ, it provides emotional equipoise when under pressure, it engenders resoluteness in our wills and vision for our imaginations, and it energizes our bodies with physical resiliency.

Zephaniah gives the secret of lasting strength. It is received in silent receptive communion with the Lord: "Be silent in the presence of the Lord God" (Zephaniah 1:7). What we discover in our silence becomes the source of our strength. Note the glorious progression in our verse for today. First, the Lord rejoices over us with gladness. In spite of all our failures, He has chosen to be our God and to cherish us. Think of it! God and all the company of heaven are rejoicing over us! This gives us the confidence of silent strength. We belong to God—He's redeemed us in Christ and placed His Spirit in us. He'll never give up on us.

Alone with Him, next the Lord quiets us with His love. The unqualified, indefatigable love of the Lord gives us silent confidence, security, and peace. There's no need to prove ourselves or blow our own horns. We can live with calm, winsome joy. And knowing that the Lord rejoices over us frees us to rejoice in Him. The Hebrew word for "rejoice" means "to spin around." Our hearts pirouette with praise as we hear God's song, more profound than audio sound: "This is My beloved person in whom I am pleased." Have you heard the song of silent strength?

Today's Thought: I commit this day and all of this new year to live in the silent strength of constant communion, confirming confidence, and consistent courage of my mighty God.

January 2 Habakkuk 3:17-19

Yet I will rejoice in the Lord, I will joy in the God of my salvation. The Lord God is my strength (Habakkuk 3:18,19).

The Pirouetting Heart

One Sunday I began a message on our verses for today from Habakkuk by leaping and spinning around. It was a physical dramatization of the Hebrew word "rejoice." As I mentioned yesterday, the word means "to leap for joy and spin about in exultation." There are times when our hearts leap and pirouette with sheer joy. Habakkuk's experience of joy did that for him.

We might expect that this was a particularly happy time for the prophet. No, it was a *joyous* time. And there's a great difference between happiness and joy. Happiness is dependent on having no problems or concerns; joy is having faith in God in spite of anything. Habakkuk had been through a profound experience with God. He dared to question honestly what God was doing with His people and why He was allowing the growing strength of the Chaldean enemy. Then the prophet was silent. The Lord gave him the benchmark truth that the just shall live by faith in Him alone. There would be trouble ahead as God judged the apostasy of His people with an enemy invasion, but Habakkuk would trust in Him.

The prophet of faith *heaps* up all that will happen and in spite of it all, *leaps* for joy. Habakkuk shifts his faith from trust in circumstances to trust in God. It is then that he can say the Lord is his strength. His heart not only pirouettes in joy, but is also given strength in weakness, light-footed security like the deer, and elevated vision for the future.

Today's Thought: Focus on God, His just judgments, and His indefatigable love. Joy will surge in you and new strength will flow.

The joy of the Lord is your strength (Nehemiah 8:10).

"Rejoyed"

A reassuring theme throughout this daily devotional guide is that there is an inseparable relationship between joy and strength. This is one of the major themes of the Bible and the key to living in the flow of supernatural energy. We were meant to be the riverbed for the flow of the Spirit of the Lord. Joy and the energy-releasing strength it produces is not something we can create. We only have a choice to allow the Spirit to flow through the trench of our hearts that has been excavated by life's challenges and difficulties. Want joy and strength? Let the river of the Spirit fill and then overflow the banks of your heart.

Nehemiah expresses this in a pointed one-liner: "The joy of the Lord is your strength." In the difficult times of rebuilding the wall of Jerusalem after the exile, only the Lord could give the people what they needed to persist and endure. And when the work was completed, not even the rebuilt wall was to be a lasting source of joy. There would be new challenges in which joy and its inseparable companion—strength—would be needed. Let me coin a word: God "rejoys" us. That's how He restrengthens us. First comes renewed grace—unqualified love. Then joy bursts forth from this acceptance, forgiveness, and reconciliation. The thinking brain becomes focused on trusting God's faithfulness. It triggers the release of energy in the body. Our bodies cooperate with the divine energies of the Spirit. We are no longer fighting against God but going with the flow!

Today's Thought: Before I do anything else today, I will get "rejoyed"—for the joy of the Lord is my strength!

January 4 — Psalm 18:1-3

My God, my strength, in whom I will trust; my shield and the horn of my salvation, my stronghold (Psalm 18:2).

The Secret of Silent Strength

"He's got a kind of silent strength—know what I mean?"

I did know what the woman meant. Her comment about a mutual friend's courage in troublesome times was on target. The man is of normal height, yet he always stands tall spiritually. He's not very muscular, but he has broad shoulders when it comes to bearing other people's burdens. He spends himself, yet he never seems spent.

One day I asked the man the secret of his strength. "Lots of time with the Stronghold!" he responded with a twinkle in his eye. Then he confided that his life verse is "My God, my strength, in whom I will trust; my shield and the horn of my salvation, my stronghold" (Psalm 18:2). No wonder the man is distinguished for silent strength!

In the Old Testament, the word "stronghold" meant a place of secure refuge, unassailable by enemies. Eventually "stronghold" became one of the descriptive designations of the nature of God Himself. David frequently spoke of Him as his stronghold. Psalm 18 was written about a time when David escaped from his enemies and renewed his strength through time with the Lord.

In times of trouble or great challenges there are three things to do: head for the stronghold, hold onto the goodness of God, and hope in the promises of God.

It works—I know. For 40 years, I've never found the Stronghold to fail. In the stronghold of the Lord's presence I rediscover the stronghold of His love and power in my life. I could not have made it without time each morning in the stronghold and then a constant return all through the day.

Today's Thought: "The night is given to us to take a breath, to pray, to drink deep at the fountain of power. The day, to use the strength which has been given us, to go forth to work with it till the evening" —Florence Nightingale.

They go from strength to strength (Psalm 84:7).

From Strength to Strength

Thomas Fuller once prayed, "Lord, lighten the load or strengthen my back." Sometimes the Lord does lighten the load by taking from us a portion of what has been too heavy to carry, but most often He strengthens us to be able to carry what He has called us to do. But yesterday's strength will not suffice for today's burdens. God's strength is given in daily portions. We dare not depend on yesterday's prayers, inspiration, or insight.

Psalm 84 gives us a guide for receiving strength for today. The psalm expresses the longing of the psalmist to go to Jerusalem to the temple and describes the pilgrimage. For us, all of life is a pilgrimage toward God's plan and purpose for us. And along the way He gives us strength for each day.

"Blessed is the man whose strength is in You." The Hebrew word for "strength" here comes from the verb "to seek refuge." When our heart is set on pilgrimage, as the psalmist puts it, we can depend on the Lord's presence and protection. He is the constant source of our strength.

The Valley of Baca in the psalm refers to an arid, dry, thirsty valley a pilgrim to Jerusalem would have to pass through. We face our own Valleys of Baca in times of difficulty. But it's in those very valleys that we can count on the replenishment of strength. We can live expectantly. "They make it a spring; the rain also covers it with pools." The Hebrew word for "pools" can also mean "blessings." The promise for us is that we will go from one degree of strength to a greater surge of strength.

Today's Thought: Yesterday's strength will not suffice for today's burdens.

As your days, so shall your strength be (Deuteronomy 33:25).

Strength for the Day

Yesterday we claimed the stamina of ever-increasing strength. We stressed the importance of not depending on the strength of the past, but receiving fresh strength for each day. Today's Scripture emphasizes the reason why this is so important. All our days are different; each has its own unique challenges and opportunities. The blessing Moses gave to the tribe of Asher helps us take our next step in understanding how the Lord strengthens us: "Your sandals shall be iron and bronze; as your days, so shall your strength be" (Deuteronomy 33:25).

Another way of putting this promise would be, "Whatever each new day dishes out, the Lord's strength will be perfectly suited for the need." He is wonderfully original in the way He strengthens us. The "sandals of iron and bronze" in this promise tell us that the Lord's strength will enable us to stand firm and move forward with surefooted confidence.

A Hollywood actor asked me to pray for him. "What do you want me to pray?" I asked. "Pray that I will have courage to live in a world of compromise," he responded intently. We can all echo that prayer request. Today we will be tempted to compromise—if not in what we say and do, then in what we don't say or do when our faith is on the line. The Lord will give us courage if we put Him first in our lives.

The Lord's strength will also give us courage to press on. As happened to the tribe of Asher, our sandals will not wear out if we're running with the Lord toward His goals for us. There will be a chance today to step out in new obedience to the Lord.

Today's Thought: God's strength is given to people who are on the move and doing what love demands.

Your youth is renewed like the eagle's (Psalm 103:5).

A Tonic for the Tired

Think of a time when you were bone-tired. All you wanted to do was crawl into bed, pull up the covers, and put life on hold while you had a good sleep. Then you were given an opportunity to do something you really enjoy. With suddenly renewed energy you got dressed and were amazed that you weren't as tired as you thought.

Or think of a time when you were exhausted and learned that a burden you'd been carrying had been lifted or a long-standing problem was solved, and you were amazed at how rejuvenated you felt. Then you realized much of your exhaustion was caused by inner tension and conflict.

Praising God can also have a rejuvenating effect. This is how we receive the Lord's silent strength. When we really turn our unresolved problems, conflicts, and stresses over to the Lord and take delight in Him, our minds are cleared and the sympathetic adaption system of our bodies responds by releasing energy.

David rallied *all* of his faculties to praise the Lord—not just his soul, but all that was within him for all God had done for him. The floodgate of his mind was opened and his youth was renewed like the eagle's. (An eagle is renewed when it allows the jet stream to carry it higher until it soars.)

You may have started this day tired or under energy-sapping stress. Think of it—you have an appointment with the Creator and Lord of the universe. The mighty God! Praise and adore Him, give Him your burdens, and soar.

Today's Thought: "Think magnificently of God. Magnify His providence; adore His power; pray to Him frequently and incessantly. Bear Him always in your mind; teach your thoughts to reverence Him in every place, for there is no place where He is not. Worship and love God; first and last, think magnificently of God" —Paternus to his son.

January 8 Ephesians 3:14-21

That He would grant you, according to the riches of His glory, to be strengthened with might through His Spirit in the inner man (Ephesians 3:16).

The Dynamics of Strength

Ponder three dynamics of the power that is offered to us. First, we are to claim the strength of the Spirit of Christ, abiding in our inner being—our minds, emotions, and wills. The word "abide" implies more than a temporary visitation. It really means a permanent residency. Christ is the power of God within us so we may be strengthened with might.

Second, note the clear purpose of Christ's indwelling power: that we may be rooted and grounded in His love. Botanical and architectural metaphors are used. The roots of our lives are to be deeply planted in Christ's love, and our foundation on which our whole personality is to be built is that same amazing love. It is a love that is wide enough to be inclusive of all; it is long enough to find us whenever we wander; it is deep enough to reach us however far we fall; it is high enough to last forever. This is the fulfillment of Christ's prayer to the Father in the upper room before the crucifixion. He prayed that "the love with which You loved Me may be in them, and I in them" (John 17:26). Imagine! The same love given by the Father to the Son is the love that He manifests in us. This is beyond our human ability to expect, beyond our understanding—but not beyond what can and does happen.

Third, consider with amazement the goal of this empowering of love. It is so that we "may be filled with all the fullness of God." The preposition "with" should be translated as "unto." God's fullness, revealed in Christ, is the standard—the level—to which we can expect to grow in this life and throughout eternity.

With this power at work in us we can supersede the normal levels of our ability to think about what is possible and our usual expectation of what to ask. We can have boldness to ask for the full measure of the elements of power Paul has described.

Today's Thought: Today I will claim the strength of the indwelling Spirit of Christ.

Be still, and know that I am God (Psalm 46:10).

Let Go!

What keeps you from being quiet inside? Fear of failure? Worry over what might happen? Distress over projects you desperately want to succeed? Loved ones about whom you're concerned? Money? Conflicts with people? Or is it just the habit of being anxious that seems impossible to break?

We read the words, "Be still, and know that I am God," and yet find inner stillness elusive. We feel we have to *do* something to keep life from falling apart—and we're right. But it's *what* we do that makes all the difference. In Hebrew the word "still" is not passive, but active. It carries the implications of "let loose, leave off, let go."

Psalm 46 was written after a grave crisis in Jerusalem. In 701 BC the city had been under Assyrian siege for weeks. They planned to take the city at dawn. And then just before dawn the Assyrians retreated and the city of Jerusalem was saved. This psalm commemorates this mighty intervention. If God could do that, the people had a basis for letting go of fear for the future.

And so have we. We look back to Calvary, Easter morning, and Pentecost, and we know that our God is mighty. Then we think of all the times He has helped us in our just-before-dawn crises. So it comes down to whether we are willing to believe that He will act if we are still and let go. The reason we can be still is because of Yahweh. His name means "to make happen." Our God makes things happen. That's why we can give Him control over whatever keeps us in turmoil inside. Why not today?

Today's Thought: A little boy got his hand caught in a vase trying to reach a penny at the bottom. He got the penny, but clutched it in his hand. With his hand clutched he could not remove it from the narrow-necked vase. The vase had to be broken—all because he clutched the penny. What are you clutching? Let go!

January 10 Isaiah 30:15-18

In returning and rest you shall be saved; in quietness and confidence shall be your strength (Isaiah 30:15).

Oh, Be Quiet!

Oh, be quiet!

There are two ways of saying these words. Both ways have an exclamation point. One is a command to stop talking, making noise, or arguing. The other is a consoling appeal for a person to stop straining and struggling, an offer of rest for the restless, solace for the sobbing of our souls.

One day I wanted to say, "Oh, be quiet!" in both ways. On the way to work, I stopped at a stop sign alongside a car that had the stereo system so high it actually shook with the rhythm of the hard rock. Later in the day in a counseling session with a distressed man whose life vibrated with the noise of inner conflict, I said empathetically, "Oh, be quiet . . . let the Lord hold you and quiet you with His love." You may need the same assurance as you begin this day.

We read in the promise from Zephaniah 3:17, "He will quiet you with His love." We need to go deeper in what that means. "Quiet" means "rest, silence, peace." The Hebrew really means "He will be silent in His love." Calvin translated it, "He will rest in His love." Catch the future sense. Both translations presuppose there was a time when God was not at rest. Why? Because we lost our rest through sin and God could not rest until He completed our reconciliation and established our atonement. So the promise is prophetic of Calvary. When our redemption was complete, God could rest in His love. And now He wants to press our turbulent hearts next to His quiet heart. The Lord's love is quiet because it's complete. And we can be quiet when we rest in His everlasting arms. We put God's heart to rest when we accept His forgiving love. When our hearts are in turmoil, God cannot rest until He quiets us *in* His love.

Today's Thought: There is no rest in the heart of God until He knows that we are at rest in His grace.

But without faith it is impossible to please Him, for he who comes to God must believe that He is, and that He is a rewarder of those who diligently seek Him (Hebrews 11:6).

More Than Just Staying Alive

Charlie must have been a regular customer of the diner. When he came in all of the waitresses chimed in, "Hi, Charlie, how ya doin'?"

"Just staying alive," Charlie responded with a grim, exasperated tone. "Ah, come on Charlie," one of the waitresses said, "we expect more from you than that." And Charlie responded, "Yah, I know. You and everybody else!"

As I drank my coffee, I couldn't help overhearing the conversation. People's expectations had piled up on Charlie, and he was wondering how he was going to meet them all. We can empathize with Charlie. It's not easy to please everyone. In fact, it's impossible. And it's not our calling.

Our purpose is to please God and serve people as He guides us. What can we do to please God? The author of Hebrews put it plainly: "Without faith it is impossible to please Him" (Hebrews 11:6). And yet, faith is a gift (Ephesians 2:8,9). So, God meets His expectation of us by giving us the one thing that pleases Him. By grace He saves us through Christ and then enables us to respond to His love. Even the willingness to accept the gift of faith is engendered by His Spirit. Can we resist? Of course—He's given us free will. But He persists and, when we are overcome by the desire to know Him, we'll know that He overcame our resistance.

It's a relief to know there's one Person we can please. And it's the good pleasure of His will to free us to do it. Once we know His love, we want to do what He requires. It involves emulating His very nature in serving rather than pleasing people. And this is more than just staying alive!

Today's Thought: Today I make a new commitment to please God and serve people.

January 12 Lamentations 3:21-24

His compassions fail not. They are new every morning (Lamentations 3:22,23).

A Hopeful Day

I have a friend whose morning greeting is "Have a hopeful day!" What makes for a hope-filled day? Certainly not circumstances or situations, or the reliability of people. They all are unstable sources of hope. Jeremiah had hope because he was sure of the faithfulness of God. He wrote the passage we just read after the destruction of Jerusalem, when all human hope seemed gone. But the mercies of God were new every morning. Annie Johnson Flint wrote a beautiful poem applying Jeremiah's hope to our lives. Make it your prayer and silent strength today.

Yea, "new every morning," though we may awake,
Our hearts with old sorrow beginning to ache;
With old work unfinished when night stayed our hand
With new duties waiting, unknown and unplanned;
With old care still pressing, to fret and to vex,
With new problems rising, our minds to perplex
In ways long familiar, in paths yet untrod,
Oh, new every morning the mercies of God!
His faithfulness fails not; it meets each new day
New guidance for every new step of the way;
New grace for new trials, new trust for old fears,
New patience for bearing the wrongs of the years,
New strength for new burdens, new courage for old,
New faith for whatever the day may unfold;
As fresh for each need as the dew on the sod;
Oh, new every morning the mercies of God!

Today's Thought: "What oxygen is to the lungs, hope is to the soul" —Emil Brunner.

"Not by might nor by power, but by My Spirit," says the Lord of hosts (Zechariah 4:6).

The Turning Point

There's a turning point in every situation, every relationship, every problem. It happens when we run out of human resources and turn to the Lord for His silent strength.

Zerubbabel came to a time like that. The reconstruction of the temple was going slowly. The people proved to be unreliable procrastinators, and enemies hassled the work of rebuilding. Discouragement set in. What was the leader to do?

It was at this time that the Lord gave the prophet Zechariah a very hopeful vision. He revealed to the prophet that the temple rebuilding would be completed if—only if—Zerubbabel followed the word the Lord gave to him through the prophet. The word said, "This is the word of the Lord to Zerubbabel: 'Not by might nor by power, but by My Spirit' says the Lord of hosts" (Zechariah 4:6).

This was the turning point. The might of military strength and the power of human effort were not enough. God's Spirit alone could give Zerubbabel and the people the supernatural capability to do what He had called them to do. When they turned to the Lord, the strength to endure and finish would be given.

I think of the thousands of times I've quoted these words or had them quoted to me in robing rooms before leading worship, before television tapings, during a challenging venture of faith, while praying for the sick, or when counseling a potential believer. I think of this verse constantly when I write a book or give leadership in a cause or face impossibilities. It brings me to the turning point, from trying to trusting. You may be at one of those turning points today. The Lord has brought you to it so you can discover resources in His silent strength.

Today's Thought: If we are not now in situations in which we are forced to say, "Lord, not by might nor by power, but by Your Spirit," then we probably have settled for a safe but unadventuresome life.

Who are you, O great mountain? (Zechariah 4:7).

When We Meet a Mountain

William Blake wrote, "Great things happen when men and mountains meet. . . . The rest go jostling through the streets." I say, "Magnificent things happen when people and mountains meet and Christ gave us power over defeat."

In the Scriptures, mountains are often synonyms for difficulties, obstructions, and seemingly insurmountable odds. As we saw yesterday, Zerubbabel faced the mountain of rebuilding the temple. The Lord gave him the secret of silent strength: "Not by might or by power but by My Spirit." In today's Scripture we see how the strength of the Lord will make it possible to finish the task.

Jesus taught the disciples the power of faith to remove mountains: "If you have faith as a mustard seed, you will say to this mountain, 'Move from here to there,' and it will move; and nothing will be impossible for you" (Matthew 17:20). He gives us courage to face our mountains and ask for His power to remove them. It's interesting to remember that rabbis at that time were sometimes called "mountain removers." Christ was magnificently that as He removed the mountains of sin and gave us power to deal with our daily mountains. Greatness is facing issues and standing on our convictions. When something or someone becomes an obstruction to Christ's plan for our lives, He helps us deal with the mountain. Sometimes He takes us around or over it, and sometimes He removes it—but He always helps us put it behind us.

Today's Thought: Who or what is your mountain? What is the obstruction that stands in the way of getting to the Lord's destination for your life? With Christ's power you can become a mountain remover!

If the Lord is with us, why then has all this happened to us? (Judges 6:13).

Why Does God Allow Problems?

Gideon's question to the angel expresses how we feel at times: "If the Lord is with us, why then has all this happened to us?" Hardly a day goes by that someone doesn't ask me, "If God is love, why does He allow me to have problems?"

God doesn't send problems. There are already enough to go around. The most difficult choice God ever made was to create humankind with free will so we could choose to love and glorify Him. We are not marionettes. We know what we did with our freedom: the fall, endless generations of rebellion, a world estranged from its Creator and Lord.

Many of our problems come from people who don't know or love God. Other problems are circumstantial. Still others we bring on ourselves. Problems can either make or break us. If we trust God to help us solve problems, we will grow as people and discover there is no problem too big for God. He has called us to join with Him in creatively unraveling the problems that confront us.

Actually, God came in Christ to solve our most momentous problem. He reconciled us to Himself, defeated the forces of evil, conquered death, and sent the risen Christ to be with us forever. So when we accept our salvation and Christ's present power, the biggest problems are behind us. And now, the only problems that can defeat us are those we try to handle on our own. Our challenge is to own the problem by coming to grips with it. Then we must disown the temptation to try to solve it on our own. We'll always have problems; that's life. But the Lord will give us a strategy to solve our problems and strength to endure; that's the abundant life!

Today's Thought: Today I will face my problems, unwrap them and seek to understand their component parts, spread them out before the Lord, thank Him in advance for what He's going to do, follow orders for what I am to do, and stand by to watch His miracles.

January 16 Judges 6:25–7:25

Cut down the wooden image . . . and build an altar to the Lord your God (Judges 6:25,26).

A Problem in Our Backyard

Often when we face a big problem and ask the Lord for His help, He shows us how we may have contributed to the problem. Or He puts His finger on something in our lives that has to be changed or removed so we can be His effective agent in solving the problem.

Before Gideon could be used by the Lord, he had to get rid of a problem in his own backyard. He and his father, Joash, had Baal fertility idols in their fields. They, along with most of the people of Israel, syncretized the worship of Yahweh with the Baal false gods. When the people entered Canaan, they were not trained in agriculture. They saw that the Canaanite farmers put male and female Baal shrines in their fields. The Israelites didn't stop worshiping Yahweh, they just added Baal—thus breaking the first commandment to have no other god before the Lord God.

At the same time, the Israelites were constantly harassed by the Midianites and the Amalekites who swept down upon them at harvesttime and carried off the harvest and cattle. Baal worship wasn't working. Yahweh allowed the problem of the invaders to expose the deeper problem of idol worship.

When Gideon was called to lead Israel against the Midianites, the Lord demanded that he remove the false worship of Baal from his own life before He could bless him. Gideon obeyed, rallied the troops, and won the battle—but not without the Lord. In fact, he was instructed to cut the army down to 300 men so he and all Israel would know that the Lord had secured the victory.

Problems drive us back to the Lord. Sometimes He uses the difficult time to show us anything standing between Him and us.

Today's Thought: Lord show me anything in me that would block me from receiving Your power to solve problems.

"Behold, the days are coming," says the Lord God, "that I will send a famine on the land, not a famine of bread, nor a thirst for water, but of hearing the words of the Lord" (Amos 8:11).

A Famine of Hearing

Televised newscasts bring into our homes and put on our hearts the vivid scenes of those who are dying of starvation. We have watched the process. A scarcity of food makes people acquisitive, grasping for whatever they can find to eat. This is followed by acrimony as hungry people take out their frustration on one another. Then there's agitation as they move from place to place in search of food and water. Eventually, a dull stupor is seen in their eyes set in deep, dark sockets. Finally, the monster of hunger claims its victim.

Spiritual starvation progresses much the same way. Agitation, acrimony, search for meaning in people, movements, causes, and then the dull stupor of emptiness. Long before the pulse stops, a person is dead spiritually. This is the dreadful process described by Amos in today's passage. But note, it was not a famine of the words of God but of hearing. The audio nerve in the soul of the people had been impaired by misuse and disuse. They had resisted the Lord's call for repentance, righteousness, and justice so strongly that they no longer heard. Their persistent "No!" to the Lord eventually made it impossible to say "Yes."

Today there's no lack of the Word of God being preached and taught in churches and on media. But there is a famine of hearing. Often our heart ears are blocked. The famine of hearing is because we refuse to listen and obey. Surely, that's the reason for the lack of nutrition in our lives and the signs of spiritual hunger and then starvation. I don't know about you, but this leads me to ask the Lord to heal the audio nerve of my soul. Ah, to hear and do!

Today's Thought: "Therefore whoever hears these sayings of Mine, and does them, I will liken him to a wise man who built his house on the rock" (Matthew 7:24).

He will sit as a refiner and a purifier of silver; He will purify the sons of Levi, and purge them as gold and silver, that they may offer to the Lord an offering in righteousness (Malachi 3:3).

The Refiner's Face

We speak of a person with good manners and culture as being "refined." That's well and good, but it misses the mark of the Bible's definition of "refined." Malachi describes the coming of the Messiah and His ministry as a radical process of refining the gold of character and the silver of personality.

The refining of gold and silver is how the Lord works with us. The fire under the crucible was stoked to bring adequate heat to melt the raw material with the precious metals mixed in it. When it was melted and bubbling, the dross and impurities came to the surface. The refiner would continually skim off the dross. Note that Malachi says the refiner "sits." He would sit watching and waiting. The refining would be complete when he could see his own face reflected in the molten metal. Then it would be poured out into molds to cool. Some of the brilliance would be lost. Then the purifier would begin his work. To "purify" in Hebrew, as it is used in Malachi, means to polish first with a file and then with a cloth. Finally the gold and silver would shine magnificently.

Christ is the refiner of our lives. He oversees the refining of our lives in His image. He looks for His face to be reflected in us. But then after the dross has been removed, Christ becomes the polisher, the purifier who uses the file and polishing cloth to make us shine. The problems, difficulties, and challenges we go through can be used by our Lord in His refining and purifying process.

Today's Thought: "In this you greatly rejoice, though now for a little while, if need be, you have been grieved by various trials, that the genuineness of your faith, being much more precious than gold that perishes, though it is tested by fire, may be found to praise, honor, and glory at the revelation of Jesus Christ" (1 Peter 1:6,7).

For I am the Lord, I do not change (Malachi 3:6).

Strength from the Changeless One

A little boy offered a simple prayer: "God bless Mother and Daddy, my brother and sister; and God, do take care of Yourself because if anything happens to You, we're all sunk."

Indeed we are! But isn't it wonderful that we know that nothing can happen to God. He's our one sure source of silent strength because He does not change. So we sing and pray, "O Thou who changest not, abide with me."

We can never be sure of people or our best-laid plans. If we could be, we'd make them false gods. Instead we draw strength from the changeless One so we can live in a world of change and changeable people. Often disappointments with people throw us back in the arms of the Lord. We live in the jet stream of His power rather than on the roller coaster of the highs and lows of emotional instability.

The changeless nature of God is not only a basis of comfort, but a source of challenge. He is the holy God who will not rewrite the manual for righteousness to fit our desires. He is consistent in His judgments, as well as His mercy. This gives stability to life. H. H. Farmer said, "God our Father makes absolute demands and offers absolute succor."

We don't have to pray for God to take care of Himself. He is God, and the focus of His attention is caring for us.

Today's Thought: But God hath promised
Strength for the day,
Rest for the labor,
Light for the way,
Grace for the trials,
Help from above,
Unfailing sympathy,
Undying love.
—Annie Johnson Flint

Return to Me, for I have redeemed you (Isaiah 44:22).

Eleven Crucial Words

Seven words. We've heard and said them. Sometimes they are expressed with a sigh of resignation, and other times with a sob of desperation. "I just don't know where to turn!"

In response to those seven words are eleven crucial words that provide the only solution: *When you don't know where to turn, return to the Lord.* We need to hear these 11 words at the beginning of each day and in every hour of need. To return to the Lord is to repent, and not only for the more obvious sins. We also need to repent for the pride of running our own lives, of depending on our own guts and gusto. And what about the lack of caring for people and the suffering of our society? Repentance means to turn around, to change our minds, to accept forgiveness and make a fresh start. God's constant call is "Return to Me, for I have redeemed you."

In the Old Testament there are more references to God's repentance than human repentance. The reason is that people's rebellion and willfulness brought God's righteous judgment. He could not wink at sin. But He always wanted things to be right again between Himself and His people. And God had to make the first move and provide a way for His people to repent. In a profound sense, Christ's death on the cross was God's repentance, a changing of His mind. Instead of giving us what we deserved, He redeemed us. And now we know Him as our Father who waits with outstretched arms to welcome us back home where we belong. There's no other place to turn.

Today's Thought: We repent not to be forgiven but because we know we already are.

In all your ways acknowledge Him, and He shall direct your paths (Proverbs 3:6).

The Lord Is My Pacesetter

There's enough time in every day to accomplish what the Lord wants us to do. But do I believe that? Do you?

If we really did, it would take the strain and stress out of our days. The Lord loves us and would not pile on us more than we could do. So when we become overburdened, it must be that we have planned more than He intended. We forget the times He provided the silent strength to do our work and meet a heavy schedule because we asked for His help in planning.

Some time ago a friend sent me a rendition of Psalm 23 by Toki Miyashina. It will give you peace in life's pressures.

The Lord is my Pacesetter, I shall not rush;
He makes me stop and rest for quiet intervals.
He provides me with images of stillness,
which restore my serenity;
He leads me in the ways of efficiency through
calmness of mind,
And His guidance is peace.
Even though I have a great many things
to accomplish each day,
I will not fret, for His presence is here.
His timelessness, His all importance,
will keep me in balance.
He prepares refreshment and renewal in the midst
of my activity,
By anointing my mind with His oils of tranquility.
My cup of joyous energy overflows.
Surely harmony and effectiveness shall be the
fruits of my hours,
For I shall walk in the pace of my Lord, and
dwell in His house forever.

I will not forget you. See, I have inscribed you on the palms of My hands (Isaiah 49:15,16).

Where Your Name Is Written

It seems absurd until it happens. People tell us God knows and cares about each of us. We smile inside and say to ourselves, "Well, if that kind of subjective nonsense helps them, why argue with them about how God can give individual attention to our needs. Let them swallow the placebo if they must!"

Then a cyclone of adversity or challenge hits our own lives. We swagger on doing the best we can with our own strength. Finally, when we're out of all resources, we cry out to God to help us. Then in a very specific way He steps in, does what we considered impossible, and we join the triumphant company of those who know that in His omniscience, God not only knows but acts to save His people.

At a time of great distress, God told His people that He would not forget them. "See, I have inscribed you on the palms of My hands."

My friend Steve thought the idea of a personal God was foolish sentimentality. He was concerned when his son committed His life to Christ and became an on-fire Christian. Then Steve's own life landed on the rocks in the midst of a cyclone of problems. One day Steve's son gave him a note. It had today's verse at the top and then a drawing of a hand with a letter on each finger: S.T.E.V.E. In response, Steve prayed for the first time in years. The Lord answered and eventually with the influence of his son and the help of his pastor, Steve became a Christian.

Today's Thought: "At the heart of the cyclone
Tearing the sky
And flinging the cloud and towers by
Is a place of central calm
And so is the roar of mortal things
There is a place where my spirit sings
In the hallow of God's palm."
—Edwin Markham

It shall come to pass that before they call I will answer; and while they are still speaking, I will hear (Isaiah 65:24).

The Secret Stair

My door was opened wide
Then I looked around
If any lack of service might be found,
And saw Him at my side!
He entered, by what secret stair,
I know not, knowing only He was there.

The secret stair! The Lord always has one. He comes in ways we least expect. He is Lord of circumstances, people, and possibilities we would never imagine. We've all had it happen. Problems mount and we wonder how we are going to make it. Then we are given a thought that turns out to be the key to unlock the solution to some difficulty. A friend offers to help us. A windfall arrives in the mail. Someone we feared changes his attitude. Events take a sudden turn for the good. The Lord did it!

But by far the greatest evidence of the Lord's intervention comes inside us. Suddenly, the empty wells of strength begin to fill up again. We are aware that we have courage where before we felt alone and afraid. A new perspective is given us. The only thing that matters is that we belong to the Lord and He is in charge. Our purpose is to live for Him and to serve other people.

The secret stair of the Lord leads to our hearts. A heart filled with Him is given the precious gift of expectancy. He has plans for us. He has not given up on us or our needs. We can live with hope.

Today's Thought: If the Lord could create the universe, redeem the world on the cross and make me a new creature, I do not need to doubt that He will use everything for His glory and my growth today.

Call to Me, and I will answer you, and show you great and mighty things, which you do not know (Jeremiah 33:3).

Mighty Things

Jeremiah was in prison. He needed a word from the Lord. The promise he was given has been a source of silent strength for God's people through the ages. The word "mighty" is the key word. In Hebrew it means mysterious, that which is inaccessible to human reason alone, that which only God can reveal. Jeremiah needed to know what the Lord was doing in the judgment of His people in Jerusalem. He also needed to know that there was hope for Judah after the exile. This is exactly what God gave him.

We all face times when we can't figure things out for ourselves. We can't penetrate the veil hanging over the future. Therefore we are uncertain what to do next. That's the time to call on the Lord to show us mighty things. He can inspire our minds to understand what He wills. When we put Him first in our lives and renew our commitment to serve Him, we can ask for a word of knowledge, a divine revelation which we could never come to by ourselves. Our God loves us and wants to help us do what He can see is most creative for our growth. Call. The mighty things will be revealed.

Today's Thought: "O Thou, who art the Light of minds that know Thee, the Life of souls that love Thee, and the Strength of the thoughts that seek Thee; help us to know Thee that we may truly love Thee, so to love Thee that we may fully serve Thee, whose service is perfect freedom; Through Jesus Christ our Lord. Amen" —Gelasian Sacramentary, AD 494.

And when the burnt offering began, the song of the Lord also began, with the trumpets (2 Chronicles 29:27).

Sacrifice, Trumpets, and Song

When Hezekiah became king, he instituted sweeping reforms and purified the temple that had fallen into misuse. The day of reinstituting worship in the temple was a momentous day. Picture the procession of priests and Levites, the trumpeters, players of stringed instruments, and King Hezekiah. At the altar the sacrifice for sin was offered. And at the moment the sacrifice began, the trumpets were sounded and all the people broke into a song of praise.

There are strategic times in our lives like that. They come when we must place our sacrifice on the altar. But since the ultimate sacrifice was made for us on Calvary, our sacrifice is the surrender of our lives. That sacrifice often becomes very specific as we commit our plans, projects, and programs to the Lord. Often what we want to do for the Lord gets mixed up with our own egos and willfulness. Then there comes a time when we must give up our control and self-serving efforts. The same thing is true of our hopes and dreams for people. We sometimes forget they belong to God and not to us.

When we place our cherished extensions of our self on the altar, there's a trumpet blast in heaven and all the company of heaven bursts into song. We've turned over our control and now we can live with freedom. The Lord's will be done! He knows what is best. And once the sacrifice of relinquishment is made, the Lord is able to multiply what we have been holding tightly. Have you heard the trumpets and song today?

Today's Thought: When we commit something or someone to the Lord, He gives them back to us to enjoy as His gifts.

My help comes from the Lord, who made heaven and earth (Psalm 121:2).

When You Know the Pilot

The young boy sat in the waiting lounge of the airport. When the flight was called, the lad was ushered on first. When I boarded the plane, I was pleased to discover he had the seat next to mine. He was polite in his greeting, and then went on coloring in one of those coloring books airlines provide for child passengers. Humming happily, he didn't seem to have a care in the world.

During the flight, we ran into a very bad storm that bounced the jetliner around like a kite in the wind. A woman seated across the aisle from the young man became very frightened. When she spoke to the lad, her voice was agitated, "Little boy, aren't you scared?"

"No ma'am," he replied, briefly looking up from his coloring book. "My dad's the pilot."

I leaned back in my seat. It was time for me to pray. The call to worship my Father had come from a little boy who trusted his dad. Did I trust God that way to get me through the storms of life? Yes. And I silently praised Him.

He'll get you through today and on to His plan for you and ultimately to heaven. Trust Him!

Today's Thought: "I don't know what the future holds, but I know Who holds the future" —E. Stanley Jones.

And in the morning you shall see the glory of the Lord (Exodus 16:7).

Disciples of the Dawn

We are called to be disciples of the dawn. This means that we not only seek the Lord in the morning, but also live expectantly all through the day. Every day has its dark times when we need the dawn of the Lord's intervention and inspiration.

The promise to the people of Israel was that they would see the glory of the Lord in the morning. This promise came when they were hungry and needed bread to eat. God assured them He would send nourishment. He gave them manna in the morning and meat in the evening. The most important promise, however, was that He would be with them all through the day.

It's wonderful to be able to go to sleep at night confident that the Lord will give us a new day and a fresh opportunity to tackle our problems with His help. Then the dawn of a new day comes. When we surrender the day to the Lord, we can expect a succession of dawns all day long—new strength to face the challenges that hit us. He will inspire our thinking, give us physical resiliency and resoluteness to do as He guides, and empower us to be loving and forgiving in our relationships.

I have a friend whose parting shot is always, "See you in the morning!" The Lord says, "In the morning you'll see My glory." And then He gives us morning glory all through the day.

Today's Thought: I will be a morning person all through today expecting the dawn of a new beginning in the dark nights of life.

January 28 Micah 6:1-8

What does the Lord require of you but to do justly (Micah 6:8).

Not Something, But You!

Our meditation today is the first of three on Micah 6:8, one of the most challenging verses in the Bible.

Biblical scholar James Mayes clears the way for an in-depth understanding of this verse: "It's you, not something, God wants."

In response to Micah's incisive prophecy about the apostasy of Judah, the prophet articulated what he sensed was their response: "With what shall we come before the Lord?" Should the people outdo David and Solomon in offerings or emulate pagan nations in sacrificing their firstborn? Then Micah reminds the people that they have known all along what God wants. He had told them through Moses: "And now, Israel, what does the Lord your God require of you, but to fear the Lord your God, to walk in all His ways and to love Him, to serve the Lord your God with all your heart and with all your soul" (Deuteronomy 10:12). Micah essentially reiterates this call.

First, it's to do justly. Luther said this means to keep God's Word. Specifically, it requires *doing* the commandments. It's putting into operation God's just order for relationships and society. Christ gave us the one motivating commandment that makes it possible. We are called to love God, and our neighbors as ourselves. Only those who have experienced His love by faith can do that. Christ, dwelling in us is the instigator and inspiration to do the commandments and His commandment to love.

A good exercise is to read over the Ten Commandments (Exodus 20:1-17) and Jesus' commandment (Matthew 22:37 and John 13:34) and His call to social justice (Matthew 25:31-46). Write a list of what justice demands of you. What is the Lord saying to you about what He wants you to do to live righteously?

Today's Thought: "People today know so much more than they do, with the result that they begin to question what they know."

—G. Campbell Morgan

January 29

What does the Lord require of you but . . . to love mercy (Micah 6:8).

The Bond of Mercy

"Loving mercy" gives "doing justly" depth and direction. The word for "mercy" means "covenant loyalty and faithfulness." God has chosen to be our God and to call us into the new covenant of grace. He has bound us to Himself and we are called to express our loyalty to Him in caring for others as He has cared for us.

The basic root of the Hebrew word for "mercy" comes from the same root as "womb." The unborn child of the womb is helpless. Mercy then is lovingkindness expressed to those from whom we have no possibility of gain. It's the direct opposite of bartered affection of the *quid pro quo* of "I'll do this for you; I expect you to do that for me." Mercy is given to those who have nothing to give us in return: those we have failed, or who are in difficult straits, disadvantaged, weakened, or poor and needy, as well as our "enemies."

You see, mercy is the very essence of the love that sent Jesus to redeem the world. When humankind was helplessly bound in sin, God so loved the world that He sent His Son: "God demonstrates His own love toward us" (Romans 5:8).

There's no possibility of loving mercy without having been loved with the mercy of God. But to have received it when we were helpless and to not express it is to deny our covenant with God. The Lord requires mercy. Today, make a list of those who are on your agenda for God's mercy through you.

Today's Thought: Since we never outgrow our need for mercy from God, we are forever bonded to those who need our mercy.

What does the Lord require of you but... to walk humbly with God" (Micah 6:8).

As the eyes of a maid to the hand of her mistress, so our eyes look to the Lord our God (Psalm 123:2).

An Attentive Journey

To walk humbly with God is not something separate from doing justice and loving mercy. Rather, it gives the driving force to both justice and mercy. We are called to journey with God, to emulate Him, to do what He is doing, and to do it His way.

The Hebrew word for "humbly" is *hasenea*, "attentiveness, thoughtfulness, watchfulness." Hans Walter Wolf says, "What is meant is the attentive sharing with God in the journey on which He is traveling." Walking humbly is not getting God to walk with us just to get Him to help us with our needs, but walking with Him to discern where He is going and joining Him. In the New Testament sense, it's following Jesus.

Walking attentively is the source of the ethics of election. We have been elected by God to watch Him as a servant watches his master to know what's important and how it should be done.

Silent strength is given to those who do the commandments, love the helpless as they are continually helped by God, and walk attentively. It's the only way to go!

Today's Thought: Watch God's methods, watch His ways—how He perfects whom He royally elects!

Can two walk together, unless they are agreed? (Amos 3:3).

The Talk and the Walk

Amos' question establishes his theme of cause and effect. "Can two walk together unless they are agreed?" The question strikes at the essence of our election and our discipleship. We are called to be saints, God's holy people. And we have been appointed to live holy, righteous lives.

The word "together" in Amos' question means to walk as a unit, as one. Two people walk to the same destination, at the same pace, and with the same rhythm. They also must have "agreed" to take the walk of unity, as a unit with oneness. Amos is not talking about a chance meeting between people taking a stroll, who decide to saunter together. The root word in Hebrew for "agreed" is "to fix upon," and also means "a summons to a set tribunal at a fixed time and place." The same word is translated "to betroth," indicating a mutual commitment. So the meaning is "How can two walk in oneness unless they have met and go in the same direction?"

Now we are at the heart of Amos' prophecy. Israel was elected to be God's people. But they were not walking in oneness with Yahweh. In fact, they were heading in different directions! Their talk in their religious life was out of harmony with what should have been their walk of moral and social righteousness. And Amos is quick to point out the inconsistencies in the people's attitude toward the hungry, the poor, and the disadvantaged. It is a travesty to say we belong to God and not walk with Him.

Today's Thought: "When we walk with the Lord,
in the light of His word,
what a glory He sheds on our way.
While we do His good will,
He abides with us still,
and with all who will trust and obey."
—Daniel B. Towner

February 1 Jeremiah 9:23,24

But let him who glories glory in this, that he understands and knows Me (Jeremiah 9:24).

Who Gets the Glory?

We were made to be glorifiers. We have an innate need to worship. And what we worship, we will glorify. To glory in something or someone is to magnify, extol, and ascribe honor to it or him or her. It makes all the difference for our lives who or what gets the glory.

The greatest danger is to glorify ourselves. We then become our own false gods. We are devoted to our own abilities instead of to the God who gave them to us. This is self-glorification. We give ourselves the glory that belongs to the Lord. We don't disbelieve in Him; we just don't glorify Him. The glory's already been squandered on ourselves and our accomplishments.

Jeremiah prophesied in Jerusalem at a time when the people had misplaced their glorification. God speaks through the prophet to those who glorify their wisdom, human powers, and ability to accumulate material things and money. God warned the people about giving glory to these accomplishments instead of giving it to Him. He created humankind to glorify Him and to enjoy the gifts of life as His entrusted provision.

When we don't do that, we miss life's greatest joy: to understand and know God. In these verses from Jeremiah we sense God's yearning over His people—over you and me. He has displayed His glory in His nature: He is lovingkindness, justice, and righteousness. These are the nouns of His nature that should motivate active glory. God's glory is what He has revealed and manifested of Himself. We are to glory in His glory.

Every day we must answer the question, "Who will get the glory today?" But don't miss the final words of today's verses: " 'For in these I delight,' says the Lord." He delights in blessing those who glory in Him. When we turn the spotlight off ourselves and onto Him, He will give us wisdom, strength, and enough material resources for our needs and to share with others.

Today's Thought: Today I will glorify the Lord and not myself!

For You have made him a little lower than the angels, and You have crowned him with glory and honor (Psalm 8:5).

Crowned with Glory

The psalmist caught the wonder of our potential. In Psalm 8 he reflects on the excellence of God's creation. He surveys the heavens, the moon and stars, and all that God has ordained. Then he suddenly is gripped by the sublime work of the Creator in our human nature: "What is man, that You are mindful of him, and the son of man, that You visit him?" And he blurts out a startling and stunning realization: "You have made him a little lower than the angels, and You have crowned him with glory and honor. You have made him to have dominion over the works of Your hands; You have put all things under his feet." In rapid-fire order the psalmist lists the extent of that dominion, expressing the excitement of his awe and wonder. Then with delight over God's goodness, he concludes with praise: "O Lord, our Lord, how excellent is Your name in all the earth!"

The psalmist's adoration is where we must begin our discussion of how to know and do God's will for our lives. His discovery is all the more awesome when we realize that the word "angels" in the Hebrew is really *Elohim*, "God"! That can be interpreted in three ways: God has made us rulers and leaders, or divine beings like the angels, or a little lower than Himself. Any of the three is motivation for unrestrained praise and devotion. We have been deputized by the Lord of all creation to cooperate with Him in the management of our lives and the world. This is our place and function in creation. And to enable us to fulfill our royal status, He has given us the capacity to think His thoughts after Him, to experience and express emotion, and to discern and do His will.

Today's Thought: The first step in finding the will of God for our lives is to praise Him for the endowment of the will He has given us. Praise for this gift enables us to begin with the assurance that God has a will and we have a will. The two can become one!

There is no truth or mercy or knowledge of God in the land. . . . My people are destroyed for lack of knowledge (Hosea 4:1,6).

How to Really Know God

There is nothing more important than knowledge of God. With it life is sublime; without it there's constant stress. It is the secret of true success, the source of wisdom beyond our understanding, the strength to endure in hard times. It is our ultimate goal, life's greatest privilege, and our most urgent need.

Knowledge of God—this is our purpose and passion. Many Christians admit that they do not really know God. For others, lack of knowledge of God is the cause of vacillating spirituality, inconsistency between the walk and talk of faith, and ineffective prayer. For most, inadequate knowledge of God accounts for the reluctant response to holy living and moral responsibility. Like the people of Israel to whom Hosea prophesied, truth and mercy (faithfulness and kindness) as well as social righteousness are missing because we do not know God.

What does it mean to know God and live with a knowledge of Him? It requires intimacy and integrity. God has revealed Himself in Christ. He has opened His heart for us to behold. Intimacy happens when we come to God and reveal our real selves. Knowing God begins by being real, honest, vulnerable. He meets us in Christ, His presence with us. Christ is the truth about God, the life of God, and the way to God. The more we know of Christ, the more we know of God. Christ is our guide. He shows the way for daily obedience, and we follow. We will know the truth, and living it will set us free. Humbly we can say we know God. Truth and mercy will be the mark of our integrity. Nothing is more important.

Today's Thought: I will make knowledge of God my first priority.

Ephraim is a cake unturned (Hosea 7:8).

What About Your Soggy Side?

What about your soggy side? Now, before you think that I'm either impertinent or downright insulting, let me clarify that I'm not talking about flabby muscles, or suggesting that you're all wet. What I am suggesting is that we all have a problem of being half-baked. Hosea is the source of that pithy epigram.

The picture is of flat bread that is cooked on hot stones. When the baking stones were fully heated by a red-hot fire and fully greased, dough was poured on them for cooking. It would cook quickly on one side. Then it would have to be turned for the other side to cook. If it was not turned, the one side would be a soggy, sticky, mushy, and very unappetizing mess.

Hosea used this simile for Ephraim/Israel. She was well-cooked on the side of dependence on other nations, false gods, and apostasy, but soggy on the side of obedience to God and righteous living.

When this epigram is applied to us today, it means that one side of our faith can be cooked and the other side soggy. Our soggy side is the neglected side of our faith. It's possible to be very pious but unbaked on the side of working for social justice. Or, the other way around: We can be orthodox but lack ortho-practice. So now my question is even more direct: What is your soggy side, and when are you going to turn it over?

Today's Thought: Today I will face my soggy side and stop being half-baked!

February 5 Revelation 1

He laid His right hand on me, saying to me, "Do not be afraid" (Revelation 1:17).

A Touch of Courage

"He laid His right hand on me. . . ."

That's an electrifying assertion, to say the least; a captivating claim, to say the most. Especially when we realize who said it, about whose land, when, and under what circumstances.

It happened to the apostle John, not during Jesus' ministry in Galilee or just after Pentecost, but many years later. That makes it all the more vital to us. What happened to John can happen to us. The same Lord who placed His hand on John can give us a new assurance of His presence and power today.

John was alone and in need of fresh courage to persevere. He was a political prisoner of Rome, banished by Domitian to the island of Patmos in the Aegean Sea. He was acutely aware of his aloneness, his own impotence, and his fear. His heart was broken over the persecution of his beloved fellow Christians back in Asia Minor. Sick with worry, John needed the Lord. "And He laid His right hand on me," John says.

Can this happen to you and me today? Yes! Sometimes we feel the physical touch; most often we are given a renewed conviction of the Lord's presence. This happens when we really want the Lord, surrender our concerns to Him, and are willing to leave the results to Him. His "right hand" is synonymous with His power. Ask Him for His strength. He is faithful!

Today's Thought: Today I will ask the Lord to place His right hand of power on me and live with confidence and courage.

That you may believe that Jesus is the Christ the Son of God, and that believing in Him you may have life in His name (John 20:31).

Good News About a Great Lord

Today we begin a study of the Gospel of John leading up to Easter. You may have wondered why we have begun our daily reading of the gospel at the end. The reason is that in these verses John clearly states why he wrote his gospel. The key words are "signs," "believing," and "life." The apostle selected from the many signs and miracles Jesus performed those that would stimulate faith and thus lead to new life in Him. John wanted to introduce his readers to eternal life. He set about to do this by presenting life with a capital "L," Jesus Christ.

So often we hear people advise others, "What you need is more faith," as if the quantity of our faith will change things. We don't need more faith, we need authentic faith. Faith does not exist in a vacuum. It's not conjured up by human ability. Faith is given to us as we behold Christ. The more we concentrate on Christ, the more our faith grows, not in size but in depth.

Studying the Gospel of John will show us how Christ introduced many different kinds of people to abundant and eternal life so we can meet Him anew each day ourselves. We'll behold His miracles and be encouraged to expect the mighty works He wants to do in our lives today. Our purpose is to become immersed in Christ, more deeply committed to Christ, and filled with the Spirit of God.

Christ is the answer to our needs. Zinzendorf put it clearly: "We have a great need for Christ and a great Christ for our needs!"

Today's Thought: When Carl Sandberg was in Springfield, Illinois studying Lincoln, he became so immersed in his work that one day when a friend dressed up as Lincoln to surprise Sandberg on the way to breakfast, the Lincoln buff simply said, "Good morning, Mr. President." He was not surprised at all. How much more does a concentration on Christ make meeting Him each day our joy. And He's really alive!

February 7 — John 1:1-13

In the beginning was the Word, and the Word was with God, and the Word was God. He was in the beginning with God (John 1:1).

Thinking Magnificently About Christ

Let your mind soar. Catch the magnitude and sense the majesty. Imagine eternity preceding time and creation. Now behold Christ. He was coequal with God the Father, existing in perfect oneness before creation. The Word of God.

John used a Greek philosophical term to communicate the glory of Christ, but filled an empty concept with awesome reality. The Word, *ho logos*, for the Greek, was the soul, the controlling force, the generative principle of the universe. John took a known idea to communicate an unknown reality. Christ was none other than the eternal preexistent Logos. This and so much more!

John selected *pros*, the most intimate of Greek prepositions, when he wrote that the Word, Christ, was with God. *Pros*, face to face unity. The Father was the instigator, the Son was the implementor. The Word was the agent of the Father's thought in action. The creative power and the congealing wisdom of the Father.

Scientists say creation began with the "big bang." If so, Christ was the uncreated creator of the instant when universes within universes were created. At the Father's command the Word created life on the planet earth. And when the Father said, "Let us make man in our own image," and the Word created humankind: Life Himself brought life into being. Christ the Word who brought light out of darkness was *the* Light who dwelt among us.

If we are to know Christ and experience His power, we must begin where John began. Who is Christ? The Word. The One who created the process by which we were born and who came so we could be reborn. The Light of truth to dispel our darkness. Ultimate reality. Our Lord!

Today's Thought: Today I will think magnificently about Christ, who He was in the beginning and who He is now as God with me. If He Created the universe, He can do magnificent things in my little world.

Grace and truth came through Jesus Christ. No one has seen God at any time. The only begotten Son, who is in the bosom of the Father, He has declared Him (John 1:17,18).

The Plummet of Love

Keep your thinking cap on as we continue to reflect magnificently about Christ, the Word. It will make all the difference for the silent strength we will be able to receive from Him today.

The Word through whom humankind was made came to dwell among us. He became flesh. Contrary to some Greek philosophers' ideas that the Divine was totally separated from impure human life, Christ was the God-man in human flesh. In a perfect union of the divine and human, Christ manifested the glory of God for us to behold. His fullness revealed God's grace, unqualified love and favor, and undistorted truth. The Word came from the bosom of the Father, His essential heart, so that we might know who God is and at the same time see what we can become.

John's prologue to his gospel reaches its full climax when he asserts that in Christ we have seen God. Up to the time of the incarnation no one has seen God. But Christ the Word has brought His glory, grace and truth into full view for us to behold. He has declared Him, exegeted God, brought out the truth for us to understand His nature and will. In the earliest and most reliable manuscripts of John's gospel, verse 18 in the Greek was not *monogenes Huios*, only begotten Son, but *monogenes Theos*, only begotten God!

Christ, the Word, is the plummet of love from the bosom of the Father. God with us. And now as risen Lord, He is with us to do in our lives the amazing things He did in the lives of people in John's gospel. The Only Begotten for those who may have thought God had forgotten. Behold your Christ and say with Thomas, "My Lord and my God!"

Today's Thought: Majesty, I will worship His majesty!

February 9

John 1:19-34;
3:22-36

He must increase but I must decrease (John 3:30).

He Must Increase

John the Baptist reveals a basic secret of how to receive the silent strength of Christ. I have asked you to read two passages about the Baptist because the first shows us his humble reception of Christ and the second reveals the reason why.

The Baptist was a renowned spiritual leader. He was the point person for a far-reaching revival movement. The decisive prophet stood tall in the tradition of the Old Testament prophets. He proclaimed the sovereignty of God, His requirement of absolute righteousness, and called people to repent, return to God, and be baptized. The masses flocked to the river Jordan to hear him and respond to his unmitigated message of judgment. At the height of his power, the prophet was becoming famous. He was talked about and became the center of much controversy about who he actually was. This is why the spiritual leaders of Israel came to find out who it was causing such a stir.

But John knew who he was. There was no mistake in his mind about his purpose. He was not the Christ. He knew who that was. His own cousin Jesus of Nazareth. The Baptist had known this with divine discernment for some time. John's calling was to prepare the way for Jesus' ministry and he knew it. There was no competition, no jockeying for recognition. He baptized with water but he knew a greater One than he would baptize with the Holy Spirit and with fire (Luke 3:16). The result of the Father's confirmation after Jesus' baptism by John led the prophet to an amazing expression of humility: "He must increase, but I must decrease."

This is how we receive the silent strength of Christ. Our ego must be yielded to Christ. Our calling is to yield center stage to Him. He must take charge; our control must be relinquished. So often I hear people say, "I must get rid of self." This is *not* the secret. It's letting Christ fill the self that opens us to His strength.

Today's Thought: When our imperious self-will decreases, Christ's power increases.

They followed Jesus (John 1:37).

Christ Has Double Vision

Christ calls us not because we are like anyone else, but to make us like Himself. In today's reading we see how Christ called three distinctly different personalities. "Three? I only found two—Andrew and Simon," you say. I think the unnamed man with Andrew was John himself. As in other references to himself in his gospel, he pointedly does not use his own name.

Along with Andrew, John had been a disciple of John the Baptist. The other gospels depict him as a man of strong passions. He was a man who matched the sea on which he sailed as a fisherman. He knew moments of calm interrupted by tempestuous storms, tornados of anger, swells of impetuous outbursts. And yet Jesus called him.

Andrew was an affable man, an entrepreneur of relationships. Whenever we meet him on the pages of the Gospels, he is bringing people together and introducing people to Jesus. Christ calls kind, caring, good people and makes them great people.

Andrew and John were with John the Baptist when the prophet clearly identified Jesus as the Messiah. "Behold the Lamb of God," he declared and released his disciples to follow Jesus. "What do you seek?" was Jesus' profound and penetrating question. Andrew answered with a question that indicated his and John's desire to be with the Master and learn from Him.

Andrew found his brother Simon and shared the exciting news. Simon was a natural leader, a strong take-charge kind of man. Christ had plans for him. He looked with divine double vision at the big fisherman, seeing Simon's abilities but also seeing the man He would help Simon become. The Master gave Simon a new name to focus the fisherman's potential, "You shall be called Cephas"—Peter. The name means "rock." On the rock of the faith Christ gave Peter, He would build His church.

Today's Thought: Each of us is unique and each of us has a special role in Jesus' plans that can be filled by no one else.

Follow Me (John 1:43).

Follow Me

William Barkley remarked that Christ did not say to His potential disciples, "Come, discuss Me," but, "Come, follow Me!" And Christ is still issuing His call today. Each week I see people respond to the call and they are all different personalities. In today's reading we see two more distinctly different men who became Jesus' disciples along with John, Andrew, and Peter.

Philip was more retiring than Andrew and John. He was not out with his countrymen listening to John the Baptist or, like John and Andrew, pressing to follow Jesus. The Master had to search for Philip and enlist him to be a disciple. A survey of the Gospel records reveals him to be a quiet, unimpressive man.

What did Jesus see in this man the day He sought him out and called him? The answer is indicated by what Philip subsequently said to Nathanael, "We have found Him of whom Moses in the law, and also the prophets, wrote." Philip knew his Scriptures and longed for the Messiah. Jesus honored that and made him a disciple.

Nathanael was a different breed. He was a direct, honest, open man. Jesus had been watching him. One day He observed Nathanael sitting under the fig tree, obviously a place of quiet where Nathanael was reading the Scriptures and praying. The amazing thing is that Jesus knew what he was reading. I think Nathanael was reading about Jacob in his deceitful, manipulative days before his Jabbok encounter. Why else would Jesus address Philip the way he did,"Behold, an Israelite indeed, in whom there is no guile"? This is further confirmed by what Jesus said to Nathanael after he confessed Him as the Son of God. The Lord referred to Jacob's vision of the angel and promised the new disciple the same vision of Him. Jesus liked Nathanael's integrity and guileless character.

Today's Thought: Christ calls very different kinds of people to be disciples because He wants to use our personalities and experiences to reach others who are just like us.

And when they ran out of wine, the mother of Jesus said to Him, "They have no wine" (John 2:3).

The Purpose of a Miracle

Mary had lived under a cloud of suspicion ever since Jesus had been conceived in her womb. Her pregnancy before marriage to Joseph could never be explained to friends and neighbors. Raising her Son of destiny took special care. His uniqueness was a secret they shared, talking of it in tender, intimate moments. But Mary did not fully understand the implications of what was ahead for Jesus. When He was baptized by John and He began to call His disciples, Mary was relieved. Now everyone would know what she had known for 30 years.

It was only natural that she would desire a vindicating moment when others could share her mother's natural pride. The moment came at a wedding in Cana she was attending. Out of courtesy to her, Jesus and His disciples also were invited. Then a social mishap occurred. They ran out of wine. "Now that Jesus has begun His ministry, surely He can exercise His divine power. How proud I would be," she thought. At last, she would be vindicated. "They have no wine," she said urgently to Jesus. His response seems sharp and curt. "What has that to do with me? My hour has not come." What did He mean?

Simply that her need could not be satisfied by having Him produce wine. If He performed a miracle it would not be for her vindication but for the manifestation of His glory. Having clarified this, Jesus went on to transform the water into wine for the authentic purpose of showing that He was indeed the Christ.

What does all this mean to us? That Christ's miracles and His answers to our prayers are not just for our comfort or convenience, but to increase our trust in Him as our all powerful Savior. He does do great things in little circumstances—all to bring us to trust our whole lives to Him.

Today's Thought: Christ will transform circumstances if doing so will bring us to allowing Him to transform our lives and if we want what we pray for to be to His glory.

February 13 John 2:13-25

Take these things away! Do not make My Father's house a house of merchandise (John 2:16).

The Cleansing of Our Temple

Let's go straight to the point. The issue is not that John puts the cleansing of the temple in Jerusalem earlier in Jesus' ministry than Matthew, Mark and Luke, who record it as part of Jesus' last week in Jerusalem. Nor is it crucial to spend a great deal of space discussing the corrupt commercialism of the temple in that time. What is crucial for us is what Christ would want to drive out of the temple of our lives and of our churches.

In this passage Christ exercises His divine authority as the Son of God. Today the Father has put judgment into His hands as reigning Lord of our lives and the church. In the Apostles' Creed we repeat the words "He shall come to judge the living and the dead." Not just at the second coming or at the conclusion of our physical lives, but now. Today. This moment.

Judgment is a part of love. Wouldn't it be frightening if we thought we could get away with unrighteousness? What if it didn't matter? There would be no order, no justice. If nothing mattered it would be like painting our portrait in the water. But it does matter. Christ was with the Father when the commandments were given to Moses. He has given us a new commandment to love. And He comes to expose anything that needs His judgment and forgiveness. Picture Him moving through the areas of our lives. Paul reminds us that our lives are a holy temple (1 Corinthians 6:19).

And what about the contemporary church? What would Christ affirm? What would He drive out? To what would He say "That has to go"?

Make a housecleaning list for yourself and your church and use it as a basis of your prayers of confession today.

Today's Thought: Today I will look through the rooms of my life with Christ and ask what He wants changed.

Most assuredly, I say to you, unless one is born again, he cannot see the kingdom of God (John 3:3).

Believers Need to Be Born Again

We all know what it's like to not connect in a conversation because we're using one meaning of a word and the person we're talking to is using another. In Jesus' encounter with Nicodemus the two of them were working with two very different meanings of "born again." Jesus was using the vertical meaning and Nicodemus the horizontal.

I think Nicodemus knew very well that Jesus was using the vertical meaning but purposely used the horizontal meaning to draw out Jesus. As *the* teacher (John 3:10) in Israel, Nicodemus would have been the leading scholar in the school of Gamael. He was fully aware of the concept of spiritual rebirth. It was required for a proselyte who became a Jew and was prominent in the teaching of two Greek mystery religions. What was unique about the teachings of Jesus was that He said good religious Jews needed to be born again. And so did Nicodemus!

Born again could mean from the beginning, a completely new start; it could also mean again, for a second time; or it could mean from above, from God. Nicodemus chose to use the second meaning to get at the radical thing Jesus was saying about being born again. The Lord was calling for a completely new birth for people who already believed in God. They needed a radical change of heart that He had come to make possible.

Today being born again is the great need of religious people. It is a radical transformation the Spirit works in our souls. Many who believe in Christ as Savior and Lord have never had this "birth from above." But we can't do it to ourselves; all we can do is ask God to change us when we know we can't change ourselves. More on this tomorrow.

Today's Thought: Have you been born again? When did it happen? What were the results in your new relationship and your involvement in Christ's mission in society?

February 15 — John 3:13-21

No one has ascended to heaven but He who came down from heaven, that is, the Son of Man (John 3:13).

In Which Third Are You?

A survey was taken of Christians about their understanding of being born again. All had heard the term used. One third said they had heard the term but did not have the foggiest notion of what it meant; another third said they thought they understood it but had never experienced it; and one third said that the new birth had happened in their lives. Many of the last group had experienced the new birth sometime after they had confessed Christ as Lord and Savior.

In today's passage from John, we discover the secret of how the new birth happens. Christ came down from heaven to make it possible. God loved the world and sent Jesus so that those who believe in Him might be saved. He was lifted up on the cross for the sins of the world. Those who believe in Him are given eternal life. Truly believing is the result of a rebirth. We die to ourselves and our control and the very life of Christ possesses us, fills us. We become a new person. It is more than accepting that Christ lived and died for the world in general. Rather it is His Spirit convincing us that we are loved and forgiven. And yielding our hearts and minds to Him, we begin a new life that death cannot end. It is a radical new start, a complete reorientation of our total being.

And what can we do to cooperate in being born again? Accept Christ's diagnosis that our deepest need is to make a completely new start; receive His healing forgiveness for all that is past; and surrender our new, ready, and receptive hearts to be filled with Christ's Spirit.

Now let me ask again: Have you been born again, when did it happen, and what difference has it made?

Today's Thought: The new birth may be sudden or gradual but there is always a point when we know for sure that we have been born again.

Jesus said to her, "I who speak to you am He" (John 4:26).

I Am for You

How are you today? Really. Christ knows and has sought you out to renew His relationship with you. He arranged this special time with Him. He knows and cares; wants to get in touch with the real you; has a powerful gift He wants to give you to make this a great day. How He cared for the Samaritan woman by the well shows us not only how we begin life in Christ but also how He renews us each day.

Christ begins our day by affirming our value to Him. Note how He approached the woman by the well. He was the initiator; He took it on Himself to break down the sexist and racial barriers. Christ breaks through whatever barriers we or others have built. Sometimes our barrier is guilt, other times pride; still other times an aching hurt over life.

The next thing Christ does is ask us for something. He asked the Samaritan woman for a drink of water; He simply asks us for today. "I need your help today." Our response is, "Lord you need me? How can that be?" Then He says, "If you knew who was asking you would have asked for what I have to give you today." What sensitivity the Savior has as He draws us into dialogue. Then He puts His finger on the very thing that makes us stingy receivers. Our sin, failures, habitual patterns that repeatedly scuttle our ship. "He knows!" we say to ourselves. "How foolish to think I could hide from Him."

All this is to lead to that awesome moment when we are prepared to receive His power. "I who speaks to you am He," He said to the woman, clearly declaring He was the Messiah. The words in Greek are "I am speaks to you." This is one of 22 times in the Gospels that Jesus used "I am" with the force of "Yahweh speaks to you." The God who makes things happen. The one who has all power for your day!

Today's Thought: When Jesus says "I am" it carries the force of the power of God present in Him. Have a powerful day!

February 17 John 4:43-54

Jesus said to him, "Go your way; your son lives." So the man believed the word that Jesus spoke to him, and he went his way (John 4:50).

Go Your Way!

"Go your way! Get on with life. You've given Me your problem, now trust the results to Me." In essence that is what Christ says to us each time we come to Him with a really big problem. It's not easy to carry on with our daily responsibilities without continuing to be racked with worry. "Did He really hear my prayer? Will things really work out in the way that He sees is ultimately best for me and the people for whom I've prayed?" we wonder.

The nobleman went his way believing the promise Jesus had given him. What a contrast this man was to the Galileans, Jesus' own countrymen, who demanded more signs because they would not accept His word that He was the Messiah. Put your fingers in your Bible at Matthew 8:5-13 and Luke 7:1-10 for cross-reference. In these passages it is a centurion whose servant is in need of healing. I think John used the account of the nobleman (and the account of the centurion) to contrast the man's faith with that of Israel: "Assuredly I say to you, I have not found such great faith, not even in Israel" (Matthew 8:10).

But don't miss the fact that Jesus told the nobleman what to expect. Sometimes He does this as we linger in His presence after we have made our request in prayer. We can go our way with defined expectancy. Other times all we have to go on is that He has heard us and will work out the answer in His way and in His timing.

The healing of the nobleman's son had the desired effect: he believed in Jesus. The people in Cana did not believe in Him after He had turned the water into wine. The point for us is our Lord answers our prayers in a way that leads us into deeper trust in Him, not in the answers. When asked if he believed in answers to prayer, a man responded, "Yes, but I believe lots more in the Lord who answers prayer!"

Today's Thought: I will surrender my concerns to the Lord and leave them with Him.

Do you want to be made well? (John 5:6).

Do You Want to Be Healed?

Thirty-eight years is a long time to wait for an answer to prayer. It can wilt the will, debilitate desire, exhaust expectancy. Could it be that we might not want what we had been praying for so persistently, so long?

But just imagine if you had prayed that long how you would feel if someone asked, "Do you really want the answer?" We'd be shocked, angered, and hurt, to say the least.

And yet, this is exactly the question Jesus put before the paralytic who had been carried to the Pool of Bethesda for 38 years. The belief was that the pool had healing powers at the moment an angel stirred up the water. Whoever stepped in first was healed. The paralytic's problem was he couldn't move fast enough to be the first one in the water. Or so he said.

Jesus' question to the man was, "Do you want to be made well?" After all his explanation of why he had not been healed, Jesus said, "Rise, take up your bed and walk." The man was healed. We get further insight into him, however, as the account goes on. When questioned about who healed him, he did not know! What kind of man was this who would seek healing for 38 years, be healed, and not ask who his healer was?

Jesus found the man afterward and reminded him that it was He who had healed him. "Sin no more," Jesus said. What was the man's sin? That he had been healed and did not give glory to the One who healed him. Receiving answers to our prayers is dependent on really wanting what we pray for and being willing to give the Lord the glory. Nothing is so cruel as ingratitude. Perhaps this was the paralytic's basic problem. He couldn't praise the Lord either before or after his healing.

Today's Thought: I will praise the Lord for the gift of life, for my salvation, and for all His blessings. I will thank Him before and after answered prayer, for it is He whom I seek. What He provides is secondary!

February 19 John 5:17-47

For as the Father has life in Himself, so He has granted the Son to have life in Himself, and has given Him authority to execute judgment also, because He is the Son of man (John 5:26,27).

The Problem of Authority

A successful young producer confessed the reason he was having difficulty growing in his faith. "It hit me last Sunday in church when you said, 'Everyone has to be under someone's authority. We're all accountable to living under authority. And the greater the authority we are given, the more we have to place ourselves unreservedly under Christ's authority.' I don't like living under authority. That's been my problem ever since I was a kid. Now I see that there's no way to continue as a Christian unless I accept Christ's authority as my absolute Lord. I want to do that today. Will you listen in on my prayer to be sure I go all the way?" The man has been soaring like a rocket ever since.

The Jews would not accept Jesus' authority as the Messiah and Son of God. When He healed the paralytic on the Sabbath, they accused Him of making Himself equal with God. They were right on target. He was assuming full authority as the Son of God. He was indeed the Word of God, the One who implemented the Father's will. The Jews had not accepted God's authority, and now they were wrangling with His authority as the One sent from God.

Christ's response gives us a clear mandate to accept His authority over our lives. We do this because of the witness the Father has given to Christ—the authority the Father has entrusted to Him to judge and to manage our lives—and because of the works that He has done and continues to do for us. Who is the authority over your life? Christ must be Lord of all or eventually He'll not be our Lord at all!

Today's Thought: There is no joy or strength or peace in the Christian life until we accept Christ's authority.

And Jesus took the loaves, and when He had given thanks He distributed them to the disciples, and the disciples to those sitting down; and likewise of the fish, as much as they wanted (John 6:11).

A Multiplied Lunch

I really enjoy this passage we have read for today. It's filled with drama. Picture it in your mind's eye. A multitude of 5000 people who were excited over Christ's healing miracles came to hear Him. As they approached, Jesus involved the disciples in a discussion of how they were going to feed them. He wanted to see just how much they trusted in His power to meet the needs of any situation. "Where shall we buy bread, that these may eat?" He asked Philip. Philip's response was, "Two hundred denarii worth of bread is not sufficient." Andrew's response was no more visionary. He had been talking to a lad who had brought his lunch with him—"five barley loaves and two small fish, but what are they among so many?"

I imagine at this point the lad's faith in Jesus outdistanced that of the disciples. Feel the warm exchange between Jesus and the lad. "Will you trust Me with your lunch?" Jesus probably asked. The lad, full of love and enthusiasm, gladly gave the Master what he had.

Taking the loaves and fish, Jesus prayed, thanking the Father in advance for the multiplications that would be provided. Then Jesus performed the miracle of multiplication and all were fed. To be sure they remembered this was a miracle, He told the disciples to gather up what was left.

Jesus did the miracle and made the lad a hero for being willing to share what little he had. This is the way Christ works. When we surrender our meager resources, He multiples them so we and others can be blessed.

Today's Thought: If you had been there on that day with a lunch under your cloak, would you have offered it to Jesus?

February 21 John 6:15-21

It is I; do not be afraid (John 6:20).

The Calming of Our Stormy Seas

Peter, John, Andrew, and the others had ridden out many a storm. It was part of their trade. They were men of the sea, and had an experienced respect for its temperamental nature. But this was no ordinary squall. It lasted for nine hours. And they had rowed only three or four miles by the fourth watch of the night (three to four o'clock in the morning). They seemed to make no progress at all. No wonder they were afraid.

It was when the situation looked most impossible that Jesus came to them, walking on the water. Their Friend, Teacher, Master—walking on the water! He had not allowed the crowd to make Him a king, but here He was stepping through the white-caps and the restless foam of the sea.

Then He spoke. His voice thundered with authority and power. "I am. Have no fear." It is the second *ego eimi*, "I am," assertion of Jesus in John's account. The English translations of the Greek do not catch the commanding majesty of Jesus' words. "It is I; do not be afraid," misses the force of the Greek: *Ego eimi me phobeisthe*. To me, the literal impact is, "Yahweh, have no fear!" The God of Moses' burning bush had come to the disciples in Jesus of Nazareth. The same Word by whom all things were made came walking on the angry sea as if it were asphalt. He was greater than the sea, more powerful than the wind. "I am" calmed the sea and brought the disciples to the shore safely.

Later in the day, when the multitude learned that Jesus was at Capernaum, they got into their boats and crossed the sea to find Him. "How did you get here?" they asked the Master. "We looked for you anxiously on the other side of the sea, but you were gone. You did not get into the boat with the disciples, and there is only one boat here!" Imagine how the disciples must have exchanged knowing looks at that. They knew! And so do we.

Today's Thought: Christ comes striding over the turbulent seas of our lives and says, "Yahweh, have no fear! I'm with you!"

I am the bread of life (John 6:35).

Bread that Really Satisfies

When the multitudes did not comprehend the significance of Jesus' miracle of multiplying the loaves and fishes, He had to make it undeniably clear. The Lord drew the sharp distinction between natural food, which was necessary but impermanent in value, and spiritual food, which would satisfy their deepest needs. "Most assuredly, I say to you, Moses did not give you the bread from heaven, but My Father gives you the true bread from heaven." Now the spiritual hunger of the people became acute.

It was then that Jesus proclaimed the third "I am," or *ego eimi*. He had not come to provide physical bread, but to be the bread of life. "I am the bread of life!" is stated twice, and then a third time with amplification: "I am the living bread which came down from heaven. If anyone eats of this bread, he will live forever; and the bread that I shall give is My flesh... for the life of the world."

Bread was the basic staff of life in that day. The people to whom Jesus spoke knew they could not live without its daily sustenance. He used an impelling image to teach them about their spiritual need.

What bread is for the physical body, Jesus Christ is for our hungry, aching hearts. He alone can satisfy this hunger. But just as Jesus refused to give another sign by providing more physical bread, so too He wants to do more than ease our heartaches with quick solutions. He wants to go deeper to heal the real source of our emotional pain. When we consider His triumphant *ego eimi* claim in the context of the total impact of this passage, we discover the three ways that Jesus feeds our profound hunger. The Bread of Life saves, satisfies, and strengthens.

Today's Thought: Our spiritual hunger pangs are but our response to the aroma of the fresh bread of life Christ has provided for us.

February 23 John 6:36-51

All that the Father gives Me will come to Me, and the one who comes to Me I will by no means cast out (John 6:37).

No! No!

In this promise, Jesus' double negative equals a positive. The phrase "by no means" translates "No! No!" Christ will not reject anyone who comes to Him, regardless of what they have done or been. We cannot be disqualified, except by our refusal to come. He will not cast us away—He never folds His arms in disdain. His saving arms are outstretched to you and me. Whoever will may come!

I have always appreciated the honesty of John Bunyan, author of *Pilgrim's Progress*, when he struggled to accept the full assurance of Christ's promise.

> This scripture did also most sweetly visit my soul: "And him who comes to Me I will in no wise cast out" (John 6:37). Oh the comfort that I have had from this word, "in no wise." . . . But Satan would greatly labor to pull this promise from me, telling me that Christ did not mean me and such as I, but sinners of a lower rank, that had not done as I had done. But I should answer him again, Satan, there is in this word no such exception. . . . If ever Satan and I did strive for any word of God in my life, it was for this good word of Christ—he at one end and I at the other. Oh, what work we did make! It was for this in John, I say, that we did tug and strive; he pulled, and I pulled; but God be praised, I got the better of him.

Prayerfully think of people who need this promise. Some have never come to Christ because they think they have a corner on failure. Others have drifted from the Savior they have known and loved. Others doubt and feel disqualified. And to all, Christ says, "No! No! I will not turn My back on you! Come as you are."

Today's Thought: "The soul that on Jesus hath leaned for repose I will not, I will not desert to its foes. That soul though all hell should endeavor to shake I'll never, no never, no never forsake!" (taken from "How Firm a Foundation").

Most assuredly, I say to you, unless you eat the flesh of the Son of Man and drink His blood, you have no life in you. Whoever eats My flesh and drinks My blood has eternal life, and I will raise him up at the last day (John 6:53,54).

Hope from a Hard Saying

Jesus' words brought a strong resistant response: "This is a hard saying; who can understand it?" The New English Bible puts it even more vividly: "This is more than we can stomach! Why listen to such talk?"

The people really were put off by Jesus' hard saying. It was hard for some because they didn't understand; it was hard for others because they understood all too well. For some it sounded like cannibalism. For the Jews even eating the flesh of meat from which blood had not been completely drained was forbidden. Others present might have thought Jesus was advocating some of the practices of the mystery religions. But those who understood the real meaning were challenged most of all. Perhaps these were put off more than all the others. Jesus clarified His own intent of the hard saying in verse 56: "He who eats My flesh and drinks My blood abides in Me, and I in him." The Lord was calling for complete commitment to Him and the kingdom. He wanted His followers to become one with Him.

This hard saying means the same for us—and much more. It means Christ's life-giving and healing Spirit can enter into us for the healing of our hurts, our confused thinking about ourselves and the future, and our spiritual illnesses. It also means that He who is the healing power of the world can heal our bodies and make us whole. This hard saying offers the hope of the healing of the hurts of life—physical and psychological.

Today's Thought: Christ offers us the full impact of His life, ministry, and message. His death on the cross provides us with the forgiving power of His shed blood. But most important of all, He gives us Himself in the power of His Spirit.

February 25 John 7:1-13

For even His brothers did not believe in Him (John 7:5).

The Ties that Bind

If you have ever been misunderstood or rejected by family or friends because of your faith, you will be encouraged by today's reading from John. Whatever you may have been through or are facing today, Christ knows what it's like and will give you His strength.

With the possible exception of James and Jude, at this point Jesus' brothers did not believe that He was the Messiah. But as long as He insisted on making this claim, they wondered why He didn't go to Jerusalem and declare Himself openly. Surely they knew some people had sought to kill Jesus in Judea. Were they actually counseling Him to walk into the jaws of the enemy? Had brotherly competition gone that far? Or was it because they wanted to share His recognition, even if they didn't believe He was the Son of God?

Jesus refused to bend to their pressure. He did not go with them to the feast in Jerusalem. Then, after they had gone, He went anyway. Was this vacillation? No. Jesus wanted to go to Jerusalem on His own timing and under the Father's guidance. He had to break with His brothers' efforts to control Him or manage His ministry. He went to Jerusalem secretly. He listened to what people were saying about Him and, when He was ready, He spoke openly.

Note that Jesus was gracious and courteous to His brothers. He did not draw them out into a family battle. He simply put His mission first and did what He had to do on His timing.

Today's Thought: A special salute to those who have had to pray their prayers, remain faithful to Christ, and witness with love and firmness in a family situation that is not Christian. They must find their fellowship and support outside the family. Our calling is to give them special encouragement and fellowship.

If anyone wants to do His will, he shall know concerning the doctrine, whether it is from God or whether I speak on my own authority (John 7:17).

Beyond Admiration to Adoration

As I write today's meditation, I'm seated at a desk where I study each summer at the University of Edinburgh. After reading the account of Jesus teaching at the temple during the feast, I tried to imagine what it would be like for an uneducated young man from a village in the Highlands to lecture to the faculty. If he had not been to theological school, it would be difficult to imagine him sounding like a man who had spent years in an academic setting. The faculty and student body would say, "Why listen to him? He has not got even the basics!"

But when Jesus of Nazareth spoke at the temple, the center of learning, religion, and culture, He sounded like a distinguished man of letters, yet He had never been to any of the great rabbinical schools in Jerusalem.

It was not Jesus' learned accent He wanted people to hear, but the truth He spoke. He had come from God. His intellect was not just superior—it was divine. And the only people who would be able to accept the doctrine He proclaimed were those who wanted to do God's will. So often the verse, "If anyone wants to do His will, he will know concerning the doctrine," is used to explain how to know God's will. Here the desire to know God's will is the key to accepting Christ and His revelation of God.

Jesus does not want our admiration but our adoration. He's not looking for a cheering section, but for obedient disciples. Churches are filled with many who admire Jesus but have never turned their lives over to Him. He is raiding the ranks of traditional church people and calling true disciples.

Today's Thought: Jesus is not the greatest man who ever lived; He is the only Son of God, our Lord. If we want to know God, we must begin with what He said in His Word and obey what we hear!

February 27 John 7:37-39

Out of his heart will flow rivers of living water (John 7:38).

The Inner Secret

You and I are involved in a search for the secrets of living daily in the silent strength of the Lord. Today our pilgrimage has led us to the inner secret.

On the last day of the Feast of the Tabernacles, there was a very significant ceremony. The high priest would take a golden pitcher and go down to the Pool of Siloam and fill it with water. With great dignity the pitcher was brought back by a procession that passed through the Water Gate while the people sang, "With joy you will draw water from the wells of salvation" (Isaiah 12:3). The pitcher was carried to the altar in the temple and poured out as an offering to Yahweh. Psalms 112-118—the Heilel—would be sung as the people remembered the water Yahweh gave them from the rock in the wilderness.

As they sang, suddenly Jesus' voice rang out with commanding power, "If anyone thirsts, let him come to Me and drink." Then with "I am" Yahweh authority, Christ declared that those who believed in Him would experience living water flowing from their hearts. He looked forward to the time when, after His crucifixion, resurrection, glorification, and ascension, He would return as the reigning Lord to baptize His believers with the Spirit.

This awesome promise of the living water of the Spirit is to be fulfilled in your life and mine this very day. The indwelling Spirit is the secret of silent strength. The Spirit is not just an intensification of human abilities, but the actual Spirit of the living Christ who comes from outside ourselves and enters into our minds and hearts. He quenches our spiritual thirst and gives us limitless supernatural power. It's a miracle you can expect today if you believe in Christ and have yielded your heart to be the well He fills with Himself.

Today's Thought: Draw from the well, for the more you draw the more the artesian replenishment of the Spirit will be given.

Nicodemus (he who came to Jesus by night, being one of them) said to them, "Does our law judge a man before it hears him and knows what he is doing?" (John 7:50,51).

Silent Strength that Speaks Out

Today's title may appear contradictory. How can our strength be silent if we speak? This leads us to a vital aspect of the silent strength we've been talking about in this book. The strength of the Lord within us is experienced in silence alone with Him, but it gives us courage to speak out on issues of justice and righteousness. *Christians with silent strength are not silent!* There comes a time when we must take a stand. But taking a stand is to lead people to the One who is the source of our convictions.

It was one of those times for Nicodemus. He was a member of the august Sanhedrin, the highest religious court for the Jews of the time. The Sanhedrin had met to discuss Jesus' amazing message and His astounding miracles. The Pharisees and Sadducees were divided over what to do about the claims He was making. Many of them simply could not hear what Jesus was saying because He acted as if He was equal with God.

In the heat of the debate the crucial question was asked, "Have any of the leading Pharisees believed in Him?" Nicodemus had been a secret follower of Jesus ever since that night when he learned of the necessity of being born again. He was guided by great wisdom in the way he witnessed that day in the Sanhedrin. At this point to grandstand as Jesus' disciple would have done little good. He simply would have been condemned as was Jesus, and the Pharisees and the Sadducees would have been no closer to meeting Jesus Himself. What Nicodemus wanted was for them to have an encounter with the Master as he had. In essence his question to the leaders was, "Can you judge Him without meeting Him?" This may not sound like a flaming testimony, but under the circumstances it was a stand of sheer courage.

Today's Thought: The Lord gives us wisdom to take a stand that will lead people to a confrontation with the Lord. What we say must be guided by Him, but silent strength speaks out!

March 1 John 8:1-11

But Jesus stooped down and wrote on the ground with His finger, as though He did not hear. . . . And again He stooped down and wrote on the ground (John 8:6,8).

"Drop That Stone!"

What did Jesus write in the loose, sandy soil of the ground? There have been many theories through the years. What He wrote was both for His reflection and for the crowd of accusers of the woman apprehended in the act of adultery. And what He said to them was directly related to what He wrote in the sand. With divine authority Jesus said, "He who is without sin among you, let him throw a stone at her first."

I think Jesus wrote the Hebrew letters for Yahweh in the sand. The name of God that emphasizes His grace and love; the same name of God Moses was told to use when the people asked, "Who sent you?"; the God who had given the commandments; and the God present in His Word, Christ, the "I Am," who had come to fulfill the commandments. Christ had the right to say that the one who had no sin should cast the first stone. He knew the scribes and Pharisees were trying to trap Him.

We can hear the thud, thud of the execution stones as one by one the woman's accusers dropped them, having to admit that they were not without sin. And when they had all left, and Jesus was alone with the woman, He asked her where her accusers were: "Has no one condemned you?" "No one, Lord," she said.

Then with the same divine authority, Jesus said, "Neither do I condemn you; go and sin no more." The Lord had maintained the commandment and had fulfilled it by forgiving one who had broken it.

Christ's judgment and forgiveness is all that matters. Others may criticize and condemn us, but taking it all to Him is the only way to face it, confess it, and let Him erase it. And He alone can give us the silent strength to go and sin no more. Especially if you would have been one of the accusers! Is there still a stone in your hand? Face it, confess it, let Christ remove it!

Today's Thought: Drop that stone!

I am the light of the world. He who follows Me shall not walk in darkness, but have the light of life (John 8:12).

The Light of Life

To commemorate the guidance of God there was a ceremony in the Feast of Tabernacles called the Illumination of the Temple. Four great candelabra stood in the center of the court. At the dramatic moment, these were set ablaze as a memorial to the light God had been to His people.

Allow an awesome chill of excitement to run up and down your spine as you watch Jesus walk to the center of the court and stand in the midst of the four candelabra. He speaks, and His voice rings like thunder: "I am the light of the world! He who follows Me shall not walk in darkness, but have the light of life."

Nothing could have startled and shocked the people more. It was as if He said, "God's presence was a pillar of fire for Moses and our forefathers. Now the pillar of presence is here in person. I am, *ego eimi*! Yahweh is here to be the light of life. Come, follow Me, and you will be able to walk in the light forever!"

Jesus could not have made a more astonishing claim. The word *light* was directly synonymous with God Himself. The psalmist asserted, "The Lord is my light and my salvation" (Psalm 27:1). Isaiah prophesied, "The Lord will be to you an everlasting light" (Isaiah 60:19). Micah's confession of trust was, "When I sit in darkness, the Lord will be a light to me" (Micah 7:8).

In claiming to be the light of the world, Jesus clearly declared Himself as the Messiah. There could be no question about His self-identification after that! Nor can there be for us. Jesus strides into our midnight hours with the same awesome claim: "I am the Light of the world, your life. Follow me!" Discovering our direction, discerning the Lord's will, and making our decisions all begin with living and walking in His light.

Today's Thought: Ask to be filled with the light of Christ's mind, walk in the light of Christ's guidance, live in the light of Christ's purpose and relate to others in the light of Christ's love and integrity.

If you abide in My word, you are My disciples indeed. And you shall know the truth, and the truth shall make you free (John 8:31,32).

Truth that Liberates

Christ, our Liberator, stated clearly the basis of our freedom in John 8:31-36. It is His emancipation proclamation. From it we learn the vital importance of thought as the basis of feeling freedom. A careful exposition of the entire passage becomes the authoritative, biblical foundation of a "think freedom, feel freely" thesis. Jesus said, "If you abide in My word, you are My disciples indeed. And you shall know the truth, and the truth shall make you free" (John 8:31,32).

Note the progression. We are to continue to abide. *Meinete*, from *meno*, "to abide," implies consistent, continuing abiding. We are to dwell in Christ's Word and allow that Word to dwell in us. This means what Christ has said is to be the basis of all that we think about God, life, ourselves, people, the future, death, and eternal security.

Abiding in Christ's words fills us with His truth. The word "truth" here as He uses it means "absolute reality." His clear, messianic assertion is the basis of our convictions. "I am the truth," He said with divine authority. He is "God with us," revealing the true nature of God and humankind. What He said, did, and proclaimed must become the objective standard of our beliefs, convictions, attitudes, and reactions. Bringing all thought captive to Him who is sublime truth is the source of liberated emotions. More on that tomorrow.

Today's Thought: Make a list of any area in your life where you do not feel free. Now, as you abide in Christ and His Spirit abides in you, ask Him to guide you in writing out how you are to think about each of these areas in the light of the truth He has given in His promises. Be specific. Then act and feel free.

Therefore if the Son makes you free, you shall be free indeed (John 8:36).

Free Indeed

Jesus used the idea of knowing truth in the Hebrew understanding of the Hebrew verb "to know." This was very different from the Greek idea of knowing. The Greeks thought of knowledge in terms of ideas, theories, and philosophical verities. The Hebrew meaning of knowledge went much deeper. To know something required the total involvement of the entire person. In fact, "to know" was used to describe the complete union of man and a woman in marriage—oneness of mind, heart, will, and body. This is the deeper sense in which we must consider how knowing the truth involves the thinking brain and its powers of memory, imagination, and will. Such knowing calls into action the whole nervous system, our emotions, and our physical bodies. The truth of our liberation through Christ's life, death, resurrection, and indwelling power becomes the unifying factor of our total existence.

How can this happen? It happens only as we experience the inseparable relationship between Jesus' promises: "The truth shall set you free" and "If the Son makes you free, you shall be free indeed." The truth that sets us free is Christ Himself. We cannot discover true freedom at any independent distance from Him. Dean W. R. Inge was right, "Christianity promises to make men free; it never promises to make them independent." It is in an open, honest, intimate relationship with the Truth Himself that we are set free.

Today's Thought: What distorted ideas of life keep people from being free? Am I less than the free person Christ wants me to be because of any of these debilitating ideas?

March 5 John 8:53-59

Jesus said to them "Most assuredly, I say to you, before Abraham was, I AM" (John 8:58).

Fresh Experiences

There's a great difference between the Lord of our experience and our experience of the Lord. Sometimes we become so attached to our previous experiences of Him that we miss what He is seeking to do today.

We all know people who can tell us how they became Christians or how the Lord intervened in some time of great need in the distant past. We long to ask, "What new discovery of the Lord's grace and goodness have you experienced today, yesterday, this week?" We lose our freedom in the Lord when we become proud of our past encounters with Him.

This was the problem of the leaders of Israel. When Jesus offered to set them free they touted their false confidence in their heritage as Abraham's children. So Jesus met them on their own terms. If they wanted to emulate Abraham they would have to express the patriarch's faith in God and his viable trust that made him open and responsive to God. Abraham was a friend of God, but that friendship was kept fresh with daily experiences of God. " 'Abraham believed God and it was accounted to him for righteousness.' And he was called a friend of God" (James 2:23).

Christ made the staggering assertion, "Before Abraham was, I AM." There was never a time when the Son was not. He is the timeless One who existed with the Father when Abraham was called. This was a supreme claim to Deity. Christ had authority to reveal to them their spiritual bondage to the past and set them free to experience the adventuresome faith He had engendered in Abraham of old. But they were locked into a worship of tradition and were missing the wondrous gift of new life being offered in Him in that moment.

Today's Thought: Christ has the authority to set us free of false pride over our previous experiences of His grace and give us fresh experiences of His power today. Let go of the past; today the Lord will do wondrous things!

Neither this man nor his parents sinned, but that the works of God should be revealed in him. I must work the works of Him who sent me while it is day; the night is coming when no one can work. As long as I am in the world, I am the light of the world (John 9:3-5).

The Real Issue

Is sickness caused by sin? Yes and no. Yes, sometimes we bring sickness on ourselves. And yes, unconfessed sin can debilitate healing. But, no, God does not send sickness to punish us. He may use a time of illness to bring us closer to Him, but He did not send it as retribution for sin.

How, then, can we deal with today's verses? The way the Greek is punctuated in modern versions creates the impression that the man was born blind so he could be the prop for a messianic miracle. But remember the original Greek had no punctuation marks. That was up to the translators of the text into English. G. Campbell Morgan and many others suggest the following punctuation: "Neither this man nor his parents sinned. But that the works of God should be revealed in him, I must work the works of Him who sent me while it is day."

The issue for the blind man was not who sinned but that Christ the Healer was present and could heal him. This is disarming for people today who like to define the causes of their own or others' difficulties. "What did I do to deserve this?" we ask. Or we say, "There must be a deeper cause of that person's sickness or difficulty. He probably got what he had coming." We add guilt to the suffering of the illness.

Christ asks none of these questions. He faces the reality of our need and has both compassion and the power to heal. Today, we can call on Christ for healing and pray for others' healing because we know He loves us and is ready and willing to heal.

Today's Thought: My primary calling is to put people in touch with Christ the Healer.

March 7 John 9:8-41

One thing I know: that though I was blind, now I see (John 9:25).

Twice for the Blind Man; Every Day for Us

The blind man received two healings. One of his physical eyes, the second of the eyes of his heart. When he was questioned by the Pharisees he brought forth the best witness he could in defense of Jesus for healing him on the Sabbath. The Pharisees charged, "Give God the glory! We know that this Man [Jesus] is a sinner." The blind man couldn't accept that: "Whether He is a sinner or not I do not know. One thing I know: that though I was blind, now I see."

Jesus wanted to be sure the healed man could say the same thing about the blindness of his heart. The Lord knew that the healing of the man's eyes was only the beginning of the healing he needed.

Within the hearing of the Pharisees, Jesus asked the healed man the same question the leaders needed to answer, "Do you believe in the Son of God?" The man asked life's most crucial question, "Who is He, Lord, that I may believe in Him?" Jesus now exercises His healing of the man's heart eyes. "You have both seen Him and it is He who is talking with you." The twice-healed man, seeing with both his physical eyes and the eyes of his heart said, "Lord, I believe!"

John Newton's hymn "Amazing Grace" expresses the wondrous experience of how Christ changed him from a spiritually blind and morally lost slave trader to a new man. "I once was lost but now I'm found; was blind but now I see." This is our theme song for every day. Christ heals the problem we bring Him and then heals our hearts with the gift of faith in Him. And every day of our lives He heals whatever blinds us to His truth or will for us.

Today's Thought: When I end this day, for what new healing of the eyes of my heart will I be able to sing, "I once was blind but now I see"?

I have come that they may have life, and that they may have it more abundantly (John 10:10).

Abundant Living

Jesus the Good Shepherd assures us of three crucial gifts—protection, provision, and possession.

When Jesus says that He is the door of the sheep, He has in mind the vivid image of a sheepfold with the sheep safely gathered in for the night. The entrance way had no actual door that could be closed and locked. The shepherd himself would stretch out in the entrance and guard the passageway with his own body. An invading wolf or poacher would have to deal with the shepherd who had laid down his life for the sheep. Christ protects us while we sleep and while we are awake.

Jesus identifies Himself also with the shepherd's knowledge of where to graze his sheep. He knows the danger places and the fields that have nocuous weeds harmful to the sheep. And he's always planning ahead to the next day's grazing. When a sheep nibbles its way from the flock, a good shepherd risks his life to bring it back. Jesus provides.

And our Lord knows His sheep. Like a caring shepherd He values each one. And the sheep know Him and the sound of His call. I remember vividly an experience I had in Palestine. My hiking took me to a lofty perch where I looked down on a valley filled with milling sheep and several shepherds. As the sun began to set the shepherds called out to their own flocks and the sheep separated and followed their own shepherd! Amazing. Christ knows you and me by name. We belong to Him and we know we are His possession for now and eternity. Jesus' assertion that He came to give us abundant life is in the context of His magnificent metaphors of the Good Shepherd. Abundant living is life with *the* Shepherd.

Today's Thought: I will claim the three "p's" of power today: protection, provision, possession.

Is it not written in your law, "I said, 'You are gods?' " If he called them gods, to whom the word of God came (and the Scripture cannot be broken), do you say of Him whom the Father sanctified and sent into the world, "You are blaspheming," because I said, "I am the Son of God"? (John 10:34-36).

Christ Confidence

Christ constantly gives us His esteem so we have enough ego strength to commit ourselves to Him. He knows that insecurity usually takes one of two forms: pride or defeatism. He must get through to us every day with a reaffirmation of our value as persons so we can have courage to trust Him.

The arrogant pride of the leaders of Israel who opposed Jesus was rooted in a profound insecurity. At that time, Israel was an insignificant occupied nation under the dominance of Rome. Surely this was the reason the leaders put such an emphasis on the past and in their traditions. That's all they had left! Worship became an empty ritualism that did not provide them God-inspired esteem to produce humility and openness to His grace and mercy. The leaders had lost the awesome reverence of being sons of God.

This explains why they condemned Jesus for saying He was the Son of God. Jesus' response was magnificent. He quoted Psalm 82:6, "I said, 'You are gods, and all of you are children of the Most High.'" The word for "gods" in the psalm was *elohim*, "judges, rulers, leaders." Psalm 8:5 uses the same word for angels, "For You have made him a little lower than the angels." Because the leaders depreciated their own calling, they denied Jesus His. They could not be up for His coming as Messiah because they were down on themselves.

The same thing happens to us. That's why knowing how much we mean to Christ makes us open and flexible to what He has planned for us.

Today's Thought: We have been elected to be daughters and sons of God. We are loved. This makes us secure so we don't have to resort to pride.

Then Thomas, who is called Didymus, said to his fellow disciples, "Let us also go, that we may die with Him" (John 11:16).

Christ Has a Place for Realists

History has called him Doubting Thomas. I'd much rather call him Realistic Thomas or, even better, Courageous Thomas.

Thomas was one of those people who saw things as they were. He didn't dress up reality in the costume of sentimentality. Nor did he perform as an emotional dreamer who denied the facts. He was a straightforward man of integrity and honesty. He never talked out of both sides of his mouth; when he had something to say, he said it with directness.

Didymus saw the issue of Jesus going to Bethany in response to the sad news from Mary and Martha that their brother Lazarus was dead. He knew if the Master went back into Judea the leaders of Israel would surely arrange some scheme for His demise. The other disciples tried to warn Jesus about going to Bethany, only two miles away from Jerusalem. Not Thomas. He waited for Jesus to make His decision. And when He did, he said, "All right, if He's going, let us go with Him that we may die with Him."

The next time Thomas is referred to in John's gospel is in connection with the resurrection. He had not been able to help Jesus during the trial and crucifixion. Thomas' own sense of failure kept him from the fellowship of the other disciples. When the disciples convinced him to come back, the risen Lord appeared just for Thomas.

Jesus needs realistic disciples. There may be a bit of the Thomas in you. You like to see things as they are. Christ needs you. He knows that when you really see things as He can make them, He'll have your unswerving commitment.

Today's Thought: When the Thomases of the world become Christ-centered, Christ-filled, and Christ-guided, they become disciples of the long pull.

Do you believe this? (John 11:26).

Cooperating in a Miracle

It's fascinating to see how Christ involved people in His greatest miracle. When He raised Lazarus from the dead He drew people in to take part at every stage. Many of those there at Bethany were part of His secret underground fellowship of disciples. They would become participants in the church after Pentecost. Jesus wanted people who knew how to cooperate.

The Lord began with Martha. She had to believe in more than a resurrection at the last day; she needed to know that in Christ was resurrection power. To engender her faith in Him, Christ gave another of His hope-instilling "I am" assertions. With the authority of Yahweh He said, "I am the resurrection and the life. He who believes in Me, though he may die, he shall live. And whoever lives and believes in Me shall never die. Do you believe this?" The Lord knew his friend Martha had to know that in Him was the power of God to do what might seem impossible. She would either be a channel of faith or a detriment.

The same question really was asked in another way of those whom Christ asked to roll the stone away. They, too, had to cooperate by following the Lord's command and not by saying, "Why, this is absurd!"

And once Lazarus was raised by Christ, He commanded that the people unbind his grave wrappings and set him free. Christ gets people out of the tombs of worry, doubt, and fear but needs us to help them claim the miracle. By helping to unwrap Lazarus, the people knew the miracle was real and not an illusion. They became "anything's possible now" believers.

Today's Thought: We are all living on the edge of some great thing we need Christ to do in our lives. He wants to know if we believe it can happen. "Do you believe that I am able?" His silent strength is given to those who say, "Yes."

Caiaphas, being high priest that year, said to them, "You know nothing at all, nor do you consider that it is expedient for us that one man should die for the people, and not that the whole nation should perish" (John 11:49,50).

An Expedient Equivocation

Caiaphas was a manipulator. He used his position of religious power to oppose God's power. As high priest he had very special privileges and responsibilities. It was believed that when the high priest prayed for the nation, God spoke through him. Caiaphas had not prayed for guidance about Jesus. His direction to the Sanhedrin was based on selfish concerns.

The Sanhedrin was made up of leaders of the Pharisees whose concern was the meticulous application of the details of the law, and the Sadducees, who were a political group of wealthy aristocrats who owned land. The priests were Sadducees and Caiaphas was their leader. He had succeeded his father-in-law, Annas, and served from AD 18 to AD 36. Along with his fellow Sadducees, Caiaphas was angry about the "Jesus problem." It was obvious that, after the raising of Lazarus, Jesus was becoming the popular leader of a very large movement. It would not be long before it would be disruptive and would cause a disturbance with Rome. The Romans would interpret Jesus' movement as insurrection. Peace with Rome had to be kept at any price, or the Sadducees would lose their land and wealth.

So exercising his authority as prophet and pretending he was speaking for God, Caiaphas said that it was better for one man to die than for the whole nation to perish. He did not realize the truth he had spoken. Indeed, Jesus would die for not only the nation, but for the sins of the whole world. Caiaphas wanted to save his own neck. Jesus would save the world through the death warrant Caiaphas issued that day. And because He's our Savior, we don't have to manipulate, but are called to motivate with love.

Today's Thought: I will not use God's authority to get my own way by saying, "I prayed about it."

March 13 John 12:1-11

Then Mary took a pound of very costly oil of spikenard, anointed the feet of Jesus, and wiped His feet with her hair. And the house was filled with the fragrance of the oil (John 12:3).

Broken Open and Poured Out

After a month in seclusion, Jesus came to stay with His beloved friends Lazarus, Mary, and Martha. It was six days before the Passover, and Jesus knew the time for His death had come. Jesus spent Saturday in the company of His disciples and trusted friends. We sense that they talked of all that had happened. Lazarus, the living miracle, must have entered in with sheer joy.

But grief was mingled with Mary's joy. She knew what was ahead for Jesus. The others had not been listening, but she had and knew that He would die in Jerusalem. Suddenly she could not contain herself. She had to do something to express her love and gratitude for her friend, teacher, and Lord. She leaped to her feet, went to her room and grasped a cruse filled with spikenard oil, and returned to where Jesus was seated. With abandoned adoration she broke open the cruse of precious oil and anointed Jesus' feet and wiped His feet with her hair. The fragrance of the nard oil filled the room. Mary anointed her Lord for His death.

Judas didn't like that at all. He made a pious statement about the cost of Mary's extravagant expression. He estimated the cost of the cruse at 300 denarii, a day laborer's wage for a year. "That should have been given to the poor!" he protested with fulsome magnanimity. Judas' outburst was an expression of guilt. The plot to betray Jesus was already forming in his mind. Jesus knew Mary had done a lovely thing. Really she had broken open more than the cruse; she had broken open and poured out her heart. Jesus knew that anyone who did that would also follow His command to care for the poor.

Today's Thought: True prayer is to break open our hearts and pour them out in love and adoration to our Lord. Caring for the spiritually and physically poor comes naturally after that.

Hosanna! Blessed is He who comes in the name of the Lord! (John 12:13).

Help Is Only a Hosanna Away

Today, as we look at John's account of the Triumphal Entry, I want to focus on that splendid word "hosanna." It's a word for every day of our lives. "Hosanna" expresses adoration and supplication. At the same time it praises God for His help and asks for help. "Hosanna" is a transliteration of the Hebrew word meaning "Save now!" This admonition appears prominently in Psalm 118, a processional psalm (note verse 25). During the Triumphal Entry, the pilgrims to the Passover joined Jesus' followers in praising Him. He is hailed as the long-awaited Messiah.

The word "hosanna" could well be the watchword of those who seek to be open to the silent strength of our Lord. It is our cry for help. I think of how often I've had to cry out, "Help me!"—almost every day, often every hour. And I find I'm in good company. The people I have admired most today and in history have had that plea on their lips.

We say our hosannas with a powerful perspective. The Lord answered the hosannas of the procession into Jerusalem to a greater extent than they expected: the cross for the atonement of the world, an empty tomb and a living Lord to fill our emptiness. Now we say, "Help, Lord!" And we know lasting help is on the way!

Today's Thought: Hosanna! Help, Lord! And His help is only a hosanna away.

March 15 — John 12:20-26

Unless a grain of wheat falls into the ground and dies, it remains alone (John 12:24).

The Blessing of Brokenness

There is a three-step process that takes place when we are broken by what we've done or by our impotence in life's problems and perplexities. First, confession of our failure or our need opens us to the Lord's presence and power. Second, we cry out for the Holy Spirit to fill our emptiness or inadequacy. Third, we discover the secret that brokenness—total willingness—provides the qualification for a fresh filling of the Holy Spirit. The difficulties through which we pass in this process become occasions of blessing. Our brokenness becomes the threshold of growth in a Spirit-filled life and greater freedom.

Jesus explained the secret of this in John 12:24,25: "Most assuredly, I say to you, unless a grain of wheat falls into the ground and dies, it remains alone; but if it dies, it produces much grain. He who loves his life will lose it, and he who hates his life in this world will keep it for eternal life." A grain of wheat has a hard shell protecting the wheat germ. The germ cannot grow until the shell is broken open. This happens when the grain is put into the earth. The moisture and warmth of the earth softens it, cracks it open, and the germ begins to grow. The result: the fruit of the strong stalk of wheat that grows and ripens until it is ready for the harvest.

This parabolic truth shows us how we are broken open and filled by the Spirit. At conversion to Christ, His Spirit enters us. But His abiding presence cannot grow until the shell of our preconceptions, values, and personality structure is broken open. This explains why so many Christians remain immature and do not realize the freedom of the Spirit.

Today's Thought: God loves us so much that He allows brokenness to set us free.

If anyone serves Me, let him follow Me (John 12:26).

Above All Else

Jesus called for absolute obedience. After telling the parable of the grain of wheat falling to the ground, He made an ultimate claim on us. At first it seems severe: "He who loves his life will lose it, and he who hates his life in this world will keep it for eternal life" (John 12:25). What does this mean for our growing experience of freedom? A great deal. Jesus was not calling for self-condemnation as a virtue of discipleship. The Greek word "hate" used to capture the Lord's meaning is *mison*, from *miseo*. W. E. Vine states that the word is often used to express "relative preference for one thing over another, by way of expressing either aversion from, or disregard for, the claims of one person or thing relatively to those of another, as in Matthew 6:24, and Luke 16:13, as to the impossibility of serving two masters, Luke 14:26 as to the claims of parents relatively to those of Christ; John 12:25 of disregard for one's life relatively to the claims of Christ."

The progressive breaking of the shell of willful self-control takes place as we die to our own will, plans, priorities, and goals, and accept in their place Christ, His indwelling Spirit, and His direction for our lives. This surrender and relinquishment is what brokenness that builds is all about.

And the reward? More than we dare expect or imagine. Press on to what follows Christ's call to obedience. In John 12:26 He says, "If anyone serves Me, let him follow Me; and where I am, there My servant will be also. If anyone serves Me, him My Father will honor." The promise is that we will know sublime companionship with Christ. The "honor" we will receive is to be filled with His Spirit.

Today's Thought: Welcome to the only honor roll that has lasting and ultimate meaning!

March 17 John 12:27-34

And I, if I am lifted up from the earth, will draw all peoples to Myself (John 12:32).

The Magnetic Christ

Jesus' promise focuses our attention on the magnetism of the cross. His promise was given at the conclusion of Jesus' teaching in response to the desire of certain Greeks who came to Philip asking, "Sir, we wish to see Jesus." Philip told Andrew, and in turn both told Jesus. The Master's response seems strangely inhospitable to the affirmation of the Greeks who wanted an audience with Him. Why not see them and influence the kingdoms of the world? But Jesus remembered Satan's temptation of "the kingdoms of the world and all their glory." Luke tells us, "Now when the devil had ended every temptation, he departed from Him until an opportune time" (Luke 4:13). That time had come again. The cross was before the Master, and the beguiling request of the Greeks was a tempting distraction. He would reach the Greeks, but as the crucified, risen Savior. He held firm to His calling. "And I, when I am lifted up from the earth [crucified], will draw all peoples to Myself." Greece, Rome, and the farthest reaches of civilization would learn of His magnetic power before the first century ended.

Our crucified Lord has great, impelling, lifting power. He draws us out of the quagmire of sin, gives us healing love, and sets us moving into the future with indomitable courage. And then, through Christ's cross, we are called to the way of the cross as the secret of triumphant living (Romans 6). We too are to take up the cross and follow Christ.

I overheard a woman in an ecclesiastical supply store ask for a cross. After she was shown the wide variety of liturgical crosses she said, "Oh no, I just want an everyday kind of cross." The woman's request becomes a motto for us—not an ordinary cross but Christ's cross for every day.

Today's Thought: The way of the cross is the only way, every day.

But although He had done so many signs before them, they did not believe in Him (John 12:37).

Before It's Too Late

If you're like most people, you trip over the words in verse 40 that John quotes from Isaiah 6:9,10. Would God blind people's eyes so they can't see? Would He harden their hearts so they could not understand? These words say as much about human nature as they do about God's judgment. We can resist so long that we get to a place where we can't respond. "No!" to God's overtures of love and guidance becomes a settled attitude. God created us with a free will, and that will can become hardened. It isn't that God deliberately steps in to blind our spiritual eyes or harden our hearts. We do it to ourselves.

John quotes these words from Isaiah to try to explain the rejection of the leaders of Israel of Christ. They even went so far as to say He was possessed by Satan, thus totally writing off what He said and the miracles He performed. Jesus called this the unforgivable sin. The people did not believe there was anything to confess, so there was nothing to forgive. Their hearts were hardened and their eyes were blinded by habitual patterns of rejecting the rule of God in their lives.

What's most alarming about John's account of how people reacted to Jesus in that last week are the people who believed in Christ but would not confess Him because of fear. They loved the praise of people more than God.

What does this mean for how we are to live today? Think of each day as a miniature of your whole life. Make this a day of willing obedience to the Lord. Say "yes" to His guidance and His love and forgiveness. Do that, and you'll never have to worry about the hardening of your spiritual heart.

Today's Thought: I will to be willing!

Jesus, knowing that the Father had given all things into His hands, and that He had come from God and was going to God, rose from supper and laid aside His garments, took a towel and girded Himself. After that, He poured water into a basin and began to wash the disciples' feet (John 13:3-5).

The Missing Servant

The disciples were alarmed when they arrived at the upper room where they were to celebrate the Passover with the Master. Someone was missing! They looked at one another with embarrassed glances. How could their host who had granted the use of the room there in Jerusalem have been so insensitive? There was no servant to wash their feet. Who would do it?

No wonder they were shocked when Jesus took the role of the servant and washed their feet. Peter objected. He was clever enough to know that if the Master washed his feet, he would have to wash other people's feet. Jesus became the servant to help the disciples discover that He had called them to serve the world.

Note that Jesus took the towel and basin because He knew He had come from God and was going to God. When we know we belong to God and our ultimate destiny is in Him, we can accept our calling to give ourselves away. Nothing else counts except knowing and doing what pleases Him. If our destiny and destination are settled, we can give ourselves away with abandonment. We don't need to save ourselves.

The symbols of a caring person are a towel and basin. To wash people's feet means to become their servants to help in whatever ways we can. We can experience great freedom and joy when we think of our lives, work, and relationships as opportunities to serve. Jesus said, "For I have given you an example, that you should do as I have done to you. Most assuredly, I say to you, a servant is not greater than his master; nor is he who is sent greater than he who sent him. If you know these things, happy are you if you do them" (John 13:15-17).

Today's Thought: Whom are you called to serve today?

Having received the piece of bread, he then went out immediately. And it was night (John 13:30).

And It Was Night

"And it was night." These last four words of the passage we read today describe Judas' heart as well as the time. He left the upper room and went into the night and the darkness of the betrayal of Jesus. Whatever happened to Judas, we are told that Satan entered his heart. But long before this Judas had become vulnerable.

I think Judas was an insurrectionist and a part of an active movement to overthrow Roman rule. He was zealous for Israel and wanted his people to be free of the domination of Rome. My supposition is that he saw Jesus as the potential leader of the insurrection and became His disciple because of his hopes that He would restore the kingdom to Israel. Some of the other disciples were still hoping this even after the resurrection. "Will you at this time restore the kingdom to Israel?" they asked (Acts 1:6). Along with Judas, they had a hard time accepting that Christ's kingdom was not based on political or military might.

In the week before the crucifixion, Judas got impatient. He felt that if he forced the Master's hand by precipitating an arrest, He would call down the angels and the mighty battle would begin. This would be the signal for the insurrectionists to move into action. And who would be a prominent leader? Iscariot!

Judas tried to control the uncontrollable Lord. He tried to get Jesus to fulfill his agenda. Although he betrayed the Lord for 30 pieces of silver, it wasn't the money, but a lust for power.

There's a bit of Judas in all of us. We too have our agendas for the Lord. But He won't be controlled. When we try, we betray Him in lots of little ways, and sometimes big ones. Our calling is to do things His way and on His timing.

Today's Thought: Trying to control Jesus is like trying to stop the dawn; to let Him control you is the dawn of new life!

March 21 John 13:31-35

A new commandment I give to you, that you love one another; as I have loved you, that you also love one another. By this all will know that you are My disciples, if you have love for one another (John 13:34,35).

Some Christians Aren't Easy to Love

Let's face it: Some Christians aren't easy to love. Some bug us; others frustrate us; while others differ over doctrine and church customs with us. And when it comes to issues, many want us to carry the flag for their pet cause. Add to all this the common relational problems of pride, envy, competition, and power struggles. And yet here is Jesus telling us we are to love one another as He has loved us. To make it all the more embarrassing, He tells us that the world will know whether or not we are His disciples if we exemplify His deep quality of love. His love is initiative, forgiving, caring.

Unless I miss my guess, you can name a few Christians whom you find it difficult to love quicker than I can say, "Lord, it's impossible!" So what do we do? I think the Lord knew how difficult it would be for His disciples to live His commandment. This is why He spent the rest of His discourse that Thursday night in the upper room giving the secret of how His followers would be able to do the impossible of loving one another. If it came naturally, He wouldn't have had to go to the cross to create new creatures who would be transformed and filled with His Spirit. Living on this side of Calvary and Pentecost, we realize that Christ's new commandment is impossible unless He changes our human nature and gives us the power to love. Again, think of those few people who are difficult to love, and today ask the Lord for the miracle of being able to love them. This is not too much to ask, but the task is too big to handle unless He answers.

Today's Thought: Admit the impossible and the Lord of the impossible will make it happen! Ask Him for the power and do something to express His love to those people He has put on your agenda.

Let not your heart be troubled. . . . I go to prepare a place for you. . . . I am the way (John 14:1,2,6).

When Your Heart Is Troubled

We've all had those times when problems in our lives have full impact on our inner hearts. Our hearts are troubled. We turn to Christ for help. He says to us what He said to His disciples in the upper room: "Let not your heart be troubled."

The disciples' hearts were troubled. The Greek word for "troubled" means "to be tossed to and fro"—like restless waves under the impact of a blast of wind. Jesus' assuring word is ultimately reliable: "Believe in God, believe also in Me." How does this help a troubled heart? We have a place to go with our troubled hearts—the heart of God.

The Father's house is the Father's heart. It's expansive and inclusive. When Jesus said it has many rooms or mansions, He meant that it is our true abiding place. Here the Greek word is *monai*, meaning "abiding places"—not different ones but one big enough to include all who come home to the Father through Him. And our abiding place is open now—not just at our physical death.

Jesus has prepared the place in God's heart for us. He did that on Calvary. This is what He meant when He said, "I go to prepare a place for you." It's a place of reconciliation, forgiveness, and acceptance. In that light we can appreciate Jesus' "I am" promise: "I am the way." He is the way to the heart of God paved through the sacrifice of Calvary. He takes us by the hand and shows us the way home. Until we are "at home" with the Lord in the days of our lives here and now, we will be tossed to and fro. It's inevitable; we were created to abide in His heart of love. And when we do, we are welcomed home as if we never left. An intimate communion awaits us where we can unburden all our troubles and receive strength.

Today's Thought: There's only one way to the heart of God, the way He ordained—through Jesus Christ, the Way. Let Him lead you home—now!

I am . . . the truth (John 14:6).

Truth for the Troubled

Think of all the things from which Jesus Christ, the truth, has set us free. We are free of guilt, condemning consciences, haunting memories, the insecurity of inadequacy, the frustration of self-negation, the dread of the future. Worry over death is past. We are assured of abundant life now and eternal life forever. There is nothing that can happen to or around us that Christ cannot handle. He towers over history. He is the ultimate point of reference about reality.

This is magnificently focused in one of my favorite verses from Ephesians: "Having made known to us the mystery of His will, according to His good pleasure which He purposed in Himself, that in the dispensation of the fullness of the times He might gather together in one all things in Christ, both which are in heaven and which are on earth—in Him" (Ephesians 1:9,10). Christ is the image and illumination of eternal truth. He is God's word about Himself, the liberating Word of truth that sets us free.

Christ's truth is intellectual, emotional, and relational: It reorients our thinking, becomes the basis of sorting out our feelings, and gives us a new way of relating to people with forgiveness and unqualified love. This can only happen if we come to Christ as the ultimate truth.

For something to be called the truth, it must be consistent with reality in every way. It must cover all contingencies and be universally applicable. Jesus Christ is the truth because He is reality; His revelation of God is consistent with God's essential nature, and His message is God's way for us to live with Him and with one another. There is nothing left out, no question unanswered, no eventuality not covered by what He was, said, and did.

Today's Thought: Knowing that Jesus is truth is very different from experiencing Him as truth. William Temple, the former archbishop of York and of Canterbury, said, "The ultimate truth is not a system of propositions grasped by perfect intelligence but a Personal Being apprehended by love."

I am . . . the life (John 14:6).

Our Life

In Trinity Church, Boston, there is a remarkable statue of Phillips Brooks by Saint-Gaudens. The spiritual giant stands at a pulpit with an open Bible. Behind him stands Jesus with His hand on the preacher's shoulder. The reason for Brooks' greatness is preserved for posterity. In a letter to a friend he wrote, "All experience comes to be but more and more the pressure of Christ's life upon ours. I cannot tell how personal this grows to me. He is here. He knows me and I know Him. It is no figure of speech; it is the realest thing in the world." No wonder that one of Brooks' biographers says, "He conversed with Christ as his most intimate friend. He loved his earthly friends and enjoyed their companionship, but for none of them had he such attachment as for Christ."

The last two days we have claimed Christ as the way to God and the truth about God. Today we experience the climax of His promise for times when our hearts are troubled: "I am . . . the life." Christ not only revealed how life was intended to be lived, but also offers us the strength of His own Spirit to live it to the fullest. When we are troubled we need clear direction on what to do and power to follow through. Christ provides both. He puts our troubles into perspective. Our first priority is to glorify and serve Him. Second, we ask what His love demands that we do. Then we ask for His life to surge through us as we seek to obey.

The Duke of Wellington said, "What I need is four o'clock in the morning courage." It's when we are awakened by our troubled hearts that we need Christ's life—His presence, redirection, reorientation of goals, and most of all, the assurance that when we step out to do as He has guided, His strength will sustain us. He has called us to a thrilling life of being an observer of what He is able to do with the troubles we commit to Him.

Today's Thought: When troubles awaken us, let's remember Christ never sleeps.

March 25 John 14:12-21

Most assuredly, I say to you, he who believes in Me, the works that I do he will do also; and greater works than these he will do, because I go to My Father (John 14:12).

The Greater Miracle

We are amazed at Christ's confidence in us. We are to do the works that He did. That's enough to make us wonder. But "greater works"—what did Christ mean?

He meant magnificently this: He is alive to continue His ministry through us as individuals and as the church. Start with the basics: we are to serve people, love people, forgive people. But press on. Christ has entrusted us with the power to pray for the healing of the hearts, minds, and bodies of people. Read 1 Corinthians 12. We are to claim gifts of faith, wisdom, working of miracles, and healing. These are nothing other than manifestations of Christ continuing to do through believers what He did as Jesus of Nazareth.

But what are the "greater works" we are to do? To answer this, we must ask and answer a further question. What was the one thing Christ did not do until after the atonement of the cross and the victory of the resurrection? Conversion. The transforming of people was a post-resurrection miracle. Then Christ filled His followers with His Spirit and gave them power to introduce people to Him as Savior and Lord.

This is the greater work that is the calling of every Christian. And prayer is the secret of how to do it. Jesus said, "Whatever you ask in My name, that I will do, that the Father may be glorified in the Son." We are to pray for people, pray as we share Christ with them, and pray that they will receive the gift of faith to accept Him as Savior and Lord. People who need Christ are on the top of His agenda for us. We win the right to be heard by loving, caring friendship. Then when Christ opens the way, we are privileged to share in the greatest of all miracles: helping a person live forever.

Today's Thought: People who say they have no opportunities to share what Christ means to them simply have not prayed.

Peace I leave with you, My peace I give to you; not as the world gives do I give to you. Let not your heart be troubled, neither let it be afraid (John 14:27).

Last Will and Testament

There's a wonderful story about a family gathering together in a lawyer's office to hear the reading of the will of a wealthy grandfather. Each person leans forward waiting to hear his own name and the amount of money he already has spent a thousand times over in his mind. The lawyer clears his voice and reads, "Being of sound mind, I spent it all!"

Christ's last will was very different. It might read like this: "Being of sound mind, I'm going to the cross to give you peace. It's a different quality of peace than you offer to each other in the greeting 'Shalom,' or a peace like the world people are looking for through political and military might. The peace I'm leaving you will be a peace you will have because I will take up residence in your hearts. You'll never be alone."

Christ had to distinguish His peace from the peace of the world. Anything but peace hovered just outside the upper room. In a few hours Jesus' disciples would go through the anguish of seeing Him die. Their lives would never know the absence of conflict, but they would know His presence. There would be the surging waves of opposition and hostility. And yet, Christ's people would be serene. A profound inner peace is the sure sign that we have received Christ's silent strength. There can be no peace in us unless we know that we'll have what it takes. And Christ will never let us down. We'll talk often of peace throughout this book. But for now, accept the gift for today.

Today's Thought: The will was read today. You were named as a beloved benefactor. The Savior of the world willed you the gift of peace. Being of sound mind, spend it—the supply is unlimited.

March 27 John 15:1-6

I am the vine, you are the branches. He who abides in Me, and I in him, bears much fruit; for without Me you can do nothing (John 15:5).

The Power Connection

Jesus' admonition to love is impossible without a constant flow of His Spirit into us. We cannot give away what we have not received.

The Lord gave us the secret in the powerful image of the vine and the branches. A branch separated from the vine is cut off from the life-giving sap. The Lord's warning is, "Without Me you can do nothing." We cannot love without His love moving from the vine into the branches.

The power connection is absolutely necessary. We are not called to attempt to love for His glory. Rather, we are to develop a moment-by-moment dependence upon His Spirit flowing into us and through us to people. Root and fruit are inseparably related.

What we need is a caring, sharing love. Love chooses to become involved. We need interpretation and inspiration. Someone who loves us will lift the burden by telling us what he or she discovered in suffering and what was learned in the tight places. We do not need glib phrases but truth tempered in the fires of experience.

Who in our circle of influence are suffering? Love bids us to go to them. Everything we have gone through is equipment for identifying love. Then we can share the strength the Lord provides in suffering.

Today's Thought: "I am to become a Christ to my neighbor and be for him what Christ is for me" —Martin Luther.

If you abide in Me, and My words abide in you, you will ask what you desire, and it shall be done for you (John 15:7).

"My" Shepherd

Martin Luther said that true Christianity consists in personal pronouns. There's a lovely story of a little girl who was fast asleep. When her mother and father checked in on her before they retired, they noticed a serene look on her sleeping face. They also saw that she had one hand clutched around the forefinger of her other hand. At breakfast they asked her why she fell asleep with her forefinger held so tightly. "Well," she responded, "I repeat the twenty-third Psalm before I go to sleep, like you have taught me. I keep saying it over and over again: 'The Lord is my Shepherd.' That's five words. I start counting with my little finger, and when I reach the word 'my,' I'm at my forefinger. I like 'my' best of all! He is *my* shepherd!"

I hope I never become so sophisticated that when I need clarity about the will of God and guidance for my daily decisions, I am unwilling to grasp my forefinger in personal, childlike assurance! Jesus is *my* Shepherd—He leads me through each step of the abundant, eternal life that He came to provide.

In this context, you and I can claim the promises Christ has made about prayer as the channel through which our wills become attuned to His. "If you abide in Me, and My words abide in you, you will ask what you desire, and it shall be done for you" (John 15:7). We so often leap to the second part of that promise before we meet the qualifying offer of the first part. Jesus and His words must abide in us before we can know what or how to ask. The two-part blessing contains His words, His message available to us to study in the Gospels, and His abiding presence which selects the particular truths we need in any situation and helps us clarify for what we should ask.

Today's Thought: Abiding in Christ and allowing Him to abide in us is the secret for guidance.

You did not choose Me, but I chose you and appointed you that you should go and bear much fruit, and that your fruit should remain, that whatever you ask the Father in My name He may give you (John 15:16).

Sharing Without Strain

J. Hudson Taylor, the great missionary hero and founder of the China Inland Mission, found the secret of sharing without strain. At one point in his life he was discouraged and depleted. He struggled to get more of Christ in his life. He prayed, agonized, fasted, made resolutions, read the Bible; but the serenity, vitality, and power he sought eluded him.

One day he received a letter from a caring friend. The last paragraph was an arrow of truth from God for Taylor: "Not striving to have faith," it read, "or to increase our faith, but looking to the Faithful One seems to be all we need. An abiding in the loved One entirely, from time and eternity." Hudson Taylor was amazed at his own blindness. "I'll strive no more," he said. "It was all a mistake to try to get the fullness out of Christ. He has promised to abide in me. I am part of Him. Each one of us is a limb of His body, a branch of His vine."

After that day, people noticed a change in Hudson Taylor. He labored, prayed, and disciplined himself harder than ever, but not with a sense of strain and agony. He now radiated a magnetism of love and joy, for he was no longer a man who struggled, but a man who was being used. The Lord wants the same for all of us.

Today's Thought: "Too often we attempt to work for God to the limit of our incompentency, rather than to the limit of God's omnipotency. . . . God's work done in God's way will never lack God's supplies" —J. Hudson Taylor.

Be of good cheer, I have overcome the world (John 16:33).

"Take It—It's Yours!"

I find it more difficult to have courage before a battle than during it. By "battle" I mean all the challenges, conflicts, and larger difficulties we all meet along the way. I do fairly well in the heat of the battle; it's before it that I tend to imagine more of what could go wrong than what Christ is going to make right.

Since this became a continuing problem some years ago, I worked out a saying to repeat in those anxious times of waiting: *Christ will work it out in a way that will be part of His greater plan for my life.* Sounds awfully simple, doesn't it? But without this confidence, life is simply awful, as E. Stanley Jones used to put it. That's our conviction in both our successes and setbacks when we are tempted to wonder what the Lord is allowing to happen to us or to our work for Him. Either He's in charge or He isn't. We know He is and therefore can trust that the only thing ultimately important is our relationship with Him. And this is the source of raw courage in the midst of the soul-stretching times of our lives.

Our verse for today summarizes and concludes Jesus' words to His disciples on that Thursday evening alone with them. He was honest with them—there would be tribulation. "But be of good cheer, I have overcome the world." The original words actually mean "Take courage. I have victory over the world." He said this only a few hours before the cross! For us, courage is given only by Christ, only for battles in which our faithfulness to Him and His calling is tested. He went to the cross with courage because He knew resurrection morning was coming! And today our victorious Lord doesn't work things out for the good. He works things out for the best. Courage! Take it, it's yours!

Today's Thought: We can have freedom from worry before the battle; strength in the battle; and progress toward Christ's goals as a result of the battle!

The Lord has need of it (Mark 11:3).

The Lord Has Need of It

Since we have already considered John's account of the Triumphal Entry, today let's look at it from Mark's perspective. The Triumphal Entry of Jesus into Jerusalem presents us with a paradox of power. First, Jesus was no helpless victim of what happened during the last week of His ministry. He was the producer, director, and central character in the drama. It all happened on His timing, in His way, for His greater purposes. Second, Jesus depended on the cooperative efforts of an underground network to carry out His plan.

Reading between the lines of Mark's account, we sense the atmosphere of previous planning and cooperative efforts. Palm Sunday sets before us the challenging and inspiring thought that Christ needs our help to carry out His plans. This astounding truth is underlined by one aspect of the Triumphal Entry. Jesus wanted everything He did to be in complete fulfillment of prophecy, particularly Zechariah 9:9: "Behold, your King is coming to you; He is just and having salvation, lowly and riding on a donkey, a colt, the foal of a donkey."

To accomplish this, Jesus chose to depend on a secret follower in Bethany for a colt donkey. It is obvious that it all was arranged previously. He told His disciples to go to the village, and there would be a colt tied there on which no one had sat. "Loose it and bring it to Me," Jesus said. "And if anyone says to you, 'Why are you doing this?' say, 'The Lord has need of it,' and immediately he will send it here."

The password of power for discipleship is "The Lord has need of it." All that we have and are belongs to Him. He entered Jerusalem to die on the cross so we might be set free from sin and be reconciled to God. Belonging to Him, all that we have is now at His disposal. No challenge is too great, no call too challenging.

Today's Thought: All we need to know for our service, caring, and giving is "The Lord has need of it." It's the password for discipleship.

And all Mine are Yours, and Yours are Mine, and I am glorified in them (John 17:10).

Eavesdropping on Eternity

There are few privileges of friendship as intimate as being invited to listen in on a friend's prayers. It is all the more so if those prayers include intercession for us personally and we are given the chance to hear how much our friend loves us and hopes for in our lives. We come away from the experience affirmed, encouraged, strengthened.

How would you like to be able to hear Christ pray for you? Just imagine how you would feel listening to Him talk to God about *His* vision for your life!

This was John's privilege in the upper room. He heard the Lord pray to the Father about His own ministry and the ministry He was entrusting to His disciples. If all we had was the historical record of the crucifixion and the resurrection and this prayer, we would have an abundant source of knowing who Christ is, why He came, and what we are to be in His power. Now go back and reread the prayer and put your own name in the place of the pronouns "them," "those," and "their." It is a very moving experience, especially during Holy Week. Savor every word!

The incarnation is almost finished. Christ has glorified the Father all through His ministry and now seeks to glorify Him in His death on the cross. That's how Christ viewed the crucifixion: the sublime manifestation of the glory of God that He shared with the Father.

Now the risen Christ seeks to be glorified in us. We are chosen and called to live for His glory. He longs for us to be one with the Father and experience the miracle of oneness with each other as fellow disciples. And for good reason: Christ has the world at the center of His concern. He prays for those who believe because of our oneness and our irresistible demonstration that life in Him is glorious. Now reread Christ's prayer with your church in mind.

Today's Thought: Lord, I claim what You prayed for me and the church. May it be so today.

I am He (John 18:5).

I Am He!

Christ was ready. They would not have to hunt Him down as an escaping criminal. But why the swords and spears? All the legions of heaven were available to Christ if military warfare had been God's will. I wonder if He did not smile; it was a ludicrous moment in the midst of His agony. Look at the number of soldiers sent to arrest a carpenter of Galilee! The word for "band" is *speira*, meaning 1240 calvary and 760 infantry. That's quite an expedition sent out to capture an unarmed rabbi!

When they reached the garden, Jesus stepped out from among the olive trees, defenseless and unafraid. He just had done battle with Satan and won. Knowing full well why they came and what was ahead of Him, Jesus asked, "Whom are you seeking?" (John 18:4). The answer was "Jesus of Nazareth."

Jesus' response was more than a self-identification as the man from Nazareth. With all the power of the incarnate Messiah, He thundered, "I am!" *Ego eimi* again—never spoken more forcefully than here. All the sovereignty and omnipotence of God Himself was in His voice—this was no simple declaration of human identity. It carried the unmistakable authority of the voice of God! The English translations miss the awe and wonder when *ego eimi* is translated as a gentle "I am He." Jesus' response was "Yahweh!" He answered as the One who makes things happen, the all-powerful "I am."

No wonder Judas and the soldiers drew back and fell to the ground! The original words imply that they were knocked down by the impact of His two-word reply. This was more than the determined resoluteness of a man who knew who He was because He knew what He was destined to do. This was the regal sound of a King, the Lord of all creation. It was the Word of God.

Today's Thought: The soldiers fell on the ground; we fall on our knees in adoration of Christ our Lord.

April 3

Peter answered and said to Him, ". . . I will never be made to stumble . . . even if I have to die with You I will not deny You!" (Matthew 26:33,35).

Never!

Never! It's an "almighty" word often spoken with assumed, imperious authority over ourselves or others. I hear people use this word either in proud protestation or in confession. "I would *never* do that!" they say, elevating themselves above the foibles and failures of others. And far too often I've heard people confess, "I did the one thing I promised myself I'd never do!" It's a lot easier to *say* we'll never deny our Lord than to never do it. We've all done it in big and little ways. Yesterday? Last week?

Simon Peter boldly and boastfully said that if others denied Christ, it was the one thing he would never do. But Christ understood human nature, and He knew Simon—the slippery rock on which He intended to build His church. "Will you lay down your life for My sake?" Jesus had asked. "Most assuredly, I say to you, the rooster shall not crow till you have denied Me three times." And it happened. A few hours later, Simon was asked, "Are you one of His disciples?" Three times he said what he had asserted he would never say: "I am not!" The rooster crowed long before dawn that night.

Today we deny our Lord in both what we say and do *and* in what we neglect to say and do. Our denials can be by breaking the commandments and resisting obedience to what Christ has assigned to us. What do you do when you deny the Lord and the faith? Here's a straight answer: Never use the word "never" about the Lord. Don't say, "He could never forgive this!" Rather, listen to how the Lord uses the word "never": "I will never leave you or forsake you." Everything Christ went through in His trial and crucifixion was so that we might be forgiven and have the power to declare Him rather than deny Him.

Today's Thought: Never say "never."

April 4 John 18:28–19:16

Pilate . . . was . . . afraid (John 19:8).

So Near, Yet So Far

When Jesus was turned over to Pilate, we see a very sad kind of equivocation. Pilate had embarrassing confrontations with the Jewish leaders and lost each time. He was under tremendous pressure when he tried Jesus. He lost his credibility long before Jesus was brought before him. A series of rash acts made his position with Rome very tenuous. To avoid further conflict, he allowed himself to be a participant in Caiaphas' plot. Pilate's wife had warned him to have nothing to do with the trial because of a dream she had about Jesus: "Have nothing to do with that just Man, for I have suffered many things today in a dream because of Him" (Matthew 27:19). Pilate's own instincts told him Jesus was innocent. Yet the voice of Caiaphas and the Jewish leaders pressed him into an impossible situation. When he questioned Jesus about the charge that He claimed to be a king, the Lord's reply was "You say rightly that I am a king. For this cause . . . I have come into the world, that I should bear witness to the truth. Everyone who is of the truth hears My voice" (John 18:37).

In answer to his question, Pilate got a yes and a no. Yes, Jesus was a king. No, He was not a king in Pilate's terms; His kingdom was the kingdom of God. J. B. Phillips' translation of Jesus' answer to Pilate is, "Indeed, I am!" (Mark 14:62).

Pilate is representative of those who refuse to accept the authority of Jesus because they fear the opinions and loss of approval of other people.

But we should not be too hard on Pilate. He did have the final word. He insisted on calling Jesus "King of the Jews" against their frenzied objections. As the Roman procurator, he had the final decision on what would be put on the cross above Jesus' head. Pilate wrote: "Jesus of Nazareth, the King of the Jews."

Today's Thought: Pilate, like many today, was so near yet so far—so close to becoming a believer, but so afraid.

It is finished! (John 19:30).

We Are Never Finished

Because Christ said, "It is finished!" we need not say, "I'm finished!" Christ's finished work of redemption means that we cannot be finished, defeated, or conquered by sin, fear, and anxiety. Forgiveness and deliverance from sin, reconciliation to the Father, the fulfillment of His judgment, the revelation of His grace, the manifestation of His glory—all this was accomplished. It was the end of the beginning of a new creation. And you and I are elected to receive the gift of faith to know that Christ died for us as if each of us had been the only person alive in Jerusalem that Friday. He still would have gone to the cross. Looking at it from this perspective, we are lost in wonder and praise. There is nothing that can finish us off because for each of us Christ finished our exoneration and set us free from the power of sin, Satan, and death.

Also, because Christ said, "It is finished!" in a very different way you and I are never finished. Every aspect of our personal lives, church, and society must be transformed by the power of the cross. Every vestige of pride and willfulness must be cleansed by the blood of the cross. On this Good Friday, what in your life and mine needs to be surrendered at the foot of the cross? What's still unfinished? Can we sing, "Finish then thy new creation, pure, unbounded, let us be"?

We are never finished with our calling until every person in the world has an opportunity to hear the gospel. And what of those people the Lord has put on our agenda to pour out ourselves to in affirmation, concern, and practical caring so we can communicate what the grace and forgiveness of the cross has done for us and can do for them? There's no better day than Good Friday to share with others what the cross means to us. Our work is never finished because Christ finished our redemption.

Today's Thought: Every hour is a new beginning because Christ said, "It is finished!"

April 6 1 Corinthians 15:1-11

He was buried (1 Corinthians 15:4).

Living with Half a Message

One of my favorite illustrations is of how the news of the outcome of the Battle of Waterloo was communicated to England. The message was sent by rider, by ship across the English Channel, and then by semaphore from ship to shore. The message had four words. Only the first two were communicated because a heavy fog descended suddenly. What got through was only, "W-e-l-l-i-n-g-t-o-n d-e-f-e-a-t-e-d." That's all the relay on the tower of Winchester Cathedral saw, and all he could do was pass on the sad news. England lived in disappointment for 24 hours.

Then the fog lifted and the whole message could be completed. The two missing words hidden by the fog were "t-h-e e-n-e-m-y." The whole truth was "Wellington defeated the enemy."

Between the crucifixion and the resurrection, the followers of Jesus lived with half a message. "Jesus defeated." Then on Easter morning, the other two words blazed in their hearts: "the enemy!" Jesus defeated the enemy. Death vanquished.

Often at the time of the loss of a loved one we think the enemy has won. Not so for a Christian! Or in times of difficulty we sometimes live for a time with half a message of defeat. Just wait for the fog to lift! Nothing can ultimately defeat us. We are Easter people who will live forever.

Today's Thought: The Saturday between Good Friday and Easter is a day of waiting that puts us in touch with how most of the world lives with half a message about the power of death and evil. But Easter is coming!

Then the other disciple, who came to the tomb first, went in also; and he saw and believed (John 20:8).

A *Firsthand Easter*

A clothing store in Hollywood that features used clothing worn by the stars had a sign in the window before Easter: "Get a Secondhand Hat for a Firsthand Easter!" I was so intrigued I stopped in the shop to ask the owner what he meant by a firsthand Easter. He confessed that he had just worked out a clever wording to go with secondhand hats. He was not a Christian, so I shared with him what I thought a firsthand Easter can be. It was quite a conversation about the real meaning of Easter and an opportunity to give a firsthand witness about what Christ's resurrection means to me.

John's account of the resurrection of Christ is a firsthand witness. The "other disciple" is John's way of referring to himself throughout his gospel. He was there in the upper room when Mary Magdalene burst in upon the discouraged disciples to say that Jesus was not in the tomb. We feel John's excitement as he retells how he and Peter ran to the tomb and found the empty grave clothes and believed for themselves that Christ had risen.

We all need a firsthand Easter that's more than the secondhand conviction of others or the temporary inspiration of Easter services with glorious music and the proclamation of the hope of the resurrection. An authentic Easter is one in which we meet the risen Christ personally. This requires acceptance of the cross and the forgiveness of our sins. We must pass through our own death to self with a complete surrender of our lives. Easter people are those who have had a person-to-person encounter with the living Lord. Anything less is a dull substitute.

Today's Thought: We need a firsthand heart for a firsthand Easter.

For He must reign... (1 Corinthians 15:25).

Easter in August

My most exciting Easter happened to me one August. The experience has made every day Easter for me. It was then I realized that the resurrection spells the final defeat of fear of the future.

It happened one afternoon when I was in Jerusalem. I had gone to a lonely place outside the Old City called Gordon's Garden Tomb. It is believed by many to be the authentic site of Christ's crucifixion and resurrection. My travels in Israel had brought me to the most significant places of the radical interventions of God in biblical history. I had kept this final site for last, savoring in my mind the possibility of a personal Easter in August. When I entered the garden, I climbed a long walkway to a place that looks up on a hillside. The cragged granite displays to this day an outline of the skull. Golgotha!

There I stood for what must have been an hour of refocusing in my mind's eye the excruciating suffering and pain of the cross. Then in my heart I heard the loving impact of His voice: "I did it for you, Lloyd. You are forgiven through the blood I shed here." As I walked back down into the garden below, my heart sang with gratitude—I am loved, accepted, forgiven, reconciled. Familiar hymns came to mind: "Beneath the cross of Jesus I fain would take my stand," and "There's power, power, wonder-working power in the blood of the Lamb," and "When I survey the wondrous cross." I said with Paul, "For I am determined not to know anything among you except Jesus Christ and Him crucified" (1 Corinthians 2:2).

The Lord's gentle voice sounded in my soul again: "I have allowed you to think and feel this through so that what I did here so long ago might make you more than a preacher of the resurrection—an Easter person. The same power that raised Jesus from the dead will be yours every day of your life." And in response I said out loud, "Hallelujah! Christ is risen. He is risen indeed!"

Today's Thought: Easter is every day.

Death is swallowed up in victory (1 Corinthians 15:54).

Celebrated Victory

The purpose of Easter is not to tell us we should live better lives. It is not a time for moralizing or compulsive improvement programs. Easter is the celebration of victory—Christ's and ours. So often we come to church to get insight, wisdom, and strength for our preconceived direction. We usually leave disappointed and unchanged because we want His guidance or sanction on our lives so we can be more religious. That's not Easter. The resurrection happens when people can do nothing for themselves or for God. It is when our knowledge of Jesus' life and message have driven us to cry out, "Lord, I can't do it, I can't change, I can't love, I can't forgive, I can't take it any longer!"

This is when it happens. Only then can we hear Him say, "Because I live, you shall live also!" Then we can join the magnificent procession of the Christ-encountered, Christ-liberated, Christ-healed, Christ-changed, Christ-filled people who shout the Easter refrain:

> Thanks be to God who gives us the victory
> through Jesus Christ our Lord!

Have you ever met Him? Or having met Him, have you ever felt His presence near? Or having felt His presence, have you ever experienced His resurrection lifting you up to the person He created you to be? And having experienced His resurrection, have you ever invited Him to make His postresurrection home in you? He is there for you!

Today's Thought: The contemporary Easter miracle is in your heart.

For if we have been united together in the likeness of His death, certainly we also shall be in the likeness of His resurrection (Romans 6:5).

Power of the Resurrection

The power of the resurrection is the power of personal regeneration. Resurrection spells regeneration. The two things must always be kept together: the new world and the new person. Resurrection is not just a passport to heaven, but a power to change us now. It is a present gift, not a wistful longing. Paul says he wants to know Christ and the power of his resurrection. The two are the same. To know Christ today is to come under the influence of the same power that raised Him from the dead. All life is meant to be an Eastertide full of perpetual renewal. Christ's mission is to change us and make us like Himself. What a cruel thing an example is without the power to live it. Christ is the best of all examples, but more than that, He can come within us and give us His own Spirit to fulfill the example. The result is we actually become like Him, we are able to do the things He did, and most of all, we are able to love as He loved. The resurrection is the right angle where all the disillusionment, discouragement, and disappointment with life, people, and ourselves is met with power to change us and give us a new beginning.

Today's Thought: "The resurrection means that the worst has been met and has been conquered. This puts an ultimate optimism at the center of things. No wonder the Christian in the midst of the decaying order is no pessimist. He has solid grounds for his optimism. He has got hold of unconquered and unconquerable Life!" —E. Stanley Jones.

And when He had said this, He breathed on them, and said to them, "Receive the Holy Spirit. If you forgive the sins of any, they are forgiven them; if you retain the sins of any, they are retained" (John 20:22,23).

The Power to Forgive

The disciples sat waiting in the upper room. They knew Christ was risen, but except for Mary, He had not appeared to them. Then it happened! The risen Lord came to them. He was there—alive. What a reunion it was! I imagine they began to sing, softly at first, then with gusto, "He is risen! He is risen indeed!" When the praise quieted, Christ spoke words the disciples would never forget: "As the Father has sent Me, I also send you." The room was alive with Christ's power. A mysterious quickening began in all of them. "Receive the Holy Spirit. If you forgive the sins of any, they are forgiven them; if you retain the sins of any, they are retained." The promise was a reminder of the words Jesus had spoken at Caesarea Philippi when Peter confessed Him as the Christ; the gift of the Holy Spirit was an intimation of what would happen at Pentecost.

The risen Christ has entrusted to us the power to forgive in His name. Historically, this has been called the power of absolution, which for a time in Christian history was reserved for the priesthood. Communicating forgiveness is really the calling of the priesthood of all believers. A sure sign we have experienced the Easter miracle and have been filled with the Spirit is that we are communicators of forgiveness. All Christians are charged with the responsibility to listen to people as they share their needs and confess their failures. Too often all we say is "I understand." We have the authority to say, "In the Name of the Lord Jesus, you are forgiven."

Lack of forgiveness binds people, forcing them to retain the guilt and frustration of their sins. Today's the day to accept our calling to be communicators of forgiveness.

Today's Thought: You have the power to set people free!

And Thomas answered and said to Him, "My Lord and My God!" (John 20:28).

Just for Thomas!

Thomas failed the Master in his time of need. Along with some of the others, he fled for safety when Jesus was crucified. Thomas remained alone, filled with remorse for his defection and with loneliness for the Master. He could not face the other disciples and so was not with them on the night after the resurrection when Christ appeared to them. With the charge of forgiving love ringing in their hearts, the disciples went in search of Thomas and brought the lonely disciple back into the fellowship. But Thomas the realist wanted to be sure for himself. "Unless I see in His hands the print of the nails, and put my finger into the print of the nails, and put my hand into His side, I will not believe." As usual, Thomas had to be sure.

When Christ appeared again, it was just for Thomas. Christ greeted the others, went straight to Thomas, then offered His hand and side for Thomas to touch.

This account has two powerful things to say to all of us. Christ's caring is individualized and personal. He comes for each of us. And He meets the issue of our need. Thomas's inability to believe that Christ was risen was caused by his immense guilt over his defection. Notice Thomas didn't touch the nail prints. This was unnecessary. Instead, he became one of the first to make a full confession of Christ. He was completely convinced and made no hesitation in confessing the risen Christ as his Lord and God.

Today's Thought: Christ has plans for us. He comes to give us assurance of His risen power so we can get on with His missions.

Do you love Me? . . . Feed My sheep (John 21:17).

Do You Love Me?

Suddenly it was quiet around the fire beside the Sea of Galilee. The other disciples had drifted away after breakfast. Only the resurrected Lord and Peter remained.

Peter could not lift his eyes. His heart ached with the anguish of his denial. Jesus broke the silence. "Simon, son of Jonah, do you love Me more than these?" (the fishing nets, his friends, and old life).

The words cut like a knife. Peter had said he loved the Lord and would never deny Him. Christ used Peter's own words.

Peter replied, "Yes, Lord, You know I am Your friend." The Lord has asked about love and Peter, now humiliated by his failure, replied with the word for friend. He could be sure of that.

The Lord asked the question three times, once for each of the three denials. Each time Peter protested his friendship. Finally the Lord said, "Are you really My friend? Then, feed My sheep."

The sure sign that we love Christ is that we love others with the power of His love. He comes to each of us with the chance of a new beginning. If we love Him, we will long to love as we've been loved.

As the Lord gives the day, He shows the way. He never gives us more to face in any one day than the knowledge and experience of His steadfast love will sustain.

When we begin each day with conversation with our Lord, He assures us of His never-ceasing love. Our emptiness is filled by His own Spirit of love. Each day it is new, fresh, energizing. We can start out on the adventure of each day with, "I am loved, yesterday is past, tomorrow is in His care, and I can live to the hilt today." Often the reason we find it difficult to love others is that we have not had a daily reaffirmation of Christ's faithful love.

Today's Thought: Christ dredges up the past and then washes away the debris. He heals us so He can get us moving again in loving others as He has loved us.

If I will that he remain till I come, what is that to you? You follow Me (John 21:22).

Distracting Comparisons

Christ our Lord, who is given all power and authority to reign and rule over the church, has an individual, particular plan for each of our lives. He is amazingly original in the way He works with each of us.

This makes comparisons and jealousy irrelevant. Our calling is to follow the Lord and not covet either what others have or have done. Our only goal is to keep our eyes focused on the Lord and our ears open to what He wants to do with us.

Our Scripture text makes this startlingly clear. Jesus has just given Peter a very direct challenge to feed and tend His sheep. Peter saw John close at hand. "What about him?" Didn't the Lord also have something to say to him? Jesus' response was to tell Peter that it was not his business.

This passage is autobiographical. John wrote this exchange into his gospel because of the impact it had on him and because of the crucial spiritual and relational truth it communicated. John did live longer than any of the other disciples. He had a special calling to be the pastoral overseer of the churches in Roman Asia Minor. The Lord's strategy for John's life was worked out differently than His strategy for Peter's life. Peter had his work to do; John had his. How tragic it would have been to have lost the uniqueness of either.

Putting our attention on other people's gifts, opportunities, or success breaks our concentration on the Lord. It distracts. Most of all it causes self-centered competition and eventually division. In a positive way, we need to emphasize the wondrous assurance that the Lord is up to a very exciting thing in each of us.

Today's Thought: Today I will rejoice in Christ's strategy for my life rather than being distracted by debilitating comparisons with others.

Blessed be the God and Father of our Lord Jesus Christ, who according to His abundant mercy has begotten us again to a living hope through the resurrection of Jesus Christ from the dead (1 Peter 1:3).

Eternalize

Woody Allen once said, "I don't want to achieve immortality through my work, I want to achieve immortality through not dying."

We laugh at Woody's ability to turn a humorous phrase, but actually we can't achieve immortality by either. Immortality can't be avoided. We'll all live forever spiritually. The question is where and how. Christ offers us the gift of eternal life, which is so much better than mere immortality. John 3:16 tells us Christ came that we might have eternal life. He reconciles us to God and we enter into life that never ends. Heaven begins now. Death is only a transition in our eternal life. Our resurrection, spiritual body is called from our physical body so we can press on in our growing relationship with God.

There's a sense in which we can "immortalize" a person's memory by remembering what she or he did or we can say that a person lives in our memories. But this does not say anything about where the person's spiritual soul is at the moment. We say some poets, writers, artists, or leaders are immortal. What they left behind may have a lasting quality, but some of them made no confession of faith in Christ.

Christ doesn't immortalize us; He "eternalizes" us. And it must happen in this life. Death is a demarcation line. There is no such thing as universalism—the idea that we can be saved after death. The time is now. This challenges us to be sure for ourselves and gives us a passion to lead others to Christ before it's too late.

Today's Thought: To restate Woody Allen's words: "I want to receive the gift of eternal life and know that my physical death will simply be a rising to the next phase of my relationship with God."

April 16 Colossians 1:24

I now rejoice in my sufferings for you, and fill up in my flesh what is lacking in the afflictions of Christ, for the sake of His body, which is the church (Colossians 1:24).

The Unfinished Task

The words leap out. What is lacking in the afflictions of Christ? Was His saving work on the cross incomplete? Was something left out? No, but the finished work of Calvary must be communicated to every person who does not know Christ. This means sharing the sufferings of Christ. When we really care about people, it causes heartache and sometimes heartbreak.

It is a paradox: The finished work of Calvary is "lacking" until the love of Calvary is presented to every person. When we are willing to give ourselves away and love people unqualifiedly, we will know the reality of the cross. Who is on your agenda?

A powerful story is told of Leonardo da Vinci. One day in his studio he started to work on a large canvas. He labored over it, carefully choosing the subject, arranging the perspective, sketching the outline, applying the colors, and developing the background. Then, for some unknown reason, he stopped with the painting still unfinished. He called one of his students and asked him to finish the work. The student was flabbergasted. How could he finish a painting by one of the world's truly great masters? He protested his inadequacy and insufficiency for so challenging a task. But the great artist silenced him. "Will not what I have done inspire you to do your best?" he asked.

This is really Jesus' question, isn't it? He began it all 2000 years ago. His life, message, death, resurrection, and living presence started the great painting of the redemption of the world.

He has given us the task to finish the painting. But there is a difference. Da Vinci left his student alone; Jesus never leaves us.

Today's Thought: Christ has given us the color palette and brush, and He whispers His guiding insight to us at each uncertain stroke.

But we all, with unveiled face, beholding as in a mirror the glory of the Lord, are being transformed into the same image from glory to glory, just as by the Spirit of the Lord (2 Corinthians 3:18).

Renovation in Progress

As I walked through a hotel lobby under reconstruction, I was fascinated by a sign just inside the door: "Please be patient. Renovation in progress to produce something new and wonderful."

As I stood looking at the sign, I thought, "I need a sign like that to hang around my neck for my family, friends, and fellow workers to see."

A friend of mine in Chicago has a sign on his desk that says, "There's hope for you!" I asked him what it meant. He told me those four words were what his friends in a prayer group had said to him repeatedly during a tough time when his business went belly up. Now, after he survived the crisis by trusting the Lord for his future, he had the sign made for his desk to remind himself that regardless of whatever happens, *always there's hope*. He said, "That sign is a great conversation starter. People ask what it means, and I can tell people that the Lord is in the process of making me into the person He has destined me to be. Everyone needs to be assured of that!"

Chiseled on the entryway to a little chapel on a back road in the Highlands of Scotland are some challenging words in Gaelic. Translated into English they still carry the customary directness and candor of the Highland Scot: "Come as you are, but don't leave as you came."

Jesus' gracious word is "Come to Me. I will never cast you out. But don't you expect to remain the same." We can come to Him just as we are and know that He is in the process of making "someone new and wonderful."

Today's Thought: "The most exciting discovery of our generation is the discovery that we can alter our person by altering the attitude of our mind" —William James.

The Lord Jesus Christ, our hope (1 Timothy 1:1).

Where There's Hope, There's Life

A physician I once knew had a saying he would repeat when he finished examining a patient in a hospital room. After he had checked the charts on the patient's progress, took his pulse, and discussed his condition, just before he would turn to go, he would say, "Well, where there's life, there's hope!"

I invite you to live today with a motto that is the opposite of that ambiguous prognosis: "Where there's hope, there's life!" The fact that there is physical life in us doesn't give us hope. Rather, hope gives us life. Hope enables a quality of life, it sets us free to dare, gives us confidence for daily frustrations, and supplies courage to live adventuresomely and, when the time comes, to die courageously. Jesus came to give us life—abundant and eternal. During the years of this portion of eternity, He Himself is our hope. He has defeated death and is our resurrected, living Lord. We can depend on His timely interventions to guide, strengthen, encourage, and animate us with expectation. Hope in Christ gives courage, endurance, perseverance. What He provides or withholds is always for our ultimate good, so we can trust Him.

This is not just a wonderful way to live—it's the only way to live. Why not try it today? Keep repeating our motto in all the ups and downs today: "Where there's hope, there's life!" And Hope Himself will be there—the unseen Friend with silent strength!

Today's Thought: There's always hope for *Christ is hope*, and He's present in all the ups and downs of life.

And now abide faith, hope, love (1 Corinthians 13:13).

The Floodgate of Hope

Hope is the fulcrum of faith and love. It implements faith and instigates love.

John Calvin said that hope is an "inseparable companion" of both faith and love. "When this hope is taken away, however eloquently or elegantly we discourse concerning faith, we are convicted of having none.... Hope is nothing else than the expectation of those things which faith has believed to have been truly promised by God."

Jurgen Moltmann, a German theologian, expresses the same importance of hope: "Thus in the Christian life, faith has priority, but hope the primacy. Without faith's knowledge of Christ, hope becomes a utopia and remains hanging in the air. But without hope, faith falls to pieces, becoming a faint-hearted and ultimately a dead faith. It is through faith that man finds the path of true life, but it is only hope that keeps him on that path. Thus it is that faith in Christ gives hope its assurance and hope gives faith in Christ its breadth and leads to life."

Put even more directly, hope defines the focus of faith for the present and the future and creates the channel for the flow of love. Hope helps us to see the application of the promises of God to specific problems and people and gives us a vision of what can be. It also liberates us to receive and express love as a participant with God in the realization of His will. It is impossible to truly love without hope. We must believe in a person's value and future as a child of God before we can love. When we give up hope for a person, we become incapable of loving. Hope inspires a picture of what others can be and frees us to give ourselves to them. The same is true for our personal lives. Hope sets us free to claim God's vision for our future.

Today's Thought: Without hope, faith is stunted and love is stymied.

April 20 1 Peter 1:3; 3:15

Blessed be the God and Father of our Lord Jesus Christ, who according to His abundant mercy has begotten us again to a living hope through the resurrection of Jesus Christ from the dead (1 Peter 1:3).

Always be ready to give a defense to everyone who asks you a reason for the hope that is in you (1 Peter 3:15).

Sharing Our Hope

When Deborah Kerr was filming *Quo Vadis*, she was asked by a newspaper reporter if she ever feared the lions. "No," she replied. "I have read the script!"

And so have we! We have been called to be contagious communicators of hope. Our hope is built on Jesus Christ—His cross and resurrection. We know we are loved, forgiven, and destined for heaven. Therefore we can live with the ambiguities and frustrations of life, knowing that "all things work together for good to those who love God, to those who are the called according to His purpose" (Romans 8:28).

We have entrusted our lives to a Lord who can bring good out of evil, can use all things for His glory and our growth, and who cannot be defeated by anything or anyone. Just as God could take the worst that man did at Calvary and give the best, the resurrection gives us hope not only at death but now.

Do you have a vibrant hope? Is your hope based on a source which is ultimately reliable? Has this made you a hopeful person who can infuse hope in others? People need to see what hope can do for a person. Then, when they ask why we are hopeful, we can share the real reason for our hope. Matthew Henry was right: "The ground of our hope is Christ in the world, but the evidence of our hope is Christ in the heart."

Today's Thought: "Hope is nothing more than the expectation of those things which by faith we believed to have been truly promised by God" —Moltmann.

Inasmuch then as the children have partaken of flesh and blood, He Himself likewise shared in the same, that through death He might destroy him whom had the power of death, that is the devil, and release those who through fear of death were all their lifetime subject to bondage (Hebrews 2:14,15).

The First Fear of the Last Enemy

Many of our fears are but a reflection of bondage to the fear of death. Our fear of sickness, anxiety over the loss of our faculties, and apprehension about what will happen when we die—cause so many of our lesser fears. Because we are reluctant to think about death, we don't take personally the assurances of eternal life. We put off thinking about heaven and how we will spend eternity. Therefore, though we are Christians, we continue to live with a subliminal bondage to the fear of death. The words of the author of Hebrews are pointed: "Who through fear of death were all their lifetime subject to bondage." We all know Christians like that—people who have spent their lives without a real beginning of abundant living because of the fear about the end of life.

The reigning Christ who defeated death must reign in each of us until He has put our fear of death under His feet. This is why Jesus came—"God so loved the world.... He came not to condemn... but that we should have everlasting life."

In a world like ours, reflection about death and eternal life is not a luxury reserved for the aged. The dangers of our violent world and the intrusion of crippling disease on all ages, make it a present concern beneath the surface in everyone's life.

The Lord wants to help us face this fear and put it behind us so in the assurance of eternal life forever we can live the abundant life now.

Today's Thought: "For He must reign till He has put all enemies under His feet. The last enemy that will be destroyed is death" (1 Corinthians 15:25,26).

Because of the hope which is laid up for you in heaven (Colossians 1:5).

Future Hope

The basis for future hope is the resurrection. The same power that raised Jesus from the dead is available to you and me, not only at the time of our physical death, but also in our concern over how things will work out in the future. The assurance that we are offered is that the Lord can and will intervene to pull us out of the doldrums of dread and discouragement. He steps in with power to do what we could not have imagined or dared to anticipate. I'm convinced we need a resurrection faith to trust God's will for the future.

I was privileged to be with my mother as she went through the long, hard days and nights before her life was resurrected out of her tired, paralyzed body. Physically, it was not an easy death. There were three people involved in my last conversation with her before she slipped into a coma: my mother and I—and the Lord. We prayed together. When we finished, she thanked me for my part in the conversation with the Lord. My reply was, "Mother, you taught me how to pray." She smiled and said, "Praise the Lord!"

That dear lady lived and died with the assurance of the resurrection. Many years of her life were invaded by financial needs, concern over my father's health, and the challenge of raising a family throughout the later years of the Depression. But her deep, personal relationship with Christ, whom she loved with all her heart, gave her hope in each perplexity. She expected the Lord's intervention in her needs and was not disappointed.

Long before I acknowledged His election of my life, she had claimed it and thanked God in advance that in His timing I would become a Christian. She faced my younger sister's and my dad's death with the same trust. Her own death was experienced with no fear of the future.

Today's Thought: "There are no stains on the pages of tomorrow" —Grady B. Wilson.

Fear not, for I am with you; be not dismayed, for I am your God. I will strengthen you, yes, I will help you, I will uphold you with My righteous right hand (Isaiah 41:10).

Living Without Fear

There are two basic emotions: love and fear. The potential of the first is inherited; the proclivity of the second is inculcated. We were created to love and be loved. We learn how to be afraid and to fear. In an effort to make us aware of potential dangers in life, parents teach us to be afraid. At the same time their acquired, irrational fears are passed on to us. The cycle follows from generation to generation.

How then can we overcome fear? Only by knowing we are loved and by loving. We need to know the Lord is with us, for us, and will strengthen and deliver us. This is the confidence of Isaiah in one of the Bible's most powerful "Fear not!" passages. We hear the prophet's bold assurance in the context of Christ who is God's "righteous right hand." The one at the right hand of a king wielded the power of his kingdom. Christ is the power of God with us. During His ministry, His constant word was, "Do not be afraid!" In His continuing ministry with the early church, He continued to give His fear-dispelling Spirit to the worried hearts of His followers.

The fact that there are 366 "Fear not!" assurances in the entire Bible underlines a very important fact: The Lord knows that we wrestle with fear. He wants to repattern our thinking about life so we can live without fear. There's a great difference between healthy awareness of the realities of life and the irrational panic which grips most people. We want to be careful in distinguishing between healthy preparedness for the realistic problems of life and the spiritual problem of "floating anxiety."

Today's Thought: What would it be like for you to be fearless? Do we have a clear image of that? Ask Christ to reveal it to you and then live it today.

April 24 — 1 John 4:7-21

There is no fear in love; but perfect love casts out fear, because fear involves torment. But he who fears has not been made perfect in love (1 John 4:18).

Love Liberates Us from Fear

John speaks of love that is perfect and that perfects. This means love that accomplishes its purpose in us and enables us to accomplish our purpose. Jesus said, "You must be perfect as your Father in heaven is perfect." It is the Father's purpose to help us accomplish our purpose. Our purpose is to live in His love and love people. When we focus on this goal, we discover the secret that life can be lived without fear.

We cannot really love and fear at the same time. Love and fear do not mix. When we are afraid we are feeling unloved. Fear is the alarm signal that we need to go deeper into the love of our Lord. Christ revealed the limitless extent of the loving heart of the Father. He now reigns as Lord of the church and pours out amazing love. When we focus on the object or subject of our fear, our fear grows. When we focus on the Lord and His love, the panic of fear disappears.

Jude reminds us to "keep ourselves in the love of God" (Jude 21) and then soars with his doxological assurance, "Now to Him who is able to keep you from stumbling" (Jude 24). The only way to keep in the love of God is to allow Christ, God with us, to keep us refreshed and renewed in the power of His love.

Just as love casts out fear, real love has its only source in the one who is loved. Christ came not to condemn the world but that through Him the world might know the unlimited love of God. John shows us how fear of judgment blocks this love. It is then we need to know the reassurance of Christ's forgiveness, experience His atonement, and be filled with His Spirit. It is only then, when His love casts out fear, that we are able to live with courage and confidence.

Today's Thought: The only cure for fear is love—God's love for us and our love for others.

Being confident of this very thing, that He who has begun a good work in you will complete it until the day of Jesus Christ (Philippians 1:6).

The Sure Cure for Discouragement

Paul gives us a tonic for discouragement—the only one that really works: God is at work within us. What He began when He called us, He intends to finish. We are all in the process of becoming the people He intends us to be. Sometimes we feel the process is slow and become impatient with ourselves. Then we project onto others and our circumstances the discouragement we are feeling with ourselves. The way to change the outer discouragement is to allow God to deal with our inner discouragement. This means refocusing our attention on the Lord and the "good work" He has begun *in* us and seeks to continue.

What is this good work? Paul gives us insight into what he meant in the prayer he told the Philippians he was praying for them. "And this I pray, that your love may abound still more and more in knowledge and all discernment, that you may approve the things that are excellent, that you may be sincere and without offense until the day of Christ, being filled with the fruits of righteousness which are by Jesus Christ, to the glory and praise of God" (Philippians 1:9-11).

All this is not something we are to produce for the Lord. He is doing it and will continue. Often the very things that cause us discouragement God is using as a part of our growth in His good work. Our challenge is to yield to Him and receive what He has to give.

The Lord renews our courage and enables us to enjoy what He is doing in us in spite of what may be happening around us. The result is that we can have a new hope for our tasks and challenges.

Today's Thought: The Lord never gives up on us and what He has called us to do.

But I want you to know, brethren, that the things which happened to me have actually turned out for the furtherance of the gospel (Philippians 1:12).

TBU Shot

My Scots friend Jimmie is a fine golfer and an excellent caddie. This makes his analysis of my game all the more helpful—and often downright embarrassing. Sometimes when I have a poor shot that somehow rolls somewhere close to where I intended, he says with a Scot's directness, "That's a TBU shot!"

"What do you mean by that?" I asked after hearing Jimmie use the expression for more of my shots than I would have wished. "A TBU shot is one that's terrible... but useful."

You guessed it—I found a parable in that. Think of the TBU situations in life, all the things we go through that seem awful at the time but prove to be very useful for our growth. It's a comfort to know that God can use everything. Nothing is wasted. But there are a couple of big "ifs."

One is awareness. At the end of every day we need a time to reflect on what God may want to teach us from our goofs and failures. Creative introspection under the guidance of His Spirit can lead to cleansing confession and growth in character.

The second "if" is commitment. When we face problems and ask God to help us, He has an amazing way of turning them into blessings. What seems like a terrible disappointment may be an appointment to get us to where God wants us. The last "if" is to forget the failure and press on; don't brood over it.

Paul learned to take the good and the tough times in stride because he knew Christ could use *everything.* His guards became Christians, and the Christians at Rome were encouraged by the way he trusted Christ. Everyone has TBU situations. What will they learn from us about how to get the most out of theirs?

Today's Thought: People are like tea bags. You never know their strength until they get in hot water.

For to me, to live is Christ (Philippians 1:21).

Grace for Gray Days

Paul's exhilaration to excel was based on a powerful purpose. When he wrote these dynamic words of our verse for today, he was under arrest and in confinement. Whether he lived or died physically was of little concern. For him, living then and forever was Christ. He would know more of Christ each day on earth or in heaven. Therefore he could press on!

The often missed point is that Paul expressed his central purpose in a very gray time of his life. It was a time of waiting for the next step, concern over the churches, and restlessness with the routines of confinement. And yet the shaft of light penetrating the grayness of those days was Christ Himself.

Nothing substitutes for experience. When Paul talked about Christ, he was not talking about a theory or an idea or a set of religious rules; he was talking about knowing a living Person. There has been a great deal of negativism in contemporary Christianity about Christian "experience." It has prompted some Christians to be wary of seeking or sharing a firsthand experience of Christ. Any dynamic Christianity is experience. This does not deny knowledge or service. When Paul said, "I know," it was a personal experience that transformed his life. The wonder of our faith is that Christ who is Lord of all can be experienced personally.

We all need a continuous flow of fresh grace from the Lord, a daily experience of Christ—not just for dark days. Most of our days are gray—neither exciting nor difficult, just gray. It's on those days we need an exhilarating experience of Christ. And He offers grace for gray days.

Today's Thought: This will be a great day or a gray day depending on whether we can say, "For to me, to live is Christ!"

God... has... given Him the name which is above every name (Philippians 2:9).

A Message to E.T.

Last year during Thanksgiving, a company specializing in outer space communications developed a very effective public relations program. The company set up a recording booth in New York City for people to record messages to be beamed out into space to E.T.

The moviemaking craft made E.T., that lovable character from outer space, so real that people thought of him as a living being. Young and old made him the mascot of our space age. It was not surprising when thousands of people of all ages lined up to record their messages to E.T.

What would you have recorded? What message do you have for life on other planets, if indeed there might be some species living out there somewhere?

How about this for a holiday greeting: "E.T. This is the planet Earth calling. In this Thanksgiving season we are filled with gratitude to the God of the universe for His visit to our planet to reveal Himself and to perform a cosmic atonement through Jesus Christ, His Son, our Lord. He died on the cross to reconcile all life to Himself. And He rose again! He lives now as reigning Lord of the universe. What He did for us, He can do for you. When you know Him personally, you'll know you're loved. This will bring you peace and joy!"

Thinking of what message we might send does put things into perspective. But if there were an E.T., he might wonder about the conditions on the planet Earth. "God so loved the world," but what have we done in response?

Today's Thought: It would take a car racing at top speed nine years to reach the moon; three hundred years to reach the sun; eight thousand, three hundred years to reach the planet Neptune; seventy-five million years to reach Alpha Centauri; and seven hundred million years to reach the Pole Star. And yet, Christ reigns over all and knows and cares about each of us!

Let this mind be in you which was also in Christ Jesus (Philippians 2:5).

The Greatness of Making Others Great

Humility is what most people think they have, think others should find, and would be hard-pressed to define. In Philippians 2:1-11, Paul describes humility in action in our relationships and then gives a magnificent description of how we discover and grow in its authentic quality. He presents us with a human impossibility and then offers supernatural power to make it possible.

We are staggered by the challenge of the first four verses of this passage. In essence the apostle calls us to express to others the same encouragement, love, affection, and mercy we have received from Christ. He nails this down by challenging us to do nothing from selfish ambition or conceit, "But in lowliness of mind let each esteem others better than himself. Let each of you look out not only for his own interests, but also for the interests of others."

How is that possible? Paul answers with the power source of true humility: "Let this mind be in you which was also in Christ Jesus. . . ." Here the word "mind" does not refer to Jesus' divine intelligence as much as His attitude and disposition. Then, in soaring rhetoric, the apostle launches into an explanation of Christ's humility, giving us a stirring vision of the majesty of Christ. It is this majesty which opens us to the gift of Christ's humility.

A Christian who is yielded to the indwelling Christ is receptive to moment-by-moment guidance in how to express love to others and put their needs first. The sure test that Christ's humility is being reproduced in us is that we have the greatness of making others great. Our concern is to build them up rather than ourselves.

Today's Thought: A self-made person worships his or her maker!

Work out your own salvation with fear and trembling; for it is God who works in you both to will and to do for His good pleasure. Do all things without murmuring and disputing, that you may become blameless and harmless, children of God without fault in the midst of a crooked and perverse generation, among whom you shine as lights in the world (Philippians 2:12-15).

It's a Pleasure!

There are two "works" that work in perfect harmony when we press on in our faith. The Christian works out what God is working on. We are to work out our own salvation—not as an object yet to be achieved, but as a possession to be explored and enjoyed with pleasure. This is because the indwelling Spirit is guiding the process "for His good pleasure." Life becomes a pleasure when we know God's pleasure over us. The desire to please Him comes in response to knowing His pleasure. The opposite of this is made all too clear by Paul. He talks about those who express murmuring and disputing which really means "grumbling and arguing." When we do this with God, we soon do it with others.

Knowing God's pleasure and living life as a pleasure in spite of its difficulties produces a dynamic radiance in our lives that shines. Paul calls us to live as "lights in the world." Jesus said, "You are the light of the world."

A friend of mine who is filled with Christ's Spirit responds to people with a consistent, "It's a pleasure!"

"Is it always?" I asked.

"Only when I pray my prayers and keep my eyes on Christ," he responded. Judging from the consistency of his radiance, he must pray a lot. Anything less than approaching life as a pleasure will eventually result in grumbling and arguing. Working out our salvation is applying it to all of life.

Today's Thought: Our chief end is to glorify God and enjoy Him forever!

But you know his proven character (Philippians 2:22).

Proven Character

It's a great commendation of a person to say of him or her, "What you see is what you get." We all like people who are consistent, dependable, loyal, and trustworthy. And we appreciate those who are the same inside and out and are not working on some hidden agenda. It's usually under pressure or in the fires of adversity that we see what people really are. A person's relationships usually reveal the quality of his or her character.

Our reading through Philippians this week brings us to a passage of Paul's analysis of the character of two of his friends. In a sense he is writing letters of commendation. Wouldn't it be wonderful if someone of Paul's stature could say of you and me what he said about Timothy and Epaphroditus?

The apostle affirmed Timothy for having a proven character. The word "proven" in the Greek means "tested." Paul saw Timothy's character deepen through the years since he first introduced him to Christ at Lystra. The young man became a son in the faith. He overcame timidity and fear to become a faithful disciple of Christ and a loyal friend to Paul.

Epaphroditus was sent by the Philippians to help Paul in his time of need. His character was tested by illness while in Rome. He almost died. His greatest concern, however, was that he might cause his fellow Philippians worry. And yet, Paul affirms him as a brother, fellow worker, and one who, inspite of his own health problems, ministered to the apostle.

If we had been with Paul, what kind of letter would he have written about us? Is what people see and hear us say about our faith what they get in proven character?

Today's Thought: What have the refining fires of life produced in our character?

But what things were gain to me, these I have counted loss for Christ (Philippians 3:7).

Iffy People

The apostle Paul's ministry had been dogged by distracters. Wherever he preached the gospel and Gentiles were converted to Christ, these so-called Judaizers soon followed with their brand of legalism. Their conviction was that Gentile converts had to fulfill all the regulations and requirements of Judaism, including circumcision for the men. They were "iffy" people who put legalism before justification by faith. These troublesome people obviously were active in Philippi, causing the new Christians to question their relationship with Christ by faith alone.

In the passage we read from Philippians today, Paul confronts not only the "iffy" Judaizers, but the whole spirit of legalism. He asserts that he had met all the requirements of the law but had no confidence in them. He counted them all useless in comparison to knowing Christ. All that he had been as a religious person did not bring him to redemption until he met Christ and received the gift of faith.

Legalism is a constant distraction in any age. It's used by "iffy" people to express qualified acceptance. Secondary rules and regulations are made primary. The legalists assert that unless we meet certain practices and requirements we are not really Christians. In our day it can be certain behaviors or customs that we think are absolutely essential. We reserve our approval and acceptance until people measure up. Know any "iffy" people? Ever been one? Who are you judging with the big "if" of "If you only did this, I'd accept you"?

Today's Thought: Today I will give up the big "if."

I press toward the goal (Philippians 3:14).

Suffering from a Sunset

In F. W. Boreham's lovely little book, *Boulevards of Paradise*, he tells the story of a man strolling with his granddaughter. They met a man who poured out a long tale of woe, concluding his dismal recital with an apology based on the fact that he was suffering from a slight sunstroke.

"Grandpa," exclaimed the little girl when the intruder had shuffled off, "I do hope that you'll never suffer from a sunset!"

The point is all too clear. We suffer from a sunset before the day is ended. This is not only true for people who give up the adventure of growing spiritually and intellectually in the "sunset" years of their lives, but also for Christians of every age who stop adventuring with Christ. We are promised "life all the way up," to use scholar-preacher Paul Shearer's words. Or, in the words of poet Roselle Mercher Montgomery, "You took life on tip-toe to the very last." We can be spiritually geriatric in our twenties or forties!

The opposite is Paul's commitment to press on toward the prize of the upward call of God in Christ Jesus. The secret of that is in what comes before it in Paul's encouragement to the Philippians: "That I may know Him and the power of His resurrection. . . ." Our constant experience of the rejuvenating power of the resurrection—Christ's and ours—and the infilling of His Spirit make possible that power to press on. At wherever stage of life we find ourselves, the best is always ahead!

Today's Thought: Christ turns our sunsets into dawn.

He is able even to subdue all things to Himself (Philippians 3:21).

Christ Subdues What We Submit

We are not subdued because Christ is able to subdue. Now this may sound like a contradiction. Actually, I'm using two of the alternative meanings of "subdue." When we say a person is very subdued, we mean that he or she is unexpressive. The other meaning of "subdue" is to bring something under control, to conquer it. Christians can be joyous because Christ is able to subdue the things that cause fear, worry, and anxiety.

Paul speaks of Christians as citizens of heaven, people who belong to Christ and whose eternal destiny is secure. But we are not just heavenly-minded people who are no earthly good. Rather we are those who are experiencing Christ's transforming power now. We are under Christ's control and being formed into His nature. And we become people who spend our lives serving people and working for justice in society—all because Christ subdues.

The word "subdue" in Greek is *hupotasso*, primarily a military term meaning "to rank under or put in subjection." He has conquered death and defeated Satan. When He calls us to be His disciples, He begins our character transformation, bringing our human nature under His control.

But there's a secret to experiencing Christ's power: He subdues what we submit. Is there anything in your life, personality, or relationships that He needs to bring under His control? And are there problems you face today that you need Him to help you conquer? Surrender them to Christ. He is able and has all power to subdue.

Today's Thought: "For He must reign until He has put all enemies under His feet" (1 Corinthians 15:25).

Be of the same mind in the Lord (Philippians 4:2).

Oneness Is Not an Option

No two people contradicted the meaning of their names as much as Euodia and Syntyche. The name of Euodia meant "good or prosperous journey"; Syntyche meant "pleasant acquaintance" or "good luck." But, despite their names, these two women were causing dissension in the church at Philippi. Paul calls on them to settle their differences and for the whole church to help them.

We are not told what the problem was. If we knew, we'd be able to dismiss this passage if the conflict between these two women didn't happen to be a problem we're facing right now. So the passage has application to us for whatever differences we're experiencing with other Christians: doctrinal, ethical, ecclesiastical, or personal. At the center of the problem there's probably a struggle for power.

What's the solution? Paul is direct with Euodia and Syntyche: Be of the same mind in the Lord. Differences in personality should not separate us from unity in Christ. Our task is not to make others cookie-cutter replicas of ourselves. We are to honor the uniqueness of each person. Unity in Christ also means setting aside secondary things like denominational differences or cultural patterns. Agreement on basics is what's important. Most important of all is mutual forgiveness. Paul says, "Let your gentleness be known." Finally, together with the Christian with whom we're having a battle of wills, we need to ask Christ to invade our conversation. Ask for the mind and disposition of Christ. What would He say to both involved? The Lord is at hand. He died to make us one and will settle for nothing less.

Today's Thought: Set aside nonessentials, giving up the need to always be in control. Admit that you may not have all the answers, and reach out to the person from whom you are estranged and together reach out for Christ.

Be anxious for nothing, but in everything by prayer and supplication, with thanksgiving, let your requests be made known to God; and the peace of God, which surpasses all understanding, will guard your hearts and minds through Christ Jesus (Philippians 4:6,7).

The Peace of the Secret Place

There's peace and power in the secret place of the Most High. It's there that our lowest mood meets His highest joy. Our deepest needs are confessed to His highest vision, and our longings are released to His highest power.

There's a secret place in all of us and there's a secret place of the Most High. When the two meet, profound prayer takes place. Paul shares the secret of reaching the secret place of the Most High: supplication with thanksgiving. Thanksgiving is to think magnificently about God—who He is and what He has done. It's the door into the secret place of the Most High where we receive silent strength.

The real test of what we believe and do is how we pray. Prayer is the power source. But real prayer happens when our true selves and our deepest concerns are spread out before the Lord. Then we are ushered into the inner place of peace and power.

The result of prayer from our inner secret place in the secret place of the Most High is that the peace which is beyond our expectation fills us and then garrisons our hearts as we return to the responsibilities and challenges of life. There is continuing need in all of us to grow in our understanding and practice of prayer. Everything else depends on it!

Today's Thought: "He who dwells in the secret place of the Most High shall abide under the shadow of the Almighty. I will say of the Lord, 'He is my refuge and my fortress; My God, in Him I will trust' " (Psalm 91:1,2).

I can do all things through Christ who strengthens me. . . . And my God shall supply all your needs according to His riches in glory by Christ Jesus (Philippians 4:13,19).

Spiritual Affluence

Christ provides for what He guides. He gives us strength to do what He wants us to accomplish. What He gives us the vision to conceive and the faith to believe, He will enable us to achieve. We can do all things—everything He calls us to do—through His strength. A good translation of our verse for today is, "In union with Christ who infuses us with strength, I can do all things."

This verse is a motto for supernatural living. Christ constantly leads us to attempt what would be impossible on our own. This means we must move out beyond the limitations of our own intellect, talent, insight, experience, and training. We must venture into challenges we could not pull off on our own. Many people repeat today's verse but never realize the promise because they are limiting the possible to what they could do without Christ's strength.

Christ is the mediator between us and the riches of God in glory. Unlimited love, power, wisdom, and energy are made available to us. Christ promised strength with two qualifications: "If you ask anything in My name, I will do it. . . . If you love Me, keep My commandments" (John 14:14,15). There's the secret. His name focuses the realm of strength. It is to do His will. The commandments focus the purpose of strength: "This is My commandment, that you love one another as I have loved you" (John 15:12). When we are committed to a life of loving, sacrificial service and extending His kingdom through sharing our faith and working for social justice, we'll have strength to do all things. He will supply all our needs along the way. Christ promises spiritual affluence. Why? Because He wants to love, forgive, care, and heal through us. Are you willing?

Today's Thought: Today I will attempt something I could not accomplish without Christ's strength.

May 8 Philippians 4:14-19

Now you Philippians know also that in the beginning of the gospel, when I departed from Macedonia, no church shared with me concerning giving and receiving but you only (Philippians 4:15).

I Need You!

One of the greatest compliments a person can give is to say, "I need you!" The words melt our hearts and impel us to want to help. We all need to feel needed.

A crucial part of the ministry of sharing is to be able to admit our inadequacies and say to others, "I need you!" We can be sure that if we can't say that to others, they will probably never say it to us.

Actually, confession of our needs is an expression of healthy self-esteem. We value ourselves enough to believe that we are worthy of another's care. Those who cannot express their needs usually end up unable to help others with theirs. An honest expression of needs makes possible a healthy marriage or a creative friendship.

It is true that only God can meet our deepest needs. No human being can satisfy all of our needs. He or she was never meant to. We were created for fellowship with God. There will be a restlessness, an emptiness within us, until we rest in Him and allow Him to fill the God-shaped vacuum. The closer we grow to Him, the more we realize how much more we need Him. Yet, in His wisdom and desire that His children share His love with one another, God has ordained that aspects of our needs for Him can only be fulfilled when we seek Him together. He reserves dimensions of His power to be given as we endeavor to meet each other's needs.

Today's Thought: "Share your life, and find the finest joy man can know. Do not be stingy with your heart. Get out of yourself into the lives of others, and new life will flow into you—share and share alike" —Joseph Fort Newton.

The grace of our Lord Jesus Christ be with you (Philippians 4:23).

Grace in Our Circumstances

I asked a man how he was doing. "Not very well under the circumstances," he replied. He's a Christian, but is facing difficulties that are getting him down. We've all had times when tough circumstances made it hard for us to live our faith.

Whenever I'm tempted to get discouraged with circumstances, I turn to these last three verses of Philippians. Paul's closing remarks include a greeting from "those who are in Caesar's household." Caesar's household? Talk about difficult circumstances! Think what it would be like to be a Christian in the household of an emperor who thought he was a god and was the leader of the cult of worship of himself.

The Christians Paul is talking about were servants and soldiers who were converted to Christ. There was a strong underground movement of the followers of Christ in Rome. While Paul was a prisoner, many of his guards met the Savior through the apostle while they were guarding him. It was said that Paul's guards had to be changed repeatedly because they were all becoming Christians. Imagine being chained to that dynamic man in Christ!

Being a Christian in Rome was not only difficult; it was dangerous. But apparently those who became converts remained faithful to Christ, and the faith was spread throughout Caesar's household. They encouraged and strengthened each other as well as Paul.

The best way to live courageously in difficult circumstances is to claim that our Lord has placed us there to be His witness and to communicate His love and power. It's in trying circumstances that the grace of Christ is needed and given. So grace to you in your circumstances!

Today's Thought: Circumstances are the context of our calling and where we receive grace.

Then he called for a light, ran in, and fell down trembling before Paul and Silas (Acts 16:29).

Thank God for Crises

Thank God for crises! In them we sense our need. When things fall apart or life demands what we do not have, then we can honestly admit our need. Then the same gracious God who was with us in the crises will meet us at the point of our need.

The Philippian jailer's question to Paul is where we begin: "What must I do to be saved?"

"Nothing! You already are!" is God's gracious reply to those whose need has driven them to Him. In this context Paul could answer the jailer: "Accept the love God has offered in Jesus Christ, which you can never earn or deserve. You belong to Him. That will never change. He loves you, forgives you, accepts you. Believe that, and you will know for yourself what is already true!"

That's grace. The experience cancels out our basic motives of self-justification and reorients our whole life around the liberating secret of God's initiative of love. God has loved us all through our self-defeating efforts at independence. He has waited patiently for us to realize the love that was there all along. We respond to God not in order to receive His love, but because we already have received His love. We ask for forgiveness, a way out of a complex situation, a power to love, and a direction for the future because God is ready to give long before we are ready to receive. This kind of love will never change; He loves us as much right now as He ever will—more than we can imagine. We do not need to be good enough, faithful enough, or obedient enough to deserve it. These things will come naturally, not as prerequisites but as the result. This is the creative confidence of joyous living.

Today's Thought: We have been called by love to be God's people, to be filled with His Spirit, to communicate His love. We need nothing or no one; therefore we can use everything and serve everyone to glorify God and enjoy Him.

Martha, Martha, you are worried and troubled about many things (Luke 10:41).

Breaking the Worry Habit

While having breakfast in a hotel while on a speaking engagement, I overheard two businessmen talking.

"Well, how'd you sleep?" one asked.

"Not very well," the other replied. "I was worried whether my travel alarm clock would go off. It's been acting up lately. The batteries must be running down."

"Why not change the batteries?" his friend asked with a smile. "You must like to worry."

Are there people who like to worry? There seem to be lots of people who develop a worry habit.

Martha had the worry habit. When Jesus came to her home she was so busy with the details of preparing a meal for Him that she had no time to join her sister Mary in listening to what He had to say. What Jesus finally said to Martha is a word for worriers: "Martha, Martha, you are worried and troubled about many things. But one thing is needed, and Mary has chosen that good part, which will not be taken away from her."

In John 11, we see that Martha's worrisome nature was a pattern. When Jesus arrived after her brother Lazarus died, she was very sharp with Jesus: "Lord," she said, "if You had been here, my brother would not have died." Now there's a guilt trip! But Jesus was not put off. He engaged her in a deep conversation about the resurrection and asked her to make a response of commitment to Him. Then the Lord raised Lazarus from the tomb. After that, Martha gave up her worry over lesser things and became a committed disciple. Because of the friendship she and Mary had with Jesus, we assume she was one of "the women" referred to in Acts 1:14. After witnessing the resurrection and receiving the baptism of the Spirit, the worry habit was broken.

Today's Thought: Only one thing will break the worry habit: time with the living Lord and complete trust that He is able to work things out better than we ever imagined.

When I call to remembrance the genuine faith that is in you, which dwelt first in your grandmother Lois and your mother Eunice, and I am persuaded is in you also (2 Timothy 1:5).

The Miracle of Influence

Mother's Day is a great opportunity to think about the influence of the home in shaping—positively or negatively—a child's faith in Christ. The faith must be both taught and caught. Often all children learn from their parents' faith are the "do's and don'ts" of religion. Children learn the "oughts" but are not given the adventure of being in Christ. Life is lived by compulsion and not by conviction.

In our Scripture today we see a three-generation flow of genuine faith. Three cheers for grandmothers like Lois and mothers like Eunice.

Cheer one: Their faith was authentic. Cheer two: The faith ties and the filial ties with Timothy were intertwined in a strong bond of love in the church in their home. Timothy later became a son in the faith and a brother in the adventure of following Christ. Cheer three: They released Timothy to do the Lord's will as Paul's companion and helper. We are reminded of Lancelot's response to his mother's protective desire to keep him home and have him hunt deer like other respectable young men. "Follow the deer? Oh, Mother, no—follow Christ!"

Today's Thought: John Ruskin was right when he said that the history of a nation is not to be read in its battlefields but in its homes.

This people says, "The time has not come. . . ." Thus says the Lord of hosts: "Consider your ways!" (Haggai 1:2-5).

The Belligerent Balk

A little girl was given the big word "procrastination" to spell in the spelling bee. "P-r-o-c-r . . ." she stammered and then blurted out, "Oh, I guess I'll have to learn that tomorrow!"

Scarlet O'Hara would have identified with, "I'll think about it tomorrow—for tomorrow is another day." Procrastination.

Mark Twain said, "Do not put off until tomorrow what you can do the day after tomorrow." Bad advice. Rather, listen to Charles Dickens: "Procrastination is the thief of time. Collar him!"

Look at the word again: "pro"—put forward; "cras"—morrow. This may be the proclivity of human nature, but it has some dangerous results in our relationship with God. He wants us to do as He guides. Procrastination is the belligerent balk.

One of the classic examples of petulant procrastination in the Bible is the way the people put off work on the temple rebuilding after the exile. The work began in 536 BC and ground to a halt two years later. Pessimism led to spiritual lethargy. Soon the people became preoccupied with rebuilding their own homes and with personal pursuits. Some rationalized that the time had not come because the 70 years between the destruction and rebuilding of the temple that Jeremiah predicted was not yet complete. We can usually find some theory to support our procrastination. What the people resisted were God's specific orders to get going—stop paneling your own homes while the temple remains in ruins! Haggai was the prophet of anti-procrastination!

Think of all the times we've used circumstances to justify procrastination, taking refuge from duty by saying the right time had not come.

Today's Thought: Today is the day—let's act on one thing we've been procrastinating about.

May 14 — 2 Corinthians 6:1,2

Behold, now is the accepted time; behold, now is the day of salvation (2 Corinthians 6:2).

Keeping Up with Yesterday

More on procrastination. Allow me to ask a personal question. Is there anything we're refusing to do that God has mandated in the Bible or guided in our prayers? It's so important that we answer that question honestly and get off *dead* center today! Now is the acceptable time. The future inflow of God's silent strength is dependent on acting today.

Procrastination is really disobedience. It's questioning in the quest what God has made clear in the quiet. We are called to be God-sensitive people who can receive and follow orders. Procrastination is the expression of the coward's heart. Remember: Difficulties may be a sign that we are doing what God wants. Why would Satan be concerned about a Christian who never did anything?

A good motto is "Do all you can for whomever you can, whenever you can—for the glory of God!" Mother Teresa puts it this way: "I focus on the Lord and not the problems. Then I can deal with the problems holding the strong hand of Jesus."

Today's Thought: Procrastination is the art of keeping up with yesterday.

The time of day I do not tell as some do by the clock
Or by some distant chiming bell set on some steepled rock.
But by the progress that I see in what I have to do;
It's either "Done O'Clock" for me or
Only "Half-before through."

This hope we have as an anchor of the soul, both sure and steadfast, and which enters the Presence behind the veil (Hebrews 6:19).

The Anchor Behind the Veil

In the turbulent storms of life we have a sure and steadfast anchor that brings stability and strength. Our souls are anchored behind the veil in the heart of God.

The author of Hebrews gives us two powerful metaphors all in one word picture. The sure and steadfast anchor reminds us of the storms we must ride out in being faithful disciples. We think of Luke's description of his experience with Paul on the Adriatic Sea on the way to Rome: "Then, fearing lest we should run aground... they dropped four anchors from the stern, and prayed for day to come" (Acts 27:29). The anchor of hope holds in the night storms as we pray for the day of a new direction to come.

But the second metaphor focuses our minds on the place in which our anchor is lodged—none other than in the heart of God. The metaphor has shifted from the nautical to how near we can come to the Presence because of Christ.

We need to consider Leviticus 16:2,3. The veil of the tabernacle separated the Presence and the ark from the people. Only Aaron and the priests could enter. The veil of the wilderness tabernacle was reproduced in the temple in Jerusalem, the same veil that was torn in two at the completion of Jesus' sacrificial death for our sins on the cross (Luke 23:45).

Now through Christ we can enter the holy of holies of the presence of God with boldness (Hebrews 10:19). It is there in the intimate communion of prayer that hope is given and nurtured.

Any sailor or fisherman knows the importance of being sure the anchor is securely tied to the anchor rope or chain. The same is true for the anchor of hope. Prayer is more than throwing out the anchor. It's being held to the Presence. We can ride out any storm knowing that our anchor is secure.

Today's Thought: Prayer in the Presence gives hope for the storm.

As for you, you meant evil against me; but God meant it for good (Genesis 50:20).

Present Confidence

Joseph spoke his powerful words of faith to his guilt-ridden brothers while looking back over how God had used their evil deed to bring about good. Years before, they had stuffed him in a pit, leaving him to die. Midianite traders came by and pulled him out of the pit and eventually sold him as a slave in Egypt. But the Lord was with Joseph in Egypt. He rose to a position of power as the Pharaoh's vice-regent. Finally, during years of drought in Canaan, Joseph provided for his family in Egypt. He forgave what was done to him because he could see that God had turned their evil deed into a means of saving His people.

Now, the challenge for you and me is to say our verse for today in the midst of difficulties rather than after them. When we are hurting it is not easy to say that people or circumstances mean it for evil or selfishness or competitive pride, but God *means* it for good. The test is to express Joseph's faith in the present moment not just with twenty-twenty hindsight.

God is our loving Father. He wants only what is *ultimately* good for us. He has delegated the risen Christ to work with us to transform us, guide us each moment, and eventually get us to heaven. Jesus put it clearly: "This is the will of the Father who sent Me, that of all He has given Me I should lose nothing, but should raise it up at the last day. And this is the will of Him who sent Me, that everyone who sees the Son and believes in Him may have everlasting life; and I will raise him up at the last day" (John 6:39,40). This being the case, we can depend on the Lord to bring about His purposes even in the tough times.

Today's Thought: Lord, I trust You. You know what You're doing. You can take my mistakes and the difficulties others cause and transform them into good. Now don't let me question in the dark what You have revealed in the light. Amen.

For your Father knows the things you have need of before you ask Him (Matthew 6:8).

Even Before You Ask

A while ago in the coffee shop of the Billings, Montana, airport, the waitress had a badge on her uniform that had something most unusual on it. "I know you've got to catch a plane and that you're in a hurry. So what may I serve you?"

Now that's getting to the point! I suspect that the waitresses in the coffee shop had heard people's pressured request for a rush order so often they decided to shortcut the conversation and get right to the order. There was something honest and straightforward about this that I appreciated. And combined with the waitress' warm smile, it was a relief not to have to explain what she knew already.

I spoke at a retreat where all of the small group leaders had a badge that said, "I've got them too. What are yours?" You can imagine this started some good conversations. "What do we have in common?" people would ask. "Problems!" would be the answer. "So let's face them together and ask God for His strength." It was one of the best retreats I ever attended because people got to issues right away and prayed for each other.

Jesus said we didn't need to beat around the bush in our prayers with vain repetitions—that is, lofty phrases that hide our real need. His invitation to prayer was "For your Father knows the things you have need of before you ask Him." He's never surprised; He knows all about us. So today, hold nothing back. Pour out your heart needs. He's waiting to bless you.

Today's Thought: Prayer is not to inform God of what He knows already but to receive solutions He has already planned.

Jesus Christ is the same yesterday, today, and forever (Hebrews 13:8).

The Unchanging Christ

It is our source of comfort and courage that Jesus Christ is the same today as He was when He lived among us in the flesh. As the preexistent, eternal Word of God, the "I am," He revealed His true nature and power. He declared who He is and how He meets our deepest needs.

The awesome promise of the author of Hebrews is that what Christ was, He is now, and will be in all of our tomorrows. This gives us an unchanging center of quiet strength in a changing world. "Oh Thou who changest not, abide with me!"

He is light for our darkness; food for our hunger; peace for our pressures; forgiveness for our failures; strength for our weaknesses; the way, the truth, and the life for our confusion; the resurrection and the life for our anxieties about sickness and death. There is no human extremity unmet by the unchanging Christ.

But this great text from Hebrews also helps us deal with our memories of our yesterdays, our concern in our todays, and our uncertainties about our tomorrows. All dimensions of time are encompassed by the grace of Christ.

We vacillate, people are unreliable, and circumstances change, but the eternal Christ, the same from the beginning of creation, is our present, powerful Lord.

Today's Thought: Oh Christ, in a world of change You never change so that I can keep on changing to become all that You meant me to be.

Behold, I am setting a plumb line in the midst of My people Israel (Amos 7:8).

Anything Out of Plumb?

Recently, a friend of mine who is an excellent carpenter made me a plumb line just like the one Amos saw the Lord holding in his vision. It was designed after the ancient Egyptian plumbings used from the third millenium.

Two ledges of wood were joined, one above the other, at right angles to a plank. The line was attached to the top of the plank and passed through a hole in the upper ledge. If the line touched the edge of the lower ledge when stretched taut by the weight of the plumb, the wall was properly built "in plumb."

In Amos' vision the Lord was measuring the perpendicular of Israel against the horizon of His commandments and His righteousness and justice. The nation was leaning out of plumb.

I keep the model of the plumb line handy near a cross my Dad made for me. Both help me to measure my life each day. It's good to have an objective standard to guide my daily living. The Ten Commandments have not gone out of style, and Christ's call to be a servant has not been changed. Christ Himself is our plumb line. He constantly affirms our growth and challenges what needs to be changed. Having Him as our plumb line gives us an early warning system and a daily chance to confess and be different. Anything out of plumb today?

Today's Thought: I will not measure my life by anything or anyone except Christ, the plumb line of what life is meant to be and of what I can become.

So he prayed to the Lord, and said, "Ah, Lord, was not this what I said when I was still in my country? Therefore I fled previously to Tarshish; for I know that You are a gracious and merciful God, slow to anger and abundant in lovingkindness, One who relents from doing harm" (Jonah 4:2).

Tear Up Your Hit List!

Jonah suspected it all along. This is why he rejected the call to go to Nineveh in the first place. From the time he was a lad he was taught what God said to Moses about His nature: "The Lord, the Lord God, merciful and gracious, longsuffering, and abounding in goodness and truth, keeping mercy" (Exodus 34:6). The prophet repeated these words almost verbatim when he expressed his anger to God. He lived with the presupposition that God was the exclusive Lord of Israel. What he feared might happen became a reality: God extended His mercy to Jonah's enemies.

We can empathize with Jonah if we think of the persons or group of people we consider our enemies. Imagine being called to go as the Lord's messenger to those we've judged and hope we never see again. What if God used us and they responded to His love and forgiveness? Perhaps this is why it's so difficult to pray for people we dislike. God might answer our prayers! Then what would we do with our angry condemnation of people on our hit list? It's hard to love people who don't deserve it. And yet, that's what God does all the time—love the undeserving, ungrateful, unkind. And He expects no less of our attitude toward others.

The one thing Jonah would not do was repent. He kept his obstinate prejudices and exclusiveness right to the end. The Lord used him to preach repentance to the Ninevites, and his mission was a success. Now the prophet needed to experience the mercy of God for his own sin of judgmentalism. His sin was more serious than the "wickedness" of Nineveh.

Today's Thought: Today is the day to let God deal with our judgmentalism and exclusiveness so that we can receive and express mercy.

Multitudes, multitudes in the valley of decision! For the day of the Lord is near in the valley of decision (Joel 3:14).

A Decision About Our Decisions

One day while walking through a department store, I walked past the millinery department. A woman was trying to decide on a hat while her husband waited impatiently. "Decisions, decisions, decisions! Oh, how I hate decisions!" she said. Her husband responded, "If you can't make a decision about a silly hat, how are you going to decide what's important?"

Good question. But I wondered how the man had done in life's important decisions. Every day is filled with them. And they share our destiny. Winston Churchill said, "We build our houses and then our houses build us." Taking a lead from this, F. W. Boreham said, "We make our decisions and our decisions turn around and make us."

God will make a decision about our decisions. This is the thrust of the passage we read from Joel today. "Jehoshaphat" means "the Lord judges." The Valley of Jehoshaphat symbolizes the day of judgment. Each of us will have a day in that valley when the Lord will decide about what we've decided all through our lives. Five decisions will be most crucial. Did we decide to accept Christ as Lord and Savior of our lives? Were our daily decisions motivated by the desire to seek and do God's will? Did we accept daily forgiveness? Did we spend our time and energy caring for the poor, hungry, and disadvantaged? Did we do what love demands?

If you were to die today, would you have accomplished the reason for which you were born—and reborn?

Today's Thought: The only thing more important than our decisions is what the Lord decides about our decisions.

And seek the peace of the city where I have caused you to be carried away captive, and pray to the Lord for it; for in its peace you will have peace (Jeremiah 29:7).

What to Do About Social Problems

God cares profoundly about our cities. Their problems are problems on His heart. He places these problems on our hearts and on our agendas. The challenge to seek the welfare of the city in which we live and to pray for it is the calling of every Christian.

The word of the Lord through Jeremiah to the people of Israel about the place where they had been led captive in the exile has pointed application for us today. We may not have been carried away into exile, but we live where we do by God's appointment. He has placed us in the midst of problems among our associates, neighborhood, place where we work, and the community in which we live, so that He could use us as His agents to bring solutions to these problems. Christians should be on the forefront of the battle, out in the trenches battling for social justice and bringing help to the problems of their city.

Magnificent things are accomplished when Christians realize they are called to be involved in some of the problems confronting the city.

Coupled with the passage from Jeremiah, we need to remember Jesus' call to a compassionate ministry to the lost, lonely, and disadvantaged, plus key passages from the epistles about the application of our faith in human need. We are not to wring our hands over community problems, but to pray for the Lord's guidance about what He wants us to do.

Today's Thought: The Lord loves the city. Love for the Lord must involve every Christian in one of the areas of need in his or her city. Strength is given for service.

For we cannot but speak the things which we have seen and heard (Acts 4:20).

All that There Is of You

I can vividly remember one early morning of my first week in Hollywood. I took a walk to the top of Mount Hollywood. From that vantage point I could look over the city of Los Angeles and out to the Pacific. Below me I could see my church building and imagined my people in the homes, apartments, and offices below. Some were still on the streaming freeway on the way to work. Suddenly, I was gripped by the question, "What do you want to have happen to these people and their church and through it to this needy city? What's their fondest hope?" I reviewed my dream of what the church and contemporary Christians have been called to model for the world. Then I was aware there was someone else there. I felt His strong, gracious, challenging presence. "Are you ready?" He asked. "You need My power to fulfill My dream! Are you willing?"

Then a statement by William Booth came to mind:

> I will tell you the secret: God has had all that there was of me. There have been men with greater brains than I, even with greater opportunities, but from the day I got the poor of London on my heart and caught a vision of what Jesus Christ could do with me and them, on that day I made up my mind that God should have all of William Booth there was. And if there is anything of power in the Salvation Army, it is because God has had all the adoration of my heart, all the power of my will, and all the influence of my life.

It was then that I had to answer the Lord's question, "Lloyd, do I have all that there is of you?" What about you?

Today's Thought: Service with gladness is marked by availability, affirmation, and altruism. When we surrender our schedules to the Lord, He makes us available to people who need His love.

The law and the prophets were until John. Since that time the kingdom of God has been preached and everyone is pressing into it (Luke 16:16).

You Can't Be Serious!

Think of the different ways we say, "You can't be serious!" We say this in response when we are startled about what a person has said. It becomes an expression like "Oh, really?" or "Is that right?" But there are times when the expression "You can't be serious" means seriousness is lacking about a soul-sized issue.

In essence, Jesus was saying, "You can't be serious!" to the Pharisees when they trivialized His call to discipleship. He said, "The law and the prophets were until John. Since that time the kingdom of God has been preached and everyone is pressing into it." This was the concluding statement of the parable of the unjust steward and the Lord's incisive challenge, "No servant can serve two masters." He declared that the kingdom of God was at hand, manifest in Himself, the Messiah. No longer was it a future vision, but a present reality. Unlike the Pharisees, those who heard Jesus' call to enter the kingdom were intentionally responding—they were being serious—and were pressing to claim all that Jesus offered.

The Master's call is being sounded with clarity today. He is still seeking those who will be His enthusiastic, unreserved, intentional disciples. What would it mean for us to be serious about that today? Do we think of ourselves as faithful disciples? I plan to spend today as a wholehearted disciple of Christ, and invite you to join me.

Today's Thought: Today I'm going to invest my whole life, mind, soul, will, and resources into being an intentional disciple!

For Yours is the kingdom and the power and the glory forever. Amen (Matthew 6:13).

Because

My praying of the Lord's Prayer was given greater meaning when I discovered that the word "for" in the sentence, "For Yours is the kingdom and the power and the glory forever," can also mean "because." All the promises of the prayer are ours *because* we are offered life in the kingdom, power from God's Spirit, and glory in the manifestation of His presence. Let's think about that today.

God reigns. He has called us to be part of His kingdom on earth. As kingdom people we receive guidance in God's will, constant care in daily bread, forgiveness of our trespasses, help when tempted, and deliverance from the evil one.

The power God gives us is in the presence of Christ, our indwelling Lord. We are never left alone without Immanuel's watchful, encouraging, uplifting strength.

And the glory? Again, Christ is the glory of God's character, nature, attributes, and splendor manifested for us to behold. And the more we behold, worship, and obey Him, the more like Christ we become. The angels in heaven rejoice over how much like Jesus we are becoming—all because God is our Father!

Today's Thought: "But we all, with unveiled face, beholding the glory of the Lord, are being transformed into the same image from glory to glory, just as by the Spirit of the Lord" (2 Corinthians 3:18).

He will baptize you with the Holy Spirit and fire (Matthew 3:11).

When Nothing Less Will Do

The Holy Spirit and fire! John's prophecy was fulfilled on Pentecost. The fire of the Holy Spirit purifies, produces warmth, and galvanizes. When the Lord who is the Spirit takes up residence in us, He burns out the dross of anything which could make us ineffective disciples. As in the centering process of purifying metal, the impurities are brought to the surface and skimmed away.

Then, the sure sign that the Holy Spirit is at work in us is an inclusive, affirming warmth toward others.

A caring person discovers the joy of being a channel of the Holy Spirit. Inflow and outflow are perfectly matched. We are called to care and are given grace. The decision to care opens the floodgate.

When we surrender our lives to be agents of the Lord's caring in situations and for people, we admit we do not belong to ourselves. We belong to our Lord and to people who need His love; and with His perfect timing and unlimited resources, He gives us His own Spirit to match the needs. We will be given love, wisdom, and the freedom to give ourselves away.

Lastly, we are galvanized into a unity and oneness with other believers. The gift of profound fellowship occurs. This leaves us with personal questions. Are we on fire? In what ways do we quench, put out, or subdue the fire? We need the Holy Spirit when nothing less will do! J. B. Phillips said, "Every time we say, 'I believe in the Holy Spirit,' we mean that we believe that there is a living God able and willing to enter human personality and change it."

Today's Thought: "Should we feel at times disheartened and discouraged, a simple movement of heart toward God will renew our powers. Whatever He may demand of us, He will give us at the moment the strength and courage that we need" —Francois de Fenelon.

And suddenly there came a sound from heaven, as of a rushing mighty wind, and it filled the whole house where they were sitting (Acts 2:2).

Blowing on the Sails

One day while I was sailing, the wind went down and the sea became calm and flat. There was nothing to do but sit in irons and wait for the wind. "Irons" is a sailing term for a windless time of drifting. While waiting for the wind, I drifted past another sailboat that was floating aimlessly. The people on board the craft waved and made a flat of the hand gesture of complaint about the lack of wind. One man stood by the sails and blew on them.

I thought about that for a long time afterward. How like many Christians and far too many churches. Human breath blowing on the sails—no wonder we make so little progress!

The Spirit of God in Hebrew is *ruach*, meaning "breath" and "wind." At Pentecost the power of the Holy Spirit was like a mighty wind. The Spirit filled the disciples and got them moving again. What we need is a mighty wind—a fresh, bracing wind of a new Pentecost. Christ has been appointed by the Father to be the baptizer with the Spirit (Acts 2:33). Preparation for that is what Peter called for in the first Christian sermon: repentance, belief in Christ as Savior, and an admission of our need for power.

In this book we've been talking about silent strength. A daily Pentecost is the source of that. So stop blowing your own breath into the sails of your life or your church. Ask for a fresh wind to fill the sails. Without the Holy Spirit, we'll drift in irons and be lost at sea.

Today's Thought: Lord, fill the sails of the church with the wind of the Holy Spirit and begin with me. I lift my sails and am ready to receive Your Spirit!

Behold, I send the Promise of My Father upon you; but tarry . . . until you are endued with power from on high (Luke 24:49).

You Can't Take It Alone!

John R. W. Stott said, "Before Christ sent the church into the world, He sent the Spirit into the church. The same order must be observed today." When we open ourselves to caring, eventually we have more than we can take alone. All the troubled people, our sick and suffering world, the violence and hatred finally get to us. It is then that we have two alternatives, neither of which seems to work. We either decide the human need is too much to bear, or we build a wall around our hearts to become impervious to the sights and sounds of hurting people.

The third possibility is to realize we can't take it alone. We were never meant to! Our assurance is that God will never leave us alone to bear the caring of others in our own strength.

This is why a caring person also must be a praying person. We have not been asked to repeat Calvary by suffering for people, but to claim the love of the cross for people. When we cast our cares on the Lord, we discover what He wants us to do and then are freed to trust Him with the outcome.

We belong to Christ. The awesome authority He had over suffering, sin, and sickness is entrusted to us. We are not powerless victims. We are sent on a mission with the assurance of unlimited supply lines. I once asked a general why he was so successful. His answer is a good motto for a person who is called to care for others: "I knew that ultimately we would win. I never underestimated my enemy, and I kept my supply lines open."

Today's Thought: "The life which flows from Christ into a man is something different, not only in degree but also in kind. It is a new quality. There is a new creation, not just an intensification of powers already possessed, but the sudden emergence of an entirely new and original element whenever a man comes to be in Christ. He begins to live in the sphere of the post-resurrection life in Jesus" —James Stewart.

For all have sinned and fall short of the glory of God, being justified freely by His grace through the redemption that is in Christ Jesus (Romans 3:23,24).

A Heart Strangely Warmed

A leaf from John Wesley's journal explains the assurance God wants to give all of us today:

> May 4, 1837. In the evening I went very unwillingly to a Society in Altersgate, where one was reading Luther's preface to the Epistle to the Romans. About a quarter before nine, while he was describing the change which God works in the heart through faith in Christ, I felt my heart strangely warmed. I felt I did trust in Christ, Christ alone, for salvation; and an assurance was given to me that He had taken away my sins, even mine, and saved me from the law of sin and death.

Up to this time in Wesley's life, he was a troubled young man and an ineffective priest. He had failed in his missionary work in America and had realized how empty his life was when, on the return voyage in a storm, he was struck with panic while the Moravian Christians on board sang hymns peacefully. Wesley was a religious person who did not know God! What he had seen of the faith of the Moravians led him to go to Altersgate where his heart was warmed and his life was transformed.

This may be your greatest need as you begin this day. Or, if you've had a time of assurance like this, you might need renewal to face the pressures ahead today. It happens when we claim the love and forgiveness of God through Christ by faith alone and accept that we belong to Him. When we accept this and realize we are loved, our hearts will feel the warmth of the assurance. We can never qualify by our goodness but are loved unqualifiedly by grace.

Today's Thought: "Some people have just enough religion to make them uncomfortable" —John Wesley.

Be filled with the Spirit (Ephesians 5:18).

Keep on Being Filled

Paul admonished the Ephesians to "...be filled with the Spirit" (Ephesians 5:18). The verb is in the present passive imperative. It does not mean a once-for-all filling. If this were the case, the aorist form of the verb would have been used, indicating a completed action in the past. Rather, the apostle urges the Ephesians to "continue to allow the Spirit to fill you." The passive emphasizes something which is done to us rather than something we do. Every day, in each hour, when life stretches us with problems, difficulties, and challenges beyond us, we are to allow Christ to fill us with His Spirit. And when we fail or are conscious of our inadequacy, we are given a sublime chance to be broken open to a new infilling.

John Calvin in his *Institutes* says, "First we must understand that as long as Christ remains outside of us, and we are separated from Him, all that He has suffered and done for the salvation of the human race remains useless and of no value to us." Karl Barth speaks of the Spirit as "none other than the presence and action of Jesus Christ Himself; His stretched-out arm; He Himself in the power of His resurrection, i.e., in the power of His revelation as it begins in and with the power of His resurrection and continues its work from this point." The resurrected Christ fills us, gives us the gifts of the Spirit (1 Corinthians 12), transforms us with the fruit of the Spirit (Galatians 5:22,23), and enables us to become dynamic people—"...Christ in you, the hope of glory" (Colossians 1:27).

In my own experience, the gifts of the Spirit were imparted as the result of realizing that I could not make it on my own. Any evidence of the fruit of Christ's character has come when I failed on my own to produce authentic love, joy, peace, longsuffering, gentleness, and self-control.

Today's Thought: Lord fill me with your Spirit today!

Though he knew only the baptism of John (Acts 18:25).

The Man Who Had Everything

Many of us are like Apollos, the man who had everything, but needed Someone. Apollos is the patron saint of many of us in the church today. He was fervent in spirit, but not filled with the Spirit. He had training, skill, oratorical effectiveness, theological clarity, but no power. But, also like him, I believe that we long for what happened to him after his encounter with Priscilla and Aquila. They give us an effective model of relational evangelism! They began with affirmation—what B. F. Skinner would call reinforcement—and they were supportive of his efforts and gifts. But, having won the right to be heard, they pointed the way to life in Christ. The result was that Apollos was set on fire. I have always felt that the difference was in the fact that Apollos stopped trying to follow and proclaim Jesus as a historical figure—the Christ of Israel—and allowed the living Lord to dwell in him. I think he became more personal as he talked about the result of the relationship with the living Christ for the relationships of his own life. People were no longer impressed with Apollos, but infused with the living Christ.

St. Augustine was on target when he portrayed the entire Christian enterprise as that in which one loving heart sets another on fire. The gift of the Holy Spirit is the gift of fire—illumination, warmth, dynamic power for the communication of love to others. William Barclay said, "A witness is essentially a man who speaks from first-hand knowledge. He is a man who says, 'This is true and I know it.' He is a man who knows from personal experience that what he says is true; and it is impossible to stop a man like that because it is impossible to stop the truth."

Today's Thought: "Our task is to live our personal communion with Christ with such intensity as to make it contagious" —Paul Tournier.

Oh, that all the Lord's people were prophets and that the Lord would put His Spirit upon them! (Numbers 11:29).

The Gift of Prophecy

Would you like to have X-ray vision to be able to see into people's deepest hopes and hurts? Would you like to be able to discern what God wants you to say to these people when they ask for help? Would you like to have the courage to take a stand on crucial social issues and know that what you have to say is a word from the Lord?

If you have said "Yes!" to these questions, you are ready to receive the gift of prophecy. It is the gift of the Holy Spirit available to all Christians. Moses longed for the Spirit to come upon all the people so they could prophesy. Joel prophesied the day when that would happen, which was fulfilled on Pentecost. Prophecy is not foretelling but forth-telling.

Here's how it works. When the Holy Spirit dwells in us we become aware of the deepest needs in people and in situations. We are given discernment as to what the Lord wants. Then we are given the courage to speak the truth in love. The need before us brings forth the gist of prophecy from within us. It is not permanently endowed, but is given to us momentarily for needs in a person, the church, or society. We remain timid, equivocating disciples without it.

But don't ever forget that Paul knew that prophecy without love could be brash and insensitive. When we really love, we want the Lord's best for each person and circumstance. If we'll ask Him, He will help us discern what that is and communicate it with empathy and profound caring. Try it today!

Today's Thought: Being prophetic without love is insensitivity; loving without being prophetic is ineffective.

Let the word of Christ dwell in you richly in all wisdom (Colossians 3:16).

The Anointing of Wisdom

In the first few years of my Christian life I realized that though I knew Christ as my Lord and Savior, I was out of sync with Him. I bungled along doing the best I could with my innate intellectual ability. Decisions were arduous and often missed the mark. Counseling with people in spiritual need was long and exhausting. Then God led me to an in-depth study of the gifts of His Spirit. I studied the lives of great Christians in history who seemed to display a quality of wisdom in their relationships and their communication in writing and speaking. Without exception, each of those giants of the faith had gone through a pride-shattering realization of their own inadequacy, coupled with a plea that the wisdom gift of the mind of Christ be given them. Following their example, I asked a few trusted friends to come together to lay hands on me, asking God to entrust to me the gift of wisdom. That day was one of the most crucial transitions in my life. God answered my longing for a "hearing heart." Over the years I have experienced the results in more right decisions, deeper perceptions of people's needs, and greater precision in speaking truth with love and wisdom.

When Christ takes up residence in us and infuses His wisdom into us, we can tower over Solomon in all his glory! It all begins when we ask for what he asked: a hearing heart. But now, on this side of Calvary and Pentecost, what God offers in response is all the practical wisdom He gave to Solomon and the fullness of wisdom incarnate in Christ through His indwelling Spirit. He says longingly, "Ask what you wish Me to give you." Go for it! Ask for the mind of Christ, Wisdom—and everything else of any ultimate value—will be yours as well!

Today's Thought: Thank You, Lord, for Your answer to my prayer for an anointing of my mind with Your Spirit.

Because the foolishness of God is wiser than men, and the weakness of God is stranger than men (1 Corinthians 1:25).

Walk in Wisdom

The three words Paul uses to describe wisdom in action on the cross are righteousness, sanctification, and redemption. The power of God was utilized to make us right with Himself, to enable us to grow in that reconciled relationship, and to bring us back to the full value of our destiny by paying the price for our salvation through forgiveness. Our response is spelled out in our own cross. We surrender ourselves, die to impetuous self-willfulness, and are raised to live a new life. Wisdom's greatest choice is our commitment to Christ. Then each decision we make is to further this newfound righteousness in all of life. As each choice is made with the imputed wisdom He provides, we are sanctified more and more, which means being formed in the likeness of Christ Himself. The redemption which "purchased our salvation" becomes like a time-release capsule as we accept forgiveness from God and our forgiveness of ourselves and others as the only wise way to live.

The three dimensions of wisdom help us to ask crucial questions when we sort out what is best for ourselves and others. When faced with each of life's choices, we should ask, "Will it further a right relationship with the Lord? Will it enable me to grow in cross-oriented Christlikeness? Will it express gracious forgiveness, thus redeeming hostility and hatred, or will it sell back to evil a part of me that belongs to the Lord? Will this choice or decision or action move me forward to the person I am destined to be now and forever?" When we answer these questions honestly and act in accordance with clear-cut guidance from the Lord, we have used the power of intellect, knowledge of the facts, and perception of how each choice fits into His plan.

Today's Thought: "Walk in wisdom . . . redeeming the time" (Colossians 4:5).

In your patience, possess your souls (Luke 21:19).

Becoming the Person You Long to Be

In Jesus' description of the difficulties His disciples would face, He dropped this one-line, terse, and salient secret of triumphant discipleship: "In your patience, possess your souls." Some of the alternative translations and paraphrases cast light on the real meaning. But we are still left to wonder, "What did Christ mean by possessing, gaining, or winning our own souls?" Doesn't this contradict justification by faith alone? Not at all. The Lord is not talking about winning eternal life by our own effort, but an attitude toward ourselves that enables us to realize the full meaning of our status as loved and forgiven people.

Many confess they wrestle with an old life inside while trying to live the new life in Christ on the outside. Some find it difficult to rein in the stallions of inner fantasies, passions, and attitudes. Others experience great difficulty in changing their old ways of dealing with themselves. We get down on ourselves and often are engulfed with self-doubt. Still others struggle to get control of their desires, fears, and worries.

The conquest of self by the power of Christ is the biggest battle we must wage. He gives us the secret in this challenging saying. It's wrapped up in the word "patience." He's not simply advising that we be patient with ourselves, but that in patient trust in Him we are transformed from within and able to cope with the difficulties around us. When we yield to Him the reformation of the person inside us, we progressively become more like Him. Our reaction to the challenges and temptations around us reveals our true nature. The more we discover, the more we can surrender to Him and His life-changing power. When we are alarmed by the thoughts, feelings, and attitudes we still have, instead of self-condemnation or self-justification, we can ask Him to heal us.

Today's Thought: Both patience and self-control are fruit of the Spirit. They are twin-grafted branches inseparably related to the Vine. We can be the persons we long to be!

The fruit of the Spirit is love (Galatians 5:22).

Though I speak with the tongues of men and of angels, but have not love, I have become as sounding brass or a clanging cymbal (1 Corinthians 13:1).

The Gift of Love

All efforts to define love fall dumb before the apostle Paul's magnificent hymn of love in 1 Corinthians, chapter 13.

It is a description of Christ and the love He enables in us when He comes to indwell us.

The passage comes alive when it is read three ways. First, read it as Paul wrote it; next, put the word "Christ" in place of the word "love" and read it again; then, replace the word "love" with the personal pronoun "I" and read it once more. The miracle of Christ's indwelling power is that the love He revealed is exactly the love He will communicate to others through us.

As you begin this day, claim that filled with Christ's love, you can *be* love to others today. Try reading 1 Corinthians 13:1-8 with the personal pronoun now. It can be true!

"I am very patient and kind, never jealous or envious, never boastful or proud, never haughty or selfish or rude. I do not demand my own way. I am not irritable or touchy. I do not hold grudges and will hardly even notice when others do me wrong. I am never glad about injustice, but rejoice whenever truth wins out.

"When I love someone I will be loyal to him no matter what the cost. I will always believe in him, always expect the best of him, and always stand my ground in defending him. All the special gifts and powers from God will someday come to an end, but love goes on forever" (1 Corinthians 13:4-8 TLB, with first-person pronouns).

Today's Thought: With the Lord's help, that's the way I intend to live today! I will claim the fruit of the Spirit of love.

The fruit of the Spirit is . . . joy (Galatians 5:22).

And these things we write to you that your joy may be full (1 John 1:4).

Lasting Joy!

Joy is not gush or ho-ho jolliness. It is more than happiness. It is impervious to difficult situations and impossible people. Joy is an outward expression of grace, God's unmotivated love. The Greek word for "grace" is *charis* and the word for "joy" is *chara*. They both come from the same root.

Joy is the result of being loved by God. When His undeserved grace and forgiveness penetrates through the thick layers of self-doubt and self-negation, we begin to feel the surge of joy. Self-esteem and joy go together. We can joyously exclaim, "I'm glad I'm me!" This is not easy for most Christians. We find it difficult to let God love us and change our demeaning self-image. It takes a constant reminder of how much God loves us. The cross alone can balance the weighted scales loaded with self-condemnation.

There can be no joy without Christ living in us. His promises about joy are all connected to realizing a profound intimacy with Him. When we abide in Him and He in us, we know joy. Jesus Christ Himself is our joy!

Today's Thought: "Joy is the standard that flies on the battlements of the heart when the King is in residence" —R. Leonard Small.

The fruit of the Spirit is . . . peace (Galatians 5:22).

The Bond of Peace

Is it any wonder the word "peace" was so often on the lips of our Lord? Peace is one of our greatest needs. He greeted His disciples with the single word "Peace!" The early church was characterized by the greeting, "The peace of the Lord Jesus be with you!" A part of the historic Eucharist has been: *Pax tibiti*—"Peace to you!"

In Hebrew the word for "peace" is *shalom*. In Greek it is *eirene*. In Latin it is *pax*. What is this peace?

Peace is more than a state of freedom from hostility, more than harmony or a temporary truce in personal relationships.

Christ gives it to us by virtue of His indwelling presence, the presence Paul spoke of as fruit to imply a process of growth or degrees of development depending on our cooperation. The fruit of peace becomes resplendent in us when our acceptance of God's forgiveness is complete in every level of our being.

Are you at peace right now? Is there within you that quiet, that healing distillation that only the Lord can give? The meaning of the word "peace" in both Hebrew and Greek is "the knitting together, the unification of what has been broken and unraveled and disrupted." It means wholeness. In fact it is almost a synonym for "salvation," which means "oneness and wholeness and unification."

Peace is the result of the indwelling of the living Christ. Peace is not only a gift of Christ, it is Christ Himself living His life in us through the Holy Spirit. Peace is His presence in our hearts and minds. It is abiding in Christ and allowing Him to abide in us. Now we can say and mean, "Peace be with you! May the peace of the living Christ live in your hearts!"

Today's Thought: "Finally, brethren, farewell. Become complete. Be of good comfort, be of one mind, live in peace; and the God of love and peace will be with you" (2 Corinthians 13:11).

The fruit of the Spirit is . . . long-suffering (Galatians 5:23).

Living on the Lord's Timing

Are you ever troubled with impatience? Do difficult people ever test your patience? Does what they do or fail to do get to you? Are you ever upset when people you love fail to capture your vision for them? Ever get exasperated when people do not meet your expectations of what you want them to accomplish on your time schedules? And more profoundly, knowing people's potential and what the Lord can do with the life given over to His control, do you become impatient with their slow response or imperviousness?

Perhaps our problem with impatience is that we misunderstand patience. It is not acquiescence, or perpetual placidity, or feckless lack of fiber. Patience must be rooted in an overarching confidence that there is Someone in control of this universe, our world, and our life. We need to know that God does work things together for good for those who love Him. A patient person knows the shortness of time and the length of eternity. Patience is really faith in action. No wonder it is called an aspect of the fruit of the Spirit. It is one of the matchless characteristics of Christ Himself. If we would learn patience, He alone can teach us. There are many facsimiles of the virtue, but authentic patience comes as a result of our deep personal relationship with Christ.

Today's Thought: It would be disastrous to have anything that God did not deem best for us or to have what is best for us before God timed it.

The fruit of the Spirit is . . . kindness (Galatians 5:22).

What is desired in a man is kindness (Proverbs 19:22).

Whatever Happened to Kindness?

Kindness is the steadfast love of the Lord in action toward those who fail. Throughout the Old Testament the words for "steadfast love," "mercy," and "kindness" are used interchangeably. Kindness is the persistent effort of the Lord to reach His people and enable them to return to Him.

Jesus Christ was kindness incarnate. He came to express it; lived to model it; died to offer it; and returns to impart it to us in the Holy Spirit. Paul knew this from his own experience of the kindness of God in Christ. His rigid hostility toward others and himself had been melted by an unsurpassed kindness. God never demands anything of us that He is not willing to give us. It should not be surprising that the power to be kind is available under the code name "fruit." Kindness is implanted, imputed, and ingrained into the very nature of our new heredity in Christ Jesus. It is ours to develop and express along with the other character strengths inherent in the fruit of the Spirit. Kindness can now be reflected in all our relationships. We can be as merciful and gracious to others as Christ has been to us.

Today's Thought: Kindness is a sign of greatness.

The fruit of the Spirit is . . . goodness (Galatians 5:22).

Streaming to the goodness of the Lord (Jeremiah 31:12).

Good for Goodness' Sake!

When we feel that God is good—good to us despite everything we have said and done, then we know that mercy takes the shape of goodness. God's goodness is that He knows our need even before we ask Him. God's goodness is that He goes before us to show the way. God's goodness was that at the time humankind deserved it least, He came in Jesus Christ to reveal Himself and to die for the sins of the whole race. He came to make men and women good from the inside.

Goodness is an inside story. We are made good not by our efforts but by the efficacy of the atonement accomplished by Jesus Christ on the cross. Our status before God is in and through Christ. He accepts us as new creatures, made good on Calvary. We could not dare to come to God apart from the imputed goodness of our vicarious standing through the Savior. The Lord looks at us through the focused lens of Calvary. Our confidence is not in our human facsimiles of goodness, but in our relationship with Christ. We are freed from compulsive efforts to be good enough to deserve love. Instead we can live in the settled security of goodness in Christ!

The goodness of the Lord impels us to do good works. We have been conscripted to serve. Goodness does not make us "goody-goodies" but people who seek to know what is good for all and do it by Christ's power. Our title for today is a play on the words of the song, "Oh, be good for goodness' sake." Not a bad motto when we use a capital "G" and do what's good for the One whose name and nature is Goodness.

Today's Thought: "We must first be made good before we can do good" —Hugh Latimer.

The fruit of the Spirit is . . . faithfulness (Galatians 5:22).

You Can Depend on Me

The steadfast nature of the Lord is like an anchor that never pulls off the bottom. It stabilizes the ship in the midst of the storm. It is because God loves us that we know He is faithful. He cannot contradict His own nature. He Himself is unmerited, unchanging, unconditional love.

The fruit of faithfulness is a result. Faith is a primary gift of the Holy Spirit. It is the imputed gift by which we respond to what God has done for us in Jesus Christ. Belief is not our accomplishment. The same God who is Source and Sustainer of all, who dwelt in Jesus Christ for the reconciliation of the world, is the same Lord who comes to each of us to give us the capacity to claim what was done for us as the basis of our hope, now and forever. This faith leads to faithfulness, a full-grown faith which dares to believe that all things are possible. It develops as a consistency in all of life. Our faithfulness is not our human follow-through, but our trust that Christ will follow through in all of life's changes and challenges. He says, "You can depend on Me!" Can we say that to Him and to others? His dependability makes us dependable.

Today's Thought: "Oh, praise the Lord, all you Gentiles! Laud Him, all you peoples! For His merciful kindness is great toward us, and the truth of the Lord endures forever" (Psalm 117:1,2).

The fruit of the Spirit is . . . gentleness (Galatians 5:23).

The Strength of Gentleness

There is no other way to be gentle than by the name and power the Lord gives us. Authentic gentleness is one of the most miraculous manifestations of the inner power of Christ's indwelling. It requires absolute trust in His ongoing work in others. It responds to the wonder of what people have been through, not what they have done. It addresses the emerging child, often hurt and battered, in other people.

The Lord is consistently gentle with us. He stands beside us in the midst of trouble and tragedy, nursing us through it all. This is the same kind of encouragement the people around us need.

What does it mean to be gentle in life's tensions and problems? It certainly does not mean simply having a moldable, adjustable, easy lack of concern. Moses was referred to as one of the meekest men in all of Israel, and yet he marshaled the mass exodus of a diverse company of people and brought them through the wilderness to the Promised Land.

When we are truly meek, we know who we are because we know to whom we belong. We do not have to be defensive or justify ourselves any longer. We know we are loved and are therefore free to love and free to be the unique, special, unreproducible wonders that God meant us to be. Once defensive pride is taken from us by an authentic experience of humility, we are able to treat others like God treated us.

Today's Thought: Only a person who is unsure of himself and Christ is afraid to be gentle. Lording it over others is a sure sign we need the Lord.

The fruit of the Spirit is... self-control (Galatians 5:23).

Self-Control That Focuses the Wind

Self-control, the last fruit of the Spirit, is the one that makes all the rest operative. To the Greek, "self-control" meant to have "power over oneself." Paul grasped this quality from the four cardinal virtues of the Stoics and claimed it as one of the imputed vibrancies of the Holy Spirit. The Greek word, *egkrateia*, rooted in *kratos*, "strength," means to have strength to control the self. We know this is not possible until we surrender to Christ's management.

This sublime fruit of the Spirit is not negative. It does not delineate what we are against or will not do. Rather it consists of a very positive capacity to know who we are and what we will do because the Spirit is in control of our abilities and aptitudes, as well as appetites. We can have power over ourselves only when we have submitted to the Spirit's control and power in us. Christ's control is the basis of self-control.

This fruit of Christ's indwelling is more than just not flying off the handle or always being Mr. Perfect or Miss Smooth. Instead, it's being centered so that all our energies, when multiplied by the Spirit, can be used creatively rather than be squandered. A person who has the fruit of self-control becomes like a wind channel in which the power of the wind is channeled. It's silent strength that's focused to do what the Master commands.

Today's Thought: Today I will think of myself as a wind channel for the flow of the Spirit.

All things are yours (1 Corinthians 3:21).

That's Living!

One of the places I go to recapture God's dream is back to one of my favorite Scriptures. It's in that magnificent third chapter of 1 Corinthians. The Corinthians were running out of power and vision because they were enjoying the unenjoyable luxury of divisiveness and party spirit. Paul breaks the bond of the impotence in a stirring way. He reminds them of their purpose, power, and potential. "Do you not know that you are the temple of God and that the Spirit of God dwells in you?" This always reorients my perspective on the reason I am alive. Everything I need is a gift from the Holy Spirit. I don't need to use the gift. This is when I am utterly amazed at what has been provided. "For all things are yours: whether Paul or Apollos or Cephas, or the world or life or death, or things present or things to come—all are yours. And you are Christ's, and Christ is God's." Paul ticks off the amazing resources. When he talks about himself, Apollos, Cephas—leaders in the early church around whom divisive loyalties foolishly formed—I am reminded of the people who helped me find the adventure in Christ, and all the people who are His love incarnate to me. But that's not all. The world is mine to enjoy. Life is not a drudgery but a never-ending succession of God's interventions and infusions of guidance and power. Death is no longer an enemy but an anticipated transition to a fuller life. The present, therefore, can be lived as if it were the only moment I will ever have. Fear of the future is over. I cannot drift out of the sphere of His care. Even the difficulties and tragedies—the worst I or someone else can do—can be used for the best He wants for me. That's living, and I am deeply gratified. What about you?

Today's Thought: The years of our lives, however long or short they be, are for one purpose: to know God personally and to spend eternity with Him.

There was a certain man in Caesarea called Cornelius, a centurion of what was called the Italian Regiment (Acts 10:1).

The Lord Has So Much More to Give

Cornelius is the patron saint of good people who need the Holy Spirit. He is a vivid example of many fine people who need to be Spirit-filled. Often people with strong moral integrity, impeccable character and healthy self-esteem find it difficult to admit their need for rebirth and the baptism of the Spirit. Churches are filled with them. It's difficult for them to imagine that God has anything more to give them.

Not so with Cornelius. He wanted more of God. The centurion was one of the leaders of Rome's finest regiment. While on duty in Palestine, he had become a "God-fearer," the special term for a Gentile who came to believe in God. Cornelius was a generous man, built a synagogue, and prayed always. And God was pleased.

At the same time, God was preparing Peter to be willing to come to the Gentile's home in Caesarea. Actually, the Lord had a harder time getting Peter out of his Jewish exclusiveness than opening the Roman to his spiritual need. But when Peter arrived, the apostle barely got through the opening of his sermon before the Holy Spirit was poured out on Cornelius and his whole household.

Cornelius challenges all of us. We've only begun to experience God's grace and goodness. For openers, He wants to make us sure of our salvation and fill us with His Spirit. Then He wants to make us new people and get us moving in ministry. There's always a next step, and today's the day to take it. What's yours?

Today's Thought: Lord, thank You for creating in me the desire to receive more of what You want to give me.

Teach them to your children and your grandchildren (Deuteronomy 4:9).

A Father Movement

We need a father movement, and Father's Day is a good day to begin. What I have in mind is more than simply honoring fathers with parties and gifts. Rather it should be a day of calling fathers to be spiritual leaders. I'm all for women's rights and mutual submission in marriage, but men are abdicating their calling to be strong witnesses to their families. It's time for fathers to break the silence about what the Lord has done in their lives.

I talk to so many young people who have never heard their fathers say what Christ means to them or lead in family prayers. I'm not talking about lording it over a family, but making Christ the Lord of the family. Often a father's silence about his faith or what Christ has done to help him in the tough as well as the good times leads children to feel that the faith does not really matter. Children respond to intimacy. They are very curious about what makes their parents tick. If fathers can orate on "Now when I was a boy..." why not "Let me share what's really important to me. For me to live is Christ and here's why...." Often all children get from their fathers about the faith are the rules and regulations—mostly don'ts.

Father's Day produces a mixture of feelings in many fathers. Those whose children are grown hope it will be a day when, in spite of everything, they are loved as fathers, and fathers with growing children also enjoy being affirmed.

Fathers, why don't we turn it around and give a party for our children? There would be no Father's Day without them! Why not celebrate them and tell them how thankful to God we are as fathers? Use it as a day to share your faith.

Today's Thought: Nothing can happen through us that is not happening to us. Father's Day is a day for fathers to be sure they have a faith to share with their children.

For what is a man profited if he gains the whole world, and loses his own soul? Or what will a man give in exchange for his soul? (Matthew 16:26).

Finding Your True Self

The distance between our true and projected self is the breeding ground of emotional tension and agitation.

Mark Schorer's analysis of Sinclair Lewis points up what I mean. "In flight from himself, he tried to compensate by his immense vaudeville talent. He never got around to connecting his talent and his life so that he knew who he was. There was no inner certainty, no balance, no serenity, nothing between heaven and earth to which he could withdraw for quietude and healing. Because he never knew himself, he outraged himself."

That may seem a bit severe. But listen to Lewis about his own life: "I spent my life doing neither what I ought or what I wanted." That sounds like a friend of mine who commented, "Every step I take is a struggle between what I am and what I ought to be!" Shakespeare was near the truth in *Measure for Measure*: "O what man may within himself hide, though angel on the outward side." For all of us, the problem is that doing usually precedes being. John Steinbeck's Ethan was right: "Men don't get knocked out, or I mean they can fight back against big things. What kills men is erosion: they get nudged into failure." That's because there are no moorings in the heart, no criterion beyond people's opinion, no motive greater than daily schedule demands. What e. e. cummings concludes as his advice to those who would write in *The Magic Marker* is universally true: "To be nobody but yourself in a world which is doing its best, night and day, to make you everybody else—means the hardest battle which any human being can fight, and never stop fighting."

Today's Thought: We never know who we really are until we give ourselves to Christ. Losing ourselves, we find ourselves for the first time.

I will put a new spirit within them, and take the stony heart out of their flesh, and give them a heart of flesh, that they may walk in My statutes and keep My judgments and do them; and they shall be My people, and I will be their God (Ezekiel 11:19,20).

When Our Hearts Are Broken

Life, people, circumstances, unfulfilled wishes and dreams, and unrealized plans can break our hearts. Disappointment hits us all at times. We feel brokenhearted.

But look at the nature of a heart that can be broken. It must be hard or crisp to break at all. It's usually at the point where life has hardened our hearts that they are vulnerable to be broken. Pride, willfulness, determined plans for ourselves and others, and preconceptions about what should happen are areas where our hearts get hardened by self-determination. What we want is projected onto God, and we expect Him to pull it off for us. When it doesn't happen, we feel our hearts break. They break because, in Ezekiel's terms, they were "hearts of stone."

The opposite of a "heart of stone" (one set on its own will) is a "heart of flesh." Flesh throughout the Scriptures means our humanity, or humanness. When our heart of stone is removed, we are given a heart of flesh—an ability to feel the pulse of God's will and plan for us, one filled with His Spirit.

So when problems break our hearts, there's probably something deeper than the problem that needs to be broken open and filled with the Lord Himself. As a result, we feel the Lord's attitude toward the people or circumstances that have disappointed us. Instead of just feeling hurt, we discover that there is available to us deeper comfort and healing than we have ever experienced before.

Today's Thought: Disappointment is missing what we set as our appointment. It really makes way for a greater appointment—with the Lord.

It will be as though a man fled from a lion, and a bear met him (Amos 5:19).

The Lion and the Bear

There's no escaping our inescapable God. Whenever we resist doing His will or the demands of righteousness, He pursues us. Amos says it's like fleeing from a lion only to meet a bear. There's no place to hide from a God who is everywhere and knows everything.

Have you ever wanted to escape the challenge of being God's person? Has He ever called you to growth that you resisted? Instead of an approving, affirming God, you felt Him pursuing you like Frances Thompson's "hound of heaven." In life's problems, you met first the lion and then the bear.

The amazing thing is when we stop running away from God, we realize that in addition to being like a lion and a bear He really has the face of a lamb—the Lamb of God who takes away the sins of the world, yours and mine. We have experienced both sides of the nature of God. We've known His wrath when we disobeyed and we've experienced His grace when we repented.

What does God want from us? The last verse in today's Scripture reading makes it clear: "But let justice run down like water and righteousness like a mighty stream." Wholehearted commitment to personal and social righteousness is our inescapable calling. If you've been bumping into the lion and the bear these days, stop and ask God what's wrong. When the answer becomes clear, obey! The Lamb will help you—be sure of that.

Today's Thought: When nothing is going right, ask the Lord what's wrong.

And He commanded us to preach to the people, and to testify that it is He who was ordained by God to be Judge of the living and the dead. To Him all the prophets witness that, through His name, whoever believes in Him will receive remission of sins (Acts 10:42,43).

The Cutting Edge

A vital part of the continuing ministry of the reigning Christ both now and at His second coming at the end of history is judgment. We have come to think of the word "judgment" with fear and disdain. In religious circles it's associated with "fire and brimstone" preaching. The love of the Lord, not His judgment, is proclaimed. Thus the cutting edge is lost.

But you can't skim over the judgment of Christ, because it clearly is a central theme of the New Testament and the earliest creeds. Christ's basic judgment is on our response to Him as Lord and Savior. A prelude to our conversion is an experience of Christ's judgment on our lives. He said, "Most assuredly, I say to you, he who hears My word and believes in Him who sent Me has everlasting life and shall not come into judgment, but has passed from death into life" (John 5:24). Our destiny is based on our response here and now to Christ.

But after our conversion, remedial judgment continues to call us toward growth in His likeness and obedience to His moral requirements and ethical demands. Although we no longer fear an eternal judgment, we experience the judgment of the Lord's nurturing love. It shows us where we are and our need to grow. Shouldn't a Christian who has gone along with a permissive society feel judgment? And what about a believer who has never helped another person to know Christ? His eternal salvation may not be in jeopardy, but surely his maturity is. Then too, we should all feel judgment when we have little or no involvement in Christ's ministry in the needs around us. It's because our Lord loves us that He shows us what we can be.

Today's Thought: "From thence He shall come to judge the quick and the dead" —Apostles' Creed.

If we say that we have no sin, we deceive ourselves, and the truth is not in us (1 John 1:8).

True Confessions

Before we pray our prayers of confession, it is good to ask the Lord what He wants us to confess. Often our confession deals with surface issues when there may be deeper causes the Lord wants to expose and expunge. Taking time to be quiet before the Lord and asking Him to probe deeper into our hearts makes confession much more liberating. The strength of the Lord flows through a clean channel. Sometimes the channel is blocked by inner resistance or unexamined motives the Lord wants to remove. His Spirit acts like a plumber's tool, breaking up the clog in the pipes.

The word "confess" literally means "to speak the same thing." In Greek it is *homologeo*: *homos*, "same"; *lego*, "to speak." It implies to give assent, be in accord, agree with, and declare openly. Authentic confession to the Lord is telling Him what He has told us we need to confess.

The other day, I prayed my morning prayers and did not feel the sure and silent strength I usually receive. Then I realized my confession had been very glib and shallow. So I went back to prayer. "Lord, show me myself, expose any hidden sin and debilitating attitudes, any subtle resistance to Your will." In the silence, things came to mind I would not have thought of by myself—things done and said, and others I'd been putting off doing and saying. When I confessed what the Lord had placed His finger on, the flow of power returned. What is the Lord asking you to confess today?

Today's Thought: Spend as much time asking the Lord what to confess as you spend confessing.

Surely He has borne our griefs and carried our sorrows (Isaiah 53:4).

Calvary Covers It All

The old hymn "Calvary Covers All" proclaims a truth we need every day. Our reading from Isaiah 53 fills us with awe and gratitude. It helps us claim all that was on Christ's mind when He died on the cross. And every aspect was completed for us. Christ the Healer went to the cross for the healing of all the hurts of life.

Calvary covers our sins. "Surely He has borne our griefs," identifies Christ as the scapegoat. Our minds leap to Leviticus 16:22 and the scapegoat on which the sins of the people were placed before the goat was led into the wilderness. The sins were banished forever. Christ did that for us on the cross. All our transgressions and iniquities (habitual sins) can be forgiven.

Calvary covers our physical needs: "He has borne our griefs and carried out sorrows." The Hebrew word for "griefs" is *choli*, and can also mean "disease" and "sickness." "Sorrows," *makob*, means "pain" or "distress." The victorious Christ is with us now to release in us the healing power of His cross. His healing miracles during His ministry were only a portion of the unleashing of this healing power in the world. This is why we can pray for healing and gratefully anticipate His miracles.

Calvary covers what robs us of peace. The "chastisement of our peace" means the judgment for our discord and lack of peace. Paul says we now have peace with God because of the blood of Christ. When we accept that we are loved and forgiven, we are given the gift of peace.

Can you think of a single need we have today that was not dealt with by Christ on the cross? But more important, what needs do you have right now that need healing?

Today's Thought: "Calvary covers it all,
My past with its sin and stain;
My guilt and despair Jesus took on Him there,
And Calvary covers it all."
—Mrs. Walter G. Taylor

June 23 Proverbs 3:14-26

For the Lord will be your confidence, and will keep your foot from being caught (Proverbs 3:26).

Just Say "No"

E. Stanley Jones once said, "Your ability to say no determines your capacity to say yes to greater things."

The slogan of the war on drugs is "Just Say No." That admonition is needed for all of life—every day. We are constantly tempted by things we know would break the Ten Commandments. In addition, there are beguiling temptations to do what would lead us away from our primary commitment to put God first in our lives. A lot of good things can render us incapable of receiving God's best.

How can we know when to say "no"? There's no other way than through consistent communion with God. We get ready for crises before they hit—not in them. A constant surrender of our minds to think God's thoughts and our will to do His will will give us the moment-by-moment discernment about what we should do.

People with silent strength are not pushovers for the pressures of people or the subtle strategies of Satan. They know the Lord will guide and will provide the course. A good test is: "Will saying yes bring me closer to the Lord?" If not, we can be sure it's time to say "no." This involves not only the more obvious sins, but also getting so busy that we have little time left for the secret place and prayer where we receive silent strength.

Today's Thought: There is a time when we must firmly choose the course we will follow, or the relentless drift of events will make the decision for us.

Who, when he had found one pearl of great price, went and sold all that he had and bought it (Matthew 13:46).

It Was Worth It!

Right from the offset, keep one thing in mind. The twin parables of the hidden treasure are autobiographical. Christ is the ploughman who discovers the treasure and the merchant who found the pearl of great price. And you are the treasure—the pearl!

These twin parables must be understood in the context of those that preceded them. Jesus clearly identified that He, the Son of Man, was the sower of the good seed. Then, without losing a beat, He talked about the ploughman who discovered the treasure in the field and the merchant who discovered the precious pearl. Both parables have one central point: the supreme value of the treasure and the pearl. No effort is too much, no price is too high, to possess them. Even the cross, Jesus? Yes.

This is what the kingdom of heaven is all about: Christ in search of the hidden treasure of humankind buried and trampled under the hardened thoroughfares of time. Found! The price paid. Our Lord is a sharp merchant who can see the ultimate value of the pearl. He must have it! He must do whatever is required to return the valued pearl to the real Owner.

When we look at these parables this way, we are reminded that we do not first choose Christ—He chooses us. Only then can we think of the kingdom of heaven having as much value to us as we are to the Lord. You and I were worth the cross. When we know how much we mean to Christ, He and the kingdom will mean everything to us!

Today's Thought: "He found the pearl of greatest price,
My heart doth sing for joy;
And sing I must for I am His,
And He is mine for aye."
—G. Campbell Morgan

June 25 Micah 7:7-9

When I fall, I will arise (Micah 7:8).

The Power to Defy Defeat

We all trip, often stumble and sometimes fall. We make mistakes, know setbacks, and experience reversals. One of the most vital aspects of living a victorious life is discovering how to fail successfully. A successful Christian is one who does not confuse failure with defeat. We can fail and still defy defeat. *We need not be defeated by our failures.*

We experience failures of reaching some of our goals on our timetable; we know failure in our relationships when we feel we've caused or have not been able to resolve conflicts that end in a breaking of the ties that should bind; we go through times when we've failed as parents, husbands, wives, friends; our career has not worked out the way we expected; projects we longed to see completed may have been shelved; fond dreams may have become part of the ashes of the disappointments of life. It's then that we discover whether or not we have a strategy for failing without being defeated.

J. H. Jowett said, "One of the primary secrets of a victorious life is to learn how to take (defeat) failures. We are not to be too much surprised by it. Still less are we to be startled and unnerved by it. We are to be prepared for it, and we are to allow for it in our plan, and we are to regard it as an incident on the way to final triumph."

In Micah 7 there is a magnificent psalm that gives us the secret of how to fail successfully and defy defeat. It anticipates the destruction of Jerusalem at the hands of Israel's enemies. But it also puts ridiculers on notice. They are not to rejoice says Micah for, "When I fall, I will arise."

Today's Thought: Christ is the Lord of countless new beginnings, not just a second chance.

Come to Me, all you who labor and are heavy laden, and I will give you rest. Take My yoke upon you and learn from Me, for I am gentle and lowly in heart, and you will find rest for your souls (Matthew 11:28,29).

Rest for the Heavy Laden

New yokes of slavery are a beguiling temptation all through our Christian life. The self-justifying tendency in us takes on different expressions. Each false effort to make ourselves more right with the Lord has to be confronted and dealt with through a new reclaiming of His unearnable grace. This is why we need deep fellowship with Christian friends who can help us discern each new yoke of slavery and replace it with the yoke of Christ. In each instance Christ says, "Come to Me, all you who labor and are heavy laden, and I will give you rest. Take My yoke upon you and learn from Me, for I am gentle and lowly in heart, and you will find rest for your souls" (Matthew 11:28,29).

When feelings of being unfree hit me, I have to recapture these words of Christ. The idea behind this promise, I think, was a training yoke in which an older, stronger ox pulled in tandem with a younger, weaker ox. The trainee learned from the experienced beast who carried the responsibility for the weight and the direction in ploughing the furrow. Christ takes the heavy load and guides us along a straight path. But as I explain this to others, I am brought back to the fact that I assume new yokes of slavery I try to carry alone. When I get exhausted or depleted, the Savior is always waiting with a liberating offer. "Take off that yoke. Here, join Me in Mine. I'll take the burden and the weight of your need." When I accept His offer, I am flooded with a renewed sense of freedom.

Today's Thought: I will allow Christ to set the direction, the pace, the goal.

See, I have set before you an open door (Revelation 3:8).

A Day of Opportunity

Ernest Campbell has reminded us of a little-known book by Hans Sachs. There's a chapter in it entitled, "Locked in a Room with Open Doors." A boy who is obsessed with a dread of open doors is told by his brother, "One day I will tie you up in a room with all the doors open." What a vivid image! It describes our plight on some days. But we have not been tied up by someone else. We've done it to ourselves. Nathaniel Hawthorne was right: "What dungeon is so dark as one's own heart! What jailer is so inexorable as one's self!"

The risen Christ said to the church of Philadelphia, "See, I have set before you an open door" (Revelation 3:8). Think of the opportunities you have before you today. Start with the amazing opportunity to grow in your relationship with Christ. Just think of it: The Savior of the world wants to make you like Himself! Will you know more of Him at the end of this day? List the specific opportunities you will have to communicate love to and to serve people today. Christ's strength is never squandered; it's given to those who serve. Paul said, "Therefore, as we have opportunity, let us do good to all" (Galatians 6:10). In every situation, circumstance, problem, or difficulty there is an opportunity to love, forgive, give, care.

How can you live today so that at evening you will not have to say what William Hale White said about his life: "When I look back over my life and call to mind what I might have had simply for the taking, and did not take, my heart is like to break."

Pogo was wrong when he said, "We are surrounded by insurmountable opportunities." They are not insurmountable. The Lord has untied us and set us free. We can go through the open doors of opportunity.

Today's Thought: Douglas MacArthur said, "There's no security on this earth; there is only opportunity." However, we would say, "Christ is our security, and we can grasp the opportunities!"

See then that you walk circumspectly, not as fools but as wise, redeeming the time, because the days are evil. Therefore do not be unwise, but understand what the will of the Lord is (Ephesians 5:15-17).

Time Buyers

In the broadcasting world, time buyers are people who negotiate the purchase of time on radio and television stations. In a different way, every Christian is called to be a time buyer. Paul says that we are to redeem the time. Here the word "redeem" comes from the Greek verb *exagorazo*, "to buy out or buy up." The word for "time" is *kairos*, also translated as "opportunity." Following yesterday's thought, the best way to buy out the time is by making the most of every opportunity. Yesterday we prayed that we might be aware and grasp the opportunities the Lord gives us. How did you do?

These are four vital steps to be taken in buying up our opportunities:

1. Size up our strategic situation. We are where we are by the Lord's appointment. We have been placed in our neighborhood, job, church, and community to serve Him.
2. Realize the potential of relationships. We are called to love, care, and share our faith. Who among the people in our lives needs to meet Christ or receive encouragement from us?
3. Be ready for those whom the Lord has made ready. He constantly is preparing people to be open to hear what He means to you.
4. Knowledge of a need is a call of God. Don't wait around for a voice from heaven. Get cracking!

Today's Thought: Don't ever say you have no opportunities. The chances are not missing, but you may be missing the chances.

"Lord, if You are willing, You can make me clean." Then Jesus put out His hand and touched him, saying, "I am willing; be cleansed." And immediately his leprosy was cleansed (Matthew 8:2,3).

The Willingness of Christ

The significant thing about the leper's approach to Jesus was his recognition of the Master's power and the authority of His will to use that power. The man's appeal was humble and urgent. He had absolute trust that Jesus could heal him if He willed. Therefore, his petition was couched in reverence.

Matthew's account of the healing of the leper follows the Sermon on the Mount. "When He came down from the mountain, great multitudes followed Him." One of that multitude was the leper. He broke through the crowd, disregarding all the rules about the separation and exclusion of lepers from contact with others, and worshiped Christ. "Lord," he said, "if you are willing, You can make me clean." How very different than the man who said, "If you can do anything, have compassion on us."

The result was that Jesus put out His hand and touched the leper with healing power saying, "I am willing; be cleansed." Christ's willingness makes all the difference.

Now we can put the leper's healing into the broader perspective of how Jesus deals with our needs. Like the leper we press to Him with our urgent requests. Too often, however, there is not the attitude of worship and submission to His will.

The key to dynamic prayer is the attitude of the leper and his words, "If You are willing, You can." This expresses confidence in the Lord's power, but leaves the decisions with the Lord about what is ultimately best for us. Often our prayers sound like, "Do You love me or do You not? If You love me, give me what I want."

Meditation must precede supplication. There is no greater joy than to ask what the Lord has guided us to ask.

Today's Thought: In prayer, ask what to ask and then ask with confidence.

Likewise the Spirit also helps . . . for we do not know what we should pray for as we ought, but the Spirit Himself makes intercession for us (Romans 8:26).

Ask and you will receive, that your joy may be full (John 16:24).

I'm Praying for You!

The most profound expression of friendship is prayer. There are no more encouraging words we can say or hear than, "I am praying for you!" God has entrusted us with the mighty power of intercessory prayer. It is a gift. We become partners with Him in the accomplishment of His purposes in the lives of our friends.

Prayer enables us to share the pulse beat of the heart of God. The more we pray for our friends, the more we will be able to love them as He does. To intercede means to pass between, to go to God on behalf of a friend, and then to go to him or her with the blessing of the wisdom and guidance of God.

But intercessory prayer is more than convincing God of what we think our friends need. Prayer is listening with two ears: one to our friends to discern the real need beneath the surface of a problem or potential; the other to God to receive His guidance for what we are to pray. Prayer begins with God. He calls us into fellowship with Him so that He can inspire us to pray for what He is more ready to give than we are daring enough to ask. Intercessory prayer is not overcoming God's reluctance but accepting His unlimited resources.

Today's Thought: "There is nothing that makes us love a man so much as praying for him" —William Law.

The effective, fervent prayer of a righteous man avails much (James 5:16).

Caring Is Spelled P-R-A-Y-I-N-G

Most often we think of caring in terms of action; there is something we must do for a person in order for him or her to know we really care. That's true, but there is a more powerful expression of caring that comes before action and often clarifies the quality of our specific acts of caring. Being in prayer for another person is profound caring. The Lord has ordained that some of His best gifts are given when we pray for others.

Often we say, "There's nothing I can do except pray." Except pray? When we come to our heavenly Father out of concern for another, all of heaven stops to listen. Our prayers unleash the power of God for a friend or loved one. As we linger in prolonged prayer for a person, we are also given discernment about his or her needs and specific marching orders as to what is the maximum way for us to help.

Right now, in the quiet of your own prayer, spread out before the Lord the concerns you have for the people He's placed on your heart. Surrender the people and the needs to Him. He's listening—be sure of that!—and He will act.

Today's Thought: Our desire to pray is evidence that God's answer is waiting.

Pray for one another, that you may be healed (James 5:16).

Prayer Is Sharing

Prayer for others is profound sharing. It focuses our concerns about people in the heart of God. We share God's nature when we talk to Him about people, and one of the greatest gifts we can share with people is to pray for them.

We do not believe in the power of prayer, but in the power of the Lord who answers prayer. J. Edwin Hartill said, "Prayer is the slender nerve that moves the muscle of omnipotence. Prayer is simply intelligent, purposeful, devoted contact with God." Or as Clement of Alexandria put it, "Prayer is conversation with God."

In this light, tell God what is on your heart today, as one unloads one's heart to a dear friend. People who hide no secrets from each other never want for subjects of conversation; they do not weigh their words, for there is nothing to hold back. Neither do they seek for something to say; they talk out of the abundance of their hearts just what they think. This is the way we are to talk and listen to God.

Prayer is the mother tongue of the people of God. Archbishop Trench exclaimed, "Prayer is not overcoming God's reluctance; it is laying hold of His highest willingness." Listen to the Lord in prayer. Get His perspective on your concerns and problems, loved ones, and those people you need to learn to love. Spread it all out before Him. Say with Samuel, "Speak, Lord, Your servant listens."

Today's Thought: "Prayer enlarges the heart until it is capable of containing God's gift of Himself" —Mother Teresa of Calcutta.

Pray without ceasing (1 Thessalonians 5:17).

Pray Without Ceasing

Prayer is the essential key—daily and hourly prayer. In fact, making all of life a prayer puts everything into the perspective of praise, confession, intercession, and supplication.

All of life is a gift of the Lord's grace. Praising Him for all that happens to and around us, the positive and the perplexing, reminds us that He uses everything to make us open, receptive channels of His grace. When we fail, His grace abounds. We do not have to atone for ourselves—forgiveness is offered before we ask.

When we are confronted by challenges, opportunities, or difficulties, we can spread them out before the Lord and He graciously gives us exactly what we need when we need it. And then, when people's needs distress us and we are broken in our own inability to meet their needs, we are given the assurance that our prayers for them will release the power of the Lord in their problems, illnesses, and discouragements.

This is what Paul means by praying without ceasing. When we really dare to feel deeply our own and others' needs, only the Lord's grace is sufficient.

Today's Thought: Like breathing, prayer continues in every waking and sleeping moment.

"There is not in the world a kind of life more sweet and delightful than of a continual conversation with God" —Brother Lawrence.

Blessed is the nation whose God is the Lord (Psalm 33:12).

What to Do Before the Fireworks

Early in May each year the President declares a certain day as a National Day of Prayer. He calls people of all faiths to pray for him, the Congress, the Supreme Court, and our state and local leaders. In addition, I've always thought of the Fourth of July as a special day of prayer. There's no better way to celebrate the birthday of our nation.

Patriotism has not gone out of style. God calls us to be loyal citizens of the nation in which we live. Our task is not to prove that we are bigger or better than other nations, but to be all that God is calling the United States to be. He has an unfinished agenda for us. We haven't licked the problems of poverty, homelessness of so many in our cities, illiteracy, dope, crime, and the virulent spread of AIDS. And there's more.

The calling of every Christian is to be a minister. This means introducing others to Christ, but it also means social responsibility. We are to pray for guidance—for the Lord to show us the need in which He wants us to be involved. Find a need and let Him help you fill it.

On the Fourth of July a good question to ask is, "If everyone lived out his faith as a citizen the way I do, what kind of nation would we have?" So few could say, "Great!" Most would have to say that they have left the burden on someone else's shoulders.

So before the fireworks start, take time for concentrated prayer for our nation. When "God Bless America" runs through your mind, add the words "God Bless America *through me*."

Today's Thought: "If My people who are called by My name will humble themselves, and pray and seek My face, and turn from their wicked ways, then I will hear from heaven, and will forgive their sin and heal their land" (2 Chronicles 7:14).

Therefore whoever humbles himself as this little child is the greatest in the kingdom of heaven (Matthew 18:4).

Spontaneous, Responsive, Vulnerable

Picture the scene. Jesus is teaching the crowds. In the midst of the discourse, His disciples move in beside Him asking a question they surely discussed often with each other in their competitive jockeying for position with the Master and in His promised kingdom. They blurted out their top agenda question: "Who is the greatest in the kingdom of heaven?"

The Master's first answer was to call one of the children in the crowd to come to Him. We are told He "set him in the midst of them." The child scampered up onto Jesus' lap. And in this unself-conscious act of joyous response to the Master's call and the sheer delight of being close to Him, we discover the real meaning of what Jesus, holding the child, went on to say about humility.

What was the quality of that child's humility? We don't often think of children as humble. What I think the Master meant was that the child was not encumbered with inhibitions, reserve, and debilitating doubt. Long before Jesus called this child out of the crowd, I'm sure the boy and the Master had made contact. Unashamedly, he probably pushed through the crowd to be at the center circle around Jesus. Did they exchange looks, smile at each other, communicate mutual admiration? I think so! And when the child was invited to come to the Master, it was the natural next step in their growing relationship.

How quickly we lose the enthusiasm, delight, and wonderment of being a child! A vital part of humility is the unself-consciousness of a child's laughter, the freedom to have fun, the abandoned expression of excitement. "But ah," you say, "the child doesn't have the burdens and worries of an adult. He can depend on his parents to provide the necessities of life." True. But so can a child of our heavenly Father!

Today's Thought: Lord, make me spontaneous, responsive, and vulnerable again.

And I say to you, ask, and it will be given to you, seek, and you will find; knock, and it will be opened to you. For everyone who asks receives, and he who seeks finds, and to him who knocks it will be opened (Luke 11:9,10).

Christ's Secret for Solving Problems

There are creative solutions to life's biggest problems. Christ gives us the secret of finding them. He uses our imagination to show us what we would not have thought of or worked out for ourselves. But this requires persistence, importunity. It means asking, seeking, knocking—these are the three steps in using imagination in cooperation with Christ. When we ask, we surrender the problem. When we seek, we wait for Him to show us His best among the many alternatives, opening our minds to His insight. Then as His gift, He gives us an answer. It's then that we can knock, asking for the provision to accomplish what He has revealed.

We wonder why some Christians think of solutions we would not have considered. They have persisted patiently in prayer. Some are amazingly creative in what they think and say. Long prayer vigils and complete trust are the reason. They are like an inventor who waits for, searches, tests until the great "Ah-ha!" comes. Great thinkers do not give up. Often when we least expect it, the solution comes, and we know that it was worth it.

"Trust in the Lord with all your heart, and lean not on your own understanding; in all your ways acknowledge Him, and He shall direct your paths. Do not be wise in your own eyes" (Proverbs 3:5-7).

It's in response to this quality of waiting on the Lord that what Paul calls a "word of knowledge" is given by the Lord's Spirit. A supernatural insight is given and we know what should be done or communicated in a problem. Friends, families, churches, movements, all desperately need this quality of imaginative praying, thinking, and sharing.

Today's Thought: We are called to be imaginative saints.

O Lord, for your servant's sake, and according to Your own heart, You have done all this greatness (1 Chronicles 17:19).

Entrusted Greatness

Louis XIV was very specific in his will about the way he wanted his funeral to be conducted. The cathedral was to be dimly lit with only one large candle placed next to his golden coffin. The king wanted a spectacular funeral that drew attention to *his* greatness. He wanted no one to forget his proud claim, "I am the state!"

Bishop Massilon was appointed to give the eulogy. The large congregation waited in hushed silence. The bishop walked to the casket and gave his very brief eulogy—not to Louis but to God. He reached up to the candle and snuffed it out as he said, "Only God is great!"

When we focus on the greatness of our Lord and accept His blessings, our true greatness results. It is His greatness in us. All we can do is yield to the greatness He wants to be in us. Then when something great happens through us, we give Him the glory. That was King David's secret to receiving silent strength.

The reason I stress this today is that tomorrow we begin an adventure in living the Beatitudes as Jesus' eight-way test of greatness. In the next nine days we will claim Christ's greatness in us. It's all a part of the silent strength He is in us.

I have a friend who, every time I affirm or compliment him on a job well done, points his finger upward indicating he knows the source of anything great that has been accomplished through him.

Today's Thought: Whatever greatness we have is what God produces in us. Nothing will deny us of the greatness He wants for us faster than trying to be great on our own.

The Lord bless you and keep you (Numbers 6:24).

The Eight-Way Test of Great Living

One day last summer, I spent some leisurely hours walking through a burial ground next to a church in the Highlands. I came across a grave stone that caught my attention. Chiseled in the stone were the words "Here lies a great man." I thought about that epitaph for a long time afterward. What had made the man great in the eyes of his family and friends? Then I wondered, "What is true greatness and how is it achieved?"

In the Beatitudes, Jesus gave us the eight-way test of true greatness. He listed the eight character traits He wanted His disciples to possess. Jesus called those who have these qualities of greatness "blessed." The Hebrew word for "blessed," *ashere*, is a word of exclamation and affirmation: "O the blessedness of..." In the Old Testament, blessedness was inseparable from being blessed by God. It means belonging to God, being His beloved, and knowing that you are chosen, called, cherished, and cared for by Him. Blessedness is experiencing unqualified grace that is expressed by uncontainable joy.

You and I have been elected to experience the blessedness of the qualities of authentic greatness. Savor that today. We have been designed for greatness according to Christ's measurements and by His power! Each Beatitude gives us a dimension of that greatness. On closer examination, we realize that they are aspects of Christ's character. We have been blessed to be recreated in His image.

During the next eight days we are going to live the Beatitudes. For each day, I have written a devotion plus, on a second page, a morning motto that encapsulates the essence of the Beatitude so we can commit the day to living it. Then, I've included an evening evaluation to help us reflect on how we did. It's an exciting adventure in the eight-way test of great living.

Today's Thought: The word "blessed" is a special word of intimacy between the Lord and His people. Today I will live as a blessed person—chosen, called, and cherished by Him.

Blessed are the poor in spirit, for theirs is the kingdom of heaven (Matthew 5:3).

The Growing Edge

Each of the Beatitudes has three parts: the promise of greatness rooted in blessedness—being chosen, called, and cherished; the key to discovering and experiencing it; and the result it produces in our lives.

To be poor in spirit is to acknowledge that we have a need to grow. We can admit our spiritual poverty and seek the Lord's help; we can consider our powerlessness and be open to supernatural power.

The psalmist expressed the essence of what it means to be poor in spirit. "I sought the Lord, and He heard me, and delivered me from all my fears.... This poor man cried out, and the Lord heard him, and saved him out of all his troubles" (Psalm 34:4-6). Surely Jesus had this psalm in mind when He called the poor in spirit "blessed." The Hebrew word *ani* had come to mean more than material poverty. It was used for the humble and faithful. J. B. Phillips translated this first Beatitude, "How happy are the humbleminded, for the kingdom of heaven is theirs!"

Throughout His ministry, Jesus affirmed humility and warned against pride. He knew that religious pride blocked growth in greatness. That's why He affirmed the publican and exposed the pride of the Pharisee in His incisive parable. The publican could say "God be merciful to me," whereas the proud Pharisee touted his lack of need: "I thank You that I am not as other men...."

Only those who confess their need can enter the joy of the kingdom of heaven—the reign and rule of God. Abundant life now and eternal life forever is dependent on confessing our need and receiving the gift of faith.

Today's Thought: True greatness begins with and never outgrows humility.

Living the First Beatitude

Morning Motto: Today, I will claim that I am a blessed person—chosen, cherished, and called to experience the lasting joy of true greatness according to Christ's measurements. To be poor in spirit is to be humble. Authentic humility is not to be less than I am, but to confess my need for the Lord's help to be all He has destined for me to be and to do. I admit my insufficiency and inadequacy while humbly putting my trust in the Lord. Today I will prayerfully seek to know and to do the Lord's will and to grow through what He reveals in and around me. As a citizen of the kingdom of heaven under the Lord's rule, I surrender my problems and needs and thank Him in advance for what He will do in my life today.

Evening Evaluation: What kind of day have I had? Was I humble in spirit? Did I live on the growing edge? Was I quick to admit my need for the Lord? Have I grown today through what I have thought and experienced? Did pride or my need to be adequate get in the way of what the Lord wanted to teach me? Do I know more of His grace and glory than I did at the beginning of this day? In what ways did I experience the Lord's intervention and inspiration today? As I retire this night, I commit to Him all my unresolved problems and unfinished tasks. My rising in the morning will be a resurrection to another day of life in the kingdom of heaven humbly submitted to the management of Christ my King.

Blessed are those who mourn, for they shall be comforted (Matthew 5:4).

Daily Forgiveness

The blessed—the truly chosen, cherished, and called people—know they are loved in spite of their failures. Therefore, they can quickly admit their sins and receive the comfort of forgiveness rather than live in self-condemnation or self-justification. We all fail, but too few of us know how to deal with those failures. One bad day leads to a succession of bad days.

This is why it's so crucial to keep short accounts with the Lord and with others. This means seeking and expressing forgiveness as soon as we can—the same day, if possible. And when conditions in society cause us to mourn, we need to ask the Lord what He wants us to do about it and respond immediately.

This Beatitude leads to three levels of confession. When we mourn over our sins we pray, "Lord, forgive me." Then when we have been hurt or harmed by another person or see what he or she is doing with the precious gift of life, our mourning over them leads us to pray, "Lord forgive him/her."

But we are also part of a society that causes suffering. We all contribute to the lack of righteousness around us. And so we pray, "Lord, forgive us!"

Those who mourn receive comfort. That's not only the assurance of forgiveness, but also the power to change and the courage to become involved to help those who suffer. The comfort we receive is from the Comforter—the Holy Spirit. The word "comforter" means the one who stands beside, who strengthens, and who helps us in the battle.

Today's Thought: Those who mourn allow their hearts to be broken by what breaks the heart of God.

Living the Second Beatitude

Morning Motto: Greatness is living in daylight compartments. It's keeping short accounts with God, ourselves, and others. It's, whenever possible, never carrying over to the next day unconfessed sins I have committed, unforgiven hurts done to me by others, and unhealed resentments about what life has dished out to me. Therefore, today I will receive the grace of God and live as a forgiven and forgiving, empathetically caring person. To mourn is to allow my heart to be broken by what breaks the heart of God concerning others, and the world. I will be quick to seek the Lord's forgiveness for my failures and will not carry the burden of guilt. Because I am forgiven, I will quickly forgive others and seek their forgiveness. And feeling the suffering of the world, I will become an intentional disciple to bring healing and hope to other people. Throughout this day, I will claim the comfort of the Lord's presence, forgiveness, encouragement, exhortation, and power. Thus I will live an every day kind of freedom.

Evening Evaluation: Today, have I sought the Lord's forgiveness and forgiven myself as I've been forgiven by Him? Have I forgiven others and communicated love for them? Have I deeply felt the pain of the world? Now as the day comes to an end, I want to settle all my relational accounts with the Lord, myself, and others so I don't carry over a deficit that robs me of rest tonight and freedom tomorrow. My prayer this night is for tomorrow to be lived in the freedom of forgiveness. Most merciful Redeemer, Friend, and Lord, may I know You more clearly, love You more dearly, and follow You more nearly, day by day.

Blessed are the meek, for they shall inherit the earth (Matthew 5:5).

The Reins of the Reign

A dramatic scene in Tom Clancy's novel *Hunt for Red October* is when two keys are necessary to unlock the safe containing the sailing orders of the atomic submarine and the detonators of the torpedoes. When both keys were used the safe opened.

There are two key words in this third Beatitude that unlock the secret of our purpose and power. One is "meek" and the other is "inherit." They give us access to the greatness of being blessed.

Meekness is not weakness. The Hebrew word is *anaw*, used to describe a person who is moldable; one, who out of love and obedience, openly accepts the providence and guidance of God. The Greek word, *praus*, was used for an animal that was leadable by the bit and reins of its master. It also meant someone who was balanced and not given to extremes. Meekness is knowing that the Lord is our strength and being committed to following His orders. Psalm 37 is a vivid description of the meek person: doesn't fret, trusts the Lord, takes delight in Him, commits his way to Him, is willing to wait for His guidance.

Now the other key: inherit. It means to claim a possession promised by the Lord. Now we see the connection. Those who are willing to commit their lives to the Lord become inheritors of great spiritual wealth. We experience a cardinal virtue of Christ's character—"I am meek and lowly in heart," and we become "joint heirs" with Him in claiming the power given to Him by the Father to give to us. All we have to do is accept the reins of His reign in our lives.

Today's Thought: "Therefore, as the elect of God, holy and beloved, put on... meekness" (Colossians 3:12).

Living the Third Beatitude

Morning Motto: Seven days without meekness makes one W-E-A-K. Therefore, today I will live the true meaning of meekness by seeking to be a Christ-molded, Christ-led, Christ-confident person who submits to His leading and guidance. I commit this day to discover and do what He desires in my relationships and responsibilities. I will claim my spiritual inheritance as His disciple and will live joyously and expectantly in the flow of His love, power, and hope.

Evening Evaluation: Was I an open, leadable, responsive disciple today? For what positive evidence can I give thanks? In what ways did I balk at Christ's guidance or blunder in my own insight without asking for His direction? I accept forgiveness for any willful independence so that tomorrow can be different. I rest this night in complete trust and peace knowing that as I am given a new day, Christ will show the way.

Blessed are those who hunger and thirst for righteousness, for they shall be filled (Matthew 5:6).

Are You Getting What You Want?

Are you getting what you desire out of life?

The other day I was in a toy store. A little boy ran from toy to toy screaming, "I want it! I want it!" He was a junior member of the "I want it!" acquisitive society whose song is, "I want what I want when I want it!" It makes all the difference what we want.

Join me in an inward journey. Deep down inside, beneath the level of your surface wants, what is your dominant desire? What's the consuming passion of your life? And here's the rub: Are you spending your time and effort to reach this desire? Then consider: Will your desire, if you reach it, bring you true greatness?

In the fourth Beatitude, Jesus declares that the greatness of the blessed is that they desire righteousness more than a starving person longs for food and a parched person for water. God wants us to seek Him with a consuming passion. And our seeking is the result of having been found by Him. We are elected to know, love, and serve Him. Righteousness has a fourfold meaning in the Scriptures. First, it describes God's essential nature of absolute purity, truth, justice, goodness, and love. Our consuming passion is to be for God Himself. Second, righteousness is normative for knowing and doing the will of God. But we know that we, along with all humankind, sinned and rebelled against that righteousness. Third, so God sent Christ, His Righteousness, to atone for our sins and to reconcile us to Himself. Through the cross, by faith, we can receive a righteous relationship. Fourth, when we have been made right, our ultimate desire is to please God by practicing righteousness in our relationships and society. That's what God wants us to get out of life. There's no greater satisfaction than desiring what He desires for us.

Today's Thought: Greatness is being consumed by a desire for God.

Living the Fourth Beatitude

Morning Motto: As a person made right with God by grace through Christ, I commit today to be a day of righteous living. My dominant desire today, above all else, will be to seek first the kingdom of God and His righteousness in my decisions, ethics, and morality. I will hunger and thirst for righteousness today. I will feel a consuming passion to be right and reconciled with others. Not only is God's righteousness my passion, but so are people and their needs. Any person who does not know the Lord's love and any area of injustice in society becomes a part of the Lord's agenda for me.

Evening Evaluation: Did I express authentic righteousness or deny it today? In what ways did I practice righteousness and in what relationships and situations did I deny the challenge of faithfulness to my dominant desire? In what ways did I get involved in situations of human needs? How did I sense the Lord's affirmation for receiving the gift of consuming passion for His righteousness? At the end of the day, I affirm that I want to do right because I am righteous through His love and forgiveness. Tomorrow is another day and a fresh chance for a new beginning to hunger and thirst for righteousness.

Blessed are the merciful, for they shall obtain mercy (Matthew 5:7)

Multiplied Mercy

Years ago the radio comedy team of Amos and Andy kept America laughing with routines that sometimes had a deeper meaning. One time Amos told Andy how he was going to get back at a Juan he didn't like who kept slapping him on the chest. "I'm going to get even. I've put a stick of dynamite in my vest pocket. The next time he slaps me on the chest, he'll get his hand blown off!" When the laughing died down, we got the point. The same explosion would blow Amos' heart out.

Giving people what we think they deserve has the same disastrous result. Retaliation is like burning your house down to get rid of a rat. And yet, our punishment of people who have hurt or failed us is like a boomerang. We are the ones who get hurt.

In Christ, God has broken the cycle of judgment and retaliation. We have received mercy—undeserved and unearned love. In the fifth Beatitude, Jesus invites us to share His character trait of mercy. But inflow and outgo must be matched. Mercy must be given away if we want to live in its flow. This is the point of the parable of the unmerciful servant we read today.

The test of the greatness Christ offers us is to be merciful to those who do not return it. When we've endured disappointments, injustice, or hurts, we do not become bitter or sour but draw on and express mercy. This is not easy—not until we remember how merciful Christ has been to us. We are called to be a channel of divine mercy flowing through us to others. This is the source of the silent strength of greatness.

Today's Thought: Lord of mercy, thank You for recalling me to the greatness of being merciful. Help me to know what it means to lay down my life for the people around me. Then motivate me to action, so that when this day ends, I will be able to know that Your mercy has been expressed through me. Help me Lord, to be merciful!

Living the Fifth Beatitude

Morning Motto: Because I have received God's mercy, today I will seek to multiply that mercy by being merciful to others. This means getting inside a person's skin and feeling what he or she is feeling, hoping, or aching. Because God knows and cares about what's going on inside of me, I want to know and care for others. Today I will experience God's mercy, which is the basis of trust and confidence, strength and courage, hope and joy.

Evening Evaluation: How have I experienced the mercy of God today? Were there any times when I was less than merciful? Looking back, what could I have done or said differently? What can I do or express tomorrow to be a merciful person? Tonight I want to receive grace—God's outgoing love; mercy—His ingoing love; and peace—the ongoing experience. I know that receiving and giving mercy maintains the flow of grace, and peace is the abiding sense of being accepted and loved. I accept forgiveness tonight and will make a fresh start tomorrow.

Blessed are the pure in heart, for they shall see God (Matthew 5:8).

Inner Eyes

As part of an eye examination, the doctor asked me what I wanted to see. I told him I wanted to see things close at hand and also at a distance. Being nearsighted I needed a correction to see things far off. That correction would make it difficult to see things up close. The doctor's solution was to fit me with mono contact lenses. My right eye was fitted for distance and the left for up close. When the doctor had finished, I said, "Now, please do the same thing for the eyes of my heart." His reply was "You'll have to go to the Divine Physician for that!"

He was right. And Christ has given us a prescription for both seeing things at hand and seeing at a distance. Our hearts have eyes. They are our "inner eyes" with which we see God around us and discern His will for the future. But our heart eyes are often impaired because of the spiritual cataracts of willfulness and secondary loyalties.

Kierkegaard said, "Purity of heart is to will one thing." A heart that is able to see God is one in which there are no conflicting loyalties or hidden sin to cloud our vision. Purity is singleness of focused vision.

How do we purify our hearts? First, clean them out with confession. What are we holding in our hearts that contradicts our commitment to the Lord—resentments, jealousies, unconfessed sin, fantasies, plans the Lord could not bless? The second step is to invite the Holy Spirit into our hearts. He is like a lens implant that clears our vision, enabling us to see God, discern His will, and see at a distance what we are to do and be. The One who fills the heart and makes it pure.

Today's Thought: Just as the fluid in the physical eye keeps the eye cleansed, so the Holy Spirit cleanses, dilates, and retracts the vision of the spiritual eyes of the heart.

Living the Sixth Beatitude

Morning Motto: As I begin this day, I open my heart to be filled with the Holy Spirit. I want to be pure in heart so I can see God. I long for my heart to be free of the admixtures of pride, selfishness, manipulation, lust for false power, jealousy, envy, negative criticism, and resentment. Today I will accept the gifts of the Holy Spirit and live supernaturally. I will gratefully be a channel for the flow of the fruit of the Spirit—love, joy, peace, patience, kindness, goodness, faithfulness, gentleness, and self-control. And so, I expect to see God in the world, in circumstances, in people, and in the new person He is creating in me.

Evening Evaluation: How did I experience purity of heart and see God today? What inspiration, intervention, and interpretation did I receive from Him? What mixed motives did I have that prevented me from seeing God? I reaffirm my desire to be single-minded for God—to put God first in my life and make an unreserved commitment that enables me to rivet my attention upon God. I want to rest this night with a pure heart so that tomorrow I will behold more of the wonder of the grace and goodness of God.

July 15 John 14:27-31

Blessed are the peacemakers, for they shall be called sons of God (Matthew 5:9).

Going into the Family Business

A relative of mine in Minnesota began watching our television program. She rummaged through some old family photographs and found one of my dad fishing. Though the old brown-tone photo had withered with age, I could see my dad's profile clearly. One of my children said, "You look just like your father, and now I see why you like to fish."

In our relationship with our heavenly Father, we express our family likeness by manifesting the fruit of the Spirit of peace, and in doing what's important to Him: peacemaking. Jesus said, "I must be about My Father's business." He came to bring peace, made peace through the blood of the cross, and calls us to be peacemakers. Peacemaking is the family business we all share. Our Lord's last will and testament was, "Peace I leave with you, My peace I give to you."

We must have peace before we can go as peacemakers. Peace is a sure sign we have accepted our reconciliation with our Father. Peace is the result of a forgiven heart, now filled with Christ's Spirit.

When peace rules in our hearts (Colossians 3:15) we can be peacemakers. It means being the initial reconciler of conflict between us and others. Our part in the family business is to tear down walls and work constantly for understanding.

We live in a world where people and groups are at enmity. Our calling is to actively seek to resolve conflicts. We can listen to, love, and care for people on both sides without taking sides, for we stand on a third side—on the side of peace. Peacemaking is going in the family business!

Today's Thought: "I must be about My Father's business" (Luke 2:49).

Living the Seventh Beatitude

Morning Motto: God is my Father. I am at peace with Him through Christ and the forgiveness of the cross. Today I will express my family likeness in the fruit of the Spirit of peace, and will accept my calling to be a peacemaker. I will live in the flow of the peace of Christ and will seek to be a peacemaker by sharing His peace with individuals. I will be actively involved in trying to bring healing of hurts and misunderstandings between people and reconciliation of estrangement and brokenness between groups. My constant prayer will be, "Lord, make me an instrument of Your peace."

Evening Evaluation: On a scale of 1 to 10, what kind of a peacemaker was I today? Did I sow discord, fan the fires of misunderstanding between people, take sides in petty conflicts, or participate in gossip? Or did I model what it means to know Christ's peace? Did I communicate His serenity, tranquility, and joy? Was I quick to forgive, slow to judge, and resourceful in conflicts? Was I an agent of reconciliation, bringing estranged people or groups together? Tonight, I confess anything that robs me of peace so that I can receive grace and rest peacefully this night and rise in the morning with a new commitment to be a peacemaker.

July 16 — 1 Peter 4:12-19

Blessed are those who are persecuted for righteousness' sake, for theirs is the kingdom of heaven (Matthew 5:10).

For Righteousness Sake?

Two conversations—one with the man and the other about him—were very contradictory. The conversation with the man opened dramatically, "Well, now I know what it's like to be persecuted for righteousness' sake!" He told me about losing his job because of his Christian witness.

It just so happened that I knew the man's boss and knew that he also was a Christian. So I called him to get his perspective on why the man had been let go. It was a very different story. "The guy claims it was because of his Christian witness," the manager said. "That's not the case at all. In fact, he hid a lot of insubordination, incompetence, and laziness behind his pious facade. He was curt to customers, flew off the handle under pressure, and kept things in a constant turmoil. I met with him, prayed with him, and did everything to help. Someday, he's going to have to connect his convictions to his conduct!"

Some Christians are in trouble because of the proclivities of their personalities and not because of their faith. We need to be very sure it is because of righteousness sake that we're persecuted. Sometimes Christ gets blamed for our sour disposition.

It is our convictions and not us that should be the target of any persecution which happens when we take a stand on issues or go against injustice or unrighteousness. It's important to get in trouble for the right reason. Having said this, it's a sure surmise that if we're not in trouble for righteousness, we've probably become chameleons who blend into our culture rather than speaking out and becoming involved to right wrongs and being a servant to the disadvantaged, poor, and hungry. What kind of trouble are you in for righteousness' sake?

Today's Thought: Am I a winsome witness who takes a stand for what I believe?

Living the Eighth Beatitude

Morning Motto: Today I will live in constant companionship with Christ. I will seek His guidance for what I am to do and to say in each situation and relationship. Out of love for Him, I will be faithful and obedient. Under His control and with His guidance, I will speak the truth in love and take stands on issues of righteousness. I will not accept popularity at the cost of compromising my convictions. Today I want to soar like an eagle rather than blend like a chameleon. I'd rather face trouble for what's right than succeed in what's wrong. If I am misunderstood or rejected or hurt in the battle of faith, hope, and love, I will seek the healing of Christ, the Wound Healer.

Evening Evaluation: Did I follow the Lord's marching orders today? Did I remain silent when I should have taken a stand? Were my convictions compromised in any way today? From the way I acted or spoke today, would the people around me know that I belong to Christ and have put Him first in my life? When I get into trouble, is it for righteousness' sake or because of my own personality quirks, insensitivity, or ego needs? Tonight I want to move from "I want" to "Lord, what do You want?" to "Lord, I will!" If difficulties come, I will trust the Lord for His help, healing, and courage. I look forward to tomorrow with the assurance that a Christ-possessed life is uniquely endowed with power to fight His battle for what's right with Him leading each step of the way.

Living the Beatitudes in the Future: Now that you have lived the eight Beatitudes, return to them often as a way to claim the greatness the Lord has for you. You were programmed for greatness—blessed to be a blessing!

July 17 Matthew 5:13-16

You are the light of the world (Matthew 5:14).

Radiant Christians

Jesus says: "Live! Let the light of your life—the manifestation of God at work in the painful, practical, personal areas of life—shine!" We ought to be living such a radiant life that it prompts the question, "Why are you the way you are?" and opens the way for a positive answer of what God has done. There's nothing more silly than the answer to an unasked question. That's witnessing of the lowest order. But there's nothing more powerful and contagious than the answer to a sincere question about the source of our quality of life. That's witnessing of the highest order. Then we can answer in an unreligious, unjudgmental way that will communicate life and, subsequently, the Light of the World. If we are not living in such a way that people are pressing us for our key to life, then we are not truly alive.

This challenges both the old and new hypocrisy. Our purpose as light in the world is to do good works—that exposes the hypocrisy of words without actions; but the reason for the good works is to glorify God—that exposes action without words of witness. The life we live is to be clearly identified in source and substance as God's work in us. There is no such thing as a secret, uncommunicated Christianity. Either the secrecy destroys our faith or our faith destroys the secrecy.

Make a list of the people about whom you are concerned, those you know need to meet Christ personally. Beside each name write out practical acts of caring you could do to express love and affirmation. Do those "good works" today. Pray that you will be given an opportunity to share your faith with them. Watch for opportunities. Most of all, listen to them. Discover their needs and then confide how Christ has helped you in your needs. He will guide you in what you are to say. Let your light shine!

Today's Thought: Lord, I am ready and willing to share my faith in You. Make me sensitive, open, ready. Use me, Lord!

Oh, the depth of the riches both of the wisdom and knowledge of God! How unsearchable are His judgments and His ways past finding out! (Romans 11:33).

His Wonders to Perform

The great English poet William Cowper was often seized by great moments of doubt and despair. One night he had an urgent impulse to drown himself in the River Thames. He got a cab and told the driver to take him to the river. As they drove, a dense fog fell and kept the cabman from finding the river. After driving around in confusion, the cabby let Cowper out on the street. Cowper stumbled about and suddenly found himself on his own doorstep. Realizing that he had been saved from killing himself, he went inside and wrote the words to "God Moves in a Mysterious Way." He was convinced that it was God who had caused the fog to appear and save his life. What Cowper wrote will give us the courage to trust our lives to God's control today.

Today's Thought: God moves in a mysterious way
His wonders to perform;
He plants His footsteps in the sea,
And rides upon the storm.
You fearful saints, fresh courage take;
The clouds you so much dread
Are big with mercy, and shall break
In blessings on your head.
Judge not the Lord by feeble sense,
But trust Him for His grace;
Behind a frowning providence
He hides a smiling face.
His purposes will ripen fast,
Unfolding every hour;
The bud may have a bitter taste,
But sweet will be the flower.
Blind unbelief is sure to err
And scan His work in vain;
God is His own interpreter,
And He will make it plain.

For what is your life? (James 4:14).

Time to Start Living

There's a song in the Broadway musical "Pippin" which exposes the contemporary quest to squeeze all of existence into the brief years of this life. It is aptly entitled "No Time At All." The song expresses the panic of growing old and missing the delight of living. Its refrain, "Oh, it's time to start livin'," is catching and lingers on the mind long after your foot stops tapping. Though we might not agree with the values which the lyrics and chorus define as living, we respond to the urgency to start living which they communicate:

Oh, it's time to start livin',
Time to take a little from the
world we're given;
Time to take time, 'cause
Spring will turn to Fall
In just no time at all.

But what does it really mean to start living? The only satisfactory answer must include the present and eternity, or else we feverishly try to cram life into the brief span of this portion of eternity. We are all alive forever. How we live *now* determines how and where we will spend eternity.

God's will is that we really live, both now and forever. Jesus Christ came to live, reveal, and offer us both the abundant life and eternal life. You and I want both! But the second is dependent on the first. In fact, both express the same reality: Life in Christ lived to the fullest both now and beyond the comma in life we call death.

Today is the day to start living without reservations. Give Christ control of your life. Invite Him to take charge. Surrender your needs to Him. Pull out all the stops!

Today's Thought: Oh, it's time to start livin'
Time to live the abundant life
We've been given.

Whoever comes to Me, and hears My sayings and does them, I will show you whom he is like: He is like a man building a house, who dug deep and laid the foundation on the rock (Luke 6:47,48).

Start with the Basics

When we drift into an ever-increasing preoccupation with the wrong kind of thinking, we end up having used our wills so consistently for the wrong things that we find it difficult to respond to the implications of the cross for the decisions we need to make and the actions we need to take. We become our own worst enemy. Every positive thought is countered by a negative one. We think we know what we should do, but the alternatives keep us from doing anything.

The only way back to clarity of thought and resoluteness of will is to begin with the simplest, most basic things. Tell the Lord what has happened and that you want to make a new start. He has not let you go; the very reason for the desire is His grasp on your life. Then think through one basic thing each day that faithfulness to Christ creates a desire to do. Do it at all costs! Your think-willing mechanism will grow stronger. And when you are ready, He will create the desire to do some adventuresome things for His glory where only His power could pull them off.

Now in the quiet of this moment of complete openness to the Lord, ask Him to show you what you are to do today as a faithful and obedient disciple. List the challenges and opportunities you know are ahead of you. What would you do if you loved Christ with all your heart and threw caution to the wind? Unless I miss my guess, something was focused in your mind. It needn't be spectacular. Act on the guidance you have and tomorrow you will be given more.

Today's Thought: "Faith and obedience are bound up in the same bundle. He who obeys God, trusts God; and he who trusts God, obeys God" —Charles H. Spurgeon.

He became the author of eternal salvation to all who obey Him (Hebrews 5:9).

Fall in Line

Dr. Henrietta Mears, the distinguished Director of Christian Education for so many years at the Hollywood Presbyterian Church, led thousands of young people to Christ. Her ministry with college students is a benchmark for evangelism among collegians. Hundreds of them became clergy and church leaders. Several significant movements which are impacting the nation today were begun under her influence. The persistent question asked of her by people was how to find God's will for their lives. She was very direct in dispelling the mystery: "Will is the whole man active. I cannot give up my will; I must exercise it. I must will to obey. When God gives a command or a vision of truth, it is never a question of what He will do, but of what we will do. To be successful in God's work is to fall in line and do it His way."

That's quite a challenge! In this light, you and I should dare to trust the vision and direction we already have, and then act on it. That's the secret of receiving more guidance. God unfolds His will to those who have acted on what He has already revealed. The key which unlocks the clarity of His will is surrender. Our "need" always to be in control is a misuse of our will. It is defensive thought resulting in a tenacious grip on life, people, and situations. But the Lord does not attack our imperiousness. Instead, He creates the thought in us that we are at the end of our own resources and ability, and that He is willing to help us. What seems to be a desperate relinquishment is really an unbinding of our volition to allow Him to love us by doing for us what we could not do ourselves. It isn't that the Lord defeats our wills; He sets us free. And in the act of surrender, we win.

When we want God's will, we shall know as much as we are willing to act on today. More will come when this is done.

Today's Thought: "To be successful in God's work is to fall in line and do it His way" —Henrietta Mears.

Bringing every thought into captivity to the obedience of Christ (2 Corinthians 10:5).

Use Your Head

Recently in Edinburgh, Scotland, I overheard a construction worker give a pointed challenge to a fellow worker. It might be a good motto for us in using our gifts of thinking and discernment in discovering God's guidance: "Use your head, mon. Thinkin's not gone out of style!" And it's never out of style for Christians who have been on their knees and in their Bibles.

The same thing can be said for our feelings of rightness or wrongness about choices or decisions. Of course, they can be distorted by confused thinking, repressed anxieties, and unhealed prejudices. But when we make every effort to become honest, open people, God helps us bring our thinking in line with His kingdom purposes and shows us the inner tensions He wants to heal. He helps us in our prayers to deal with our hurts on a daily basis, and unpeels us like an onion, one layer at a time, until He has control of more and more of us. He wants to use our feelings in the service of His will. His goal is to make us people who feel inside whether something is best or not for us or others. When we feel strongly about something, it is good to check to see if the feeling contradicts what we know of God's will from study and prayer, as well as previous revelations from Him.

The way I've found best in approaching my feelings about things I am considering is to allow the feeling to be honored and experienced. Then I ask God to change the feeling if it's wrong or to make it even stronger if it's right.

Again, if the Lord abides in us and we abide in Him, He can guide our feelings. Consistently put your feelings at the disposal of the Lord. Then if you continue to have that inner feeling of something being wrong about a choice, don't do it!

Today's Thought: Living Lord Christ, we want our lives today to be as beautiful as they were in Your mind when You first thought of us. Amen.

Now after he had seen the vision, immediately we sought to go to Macedonia, concluding that the Lord had called us to preach the gospel to them (Acts 16:10).

The Three Lights

F. B. Meyer, the incisive biblical expositor of another generation, illustrates how to know God's will by describing an incident when he was crossing the Irish Channel on a dark, starless night.

"I stood on the deck by the captain and asked him, 'How do you know Holyhead Harbor on so dark a night as this?' He said, 'You see those three lights? Those three lights must line up behind each other as one, and when we see them so united, we know the exact position of the harbor's mouth.'"

Meyer spells out the implication. "When we want to know God's will, there are three things which always concur—the inward impulse, the Word of God, and the trend of circumstances. God in the heart, impelling you forward; God in the Book, collaborating whatever He says in the heart; and God in circumstances. Never start until all three things agree."

At this point you and I have two of those lights in line. We have the inclination, or we wouldn't be spending this time in quest of the Lord's will. We also have the clear light of the example and mighty acts of the Word incarnate. Now we need the third light of seeing what the Lord is doing in our circumstances and what He wants us to do to cooperate with Him in the accomplishment of His will. The infilling of the Spirit creates the impulse, the inspiration, and the insight we need. The indwelling Lord creates the desire to do His will, convinces us of our new life in Him, and clarifies what we are to do in specific circumstances.

There are also three precious keys to the secret of guidance: commitment of our will, freedom from dependence on contemporary values which are not rooted in Christ, and bringing our outward life into conformity with the indwelling Christ through moment-by-moment renewal of our relationship with Him.

Today's Thought: Lord, what do You want me to do?

I was not disobedient to the heavenly vision (Acts 26:19).

"Eye has not seen, nor ear heard, nor have entered into the heart of man the things which God has prepared for those who love Him." But God has revealed them to us through His Spirit (1 Corinthians 2:9,10).

God Has a Plan for Your Life

Throughout his ministry, the apostle Paul was obedient to the heavenly vision he received from the living Christ. Paul's encounter with the Lord began a long process of the total transformation of his nature. During the long years of preparation for ministry, Paul gained a clear picture of what it meant to become a new creature in Christ. He also was given the vision for the evangelization of the then-known world. His imagination was fully captured by the new man he was called to be in Christ. He became a Christ-captivated, Christ-filled, Christ-motivated, Christ-empowered person.

Paul clearly condemned the false use of the imagination in what he called "vain imaginings" of fallen man. But he also, with greater force and clarity, proclaimed the ministry of the Spirit to activate vision for what He had planned. This is worked out in several places in Paul's epistles, but most powerfully in 1 Corinthians 2. Careful consideration of this passage reveals the difference between the false and creative use of the imagination. Paul declares that he was determined to know nothing, "except Jesus Christ and Him crucified."

We are left to wonder what a brain captivated by the mind of Christ is to be like in our twentieth-century culture. Surely the mind of Christ invades all facets and faculties and functions of the brain. This is the source of a Christ-empowered imagination.

On this basis, we can pray about our decisions and plans with the full assurance that "the things which God has prepared for those who love Him" will be made clear. They will be painted vividly on the canvas of our imagination. Then with the gift of faith we can press on.

Today's Thought: Lord, use my imagination!

And He said to them all, "If anyone desires to come after Me, let him deny himself, and take up his cross daily, and follow Me" (Luke 9:23).

The Drumbeat of the Master

Henry David Thoreau said, "If a man does not keep pace with his companions, perhaps it is because he hears a different drummer. Let him step to the music which he hears, however measured or far away."

Christians march to the drumbeat of Christ. He's our "different" drummer. His will, His Kingdom, and His values set the cadences for our life. We belong first and foremost to Him. The one place He will not accept is second place. He demands absolute faithfulness and obedience. No person, position, or priority must stand in the way. He gives His strength to those who take up the cross and follow Him . . . regardless!

This leads us into an incisive inventory. In what relationships, situations, and responsibilities do we find it most difficult to march with our Drummer? It's so easy to tone down or compromise our convictions to maintain popularity. Sometimes our thinking is controlled more by culture than by Christ. Another way to discern the level of our obedience is to ask ourselves what stands in the way of living unreservedly for Christ. If we were totally committed, what would we do differently today?

Following our Drummer requires times alone with Him so we can receive His marching orders. When we do, we'll discover the meaning of another of Thoreau's metaphors: We find ourselves on "a road less traveled." But it's a road that will be traveled with and for the Master.

Today's Thought: Listen for the drumbeat.

Every good work to do His will (Hebrews 13:21).

Lead Time

Consistent, daily, hourly prayers of praise make the difference. This is why Paul stresses rejoicing always, praying without ceasing, and giving thanks in everything. All of life is to be bathed in praise. This provides the Lord with what I call creative lead time. Our praise, as the ultimate level of relinquishment, allows Him to get us ready for the decisions we must make or the next steps He wants us to take. He knows what's ahead of us and wants us to live in the flow of a constant companionship in which He can engender the wisdom we will need.

Taking advantage of creative lead time can be a source of unpressured freedom from panic for us. Often we put off talking to the Lord about a problem until the crisis deadline. We muddle with the concern and then, when the decision or choice must be made, we burst into His presence and want an immediate answer. Consistent fellowship with Him could have made this unnecessary. To be sure, there are emergencies which arise for which we need special guidance, but this can be received much more rapidly when we've been spending time in praise on a faithful, daily, hourly basis. And in the choices and decisions we know are ahead, praising God for them immediately and then waiting for the conditioning of communion with Him enables us to be sure of His will in our lives.

Today's Thought: Looking ahead I will surrender future planning and give God lead time to condition my thinking and my will.

And do not be conformed to this world, but be transformed by the renewing of your mind, that you may prove what is that good and acceptable and perfect will of God (Romans 12:2).

A Personal Will for You

When a difficult problem must be solved or a hard choice must be made, tell the Lord about it, praise Him for it, and then put off the resolution until He has full access to your mind and imagination. After the initial praise, thank Him constantly that the answer is on the way and that, in time and on time, you will know what He wants you to do.

A woman came to see me about her "unsolvable problems." When we got into the specific problems, she confessed that she did not know how to pray. We talked through the potential of praise for each of the needs. In a time of prayer with her, I asked for the anointing of the Holy Spirit on her will and imagination. She started experimenting with a kind of "release through rejoicing" prayer therapy. She is a competent executive with a large company. Her thoroughness and attention to detail were utilized in keeping a log which has become a kind of spiritual autobiography. She kept track of problems surrendered with praise. The amazing thing to her was the new freedom to imagine solutions to the very problems that had brought her to see me.

Henry Drummond once said, "There is a will of God for me which is willed for no one else besides. It is a particular will for me, different from the will He has for anyone else—a private will—a will which no one else knows about."

By the use of the word "private," the great Drummond did not mean that the will of God for each of us is separatistic, freeing us from responsibility for others. Rather, God has a personal will for each of us, as a part of the eternal purpose of God.

Today's Thought: I will seek, claim, and act on God's personal will for my life to be the unique person He intended me to be.

I delight to do Your will, O my God, and Your law is within my heart (Psalm 40:8).

Making Crucial Choices

The other day a man came to see me. He was facing some crucial decisions about a job change. "How can I know God's will for my life?" he asked urgently. My temptation was to talk over the issues involved in those decisions, pray with him, and send him on his way. I suspected that God had brought the man to the place of uncertainty about those decisions because He was up to something more profound than simply giving him detailed directions for several choices he had to make.

He wanted an answer from me right then about what he should do. My response was to share with him the wonder of his capacity to think and will. Then I told him of my own discovery that guidance in specifics comes out of consistent companionship with God. The man had never made a commitment of his will to do God's will. We did this together in the quiet of my study. Fortunately, he had two weeks before his answer about the job opportunity was due. I gave him some passages from the Bible to read and encouraged him to take a definite period each morning and evening to read and pray. His will, now committed and ready, grasped the opportunity. Filled with the enthusiasm of the realization that God was seeking to make His will known, that He had given him the capacity to respond, he left my study with the promise to return the day before his decision was due about the job.

When he returned, he was beaming. "It has been exciting to think about my will being a channel of God's will and that the desire to know God's will is because He has been tracking me so that I could listen and receive it. I've made my decision to take the job. But now I see that the decision to stay where I am or move was not the issue. God wanted me—my will—and not just the right decision. Thanks for helping me pull my anchor out of the mud!"

Today's Thought: Is my anchor in the mud?

Teach me to do Your will, for You are my God (Psalm 143:10).

Prelude to New Power

Each time we feel satisfied with false security, God allows us to go through a period of spiritual dryness and need so our confidence will not be in our own spiritual achievement but in Him alone. He is more concerned about our character than our comfort.

In this way we can accept the positive potential of our surface anxieties in life. Like hunger, anxiety alerts us to the fact that there is a need to be met within us. God will not let us go. He will disturb and alarm us about the blocks within us: areas in which we need to grow, relationships which need healing, and projects which need His guidance. Anxiety can be the prelude to new spiritual power.

A good example of this is in the life of Archbishop William Temple. He tells of an anxious, agonizing night when he had a difficult choice to make: "I tried to concentrate all my desires on knowing clearly what was God's will for me. I do not know how the hours went." He struggled with the decision until the answer was clear. The anxiety drove him back into deeper fellowship with God because he knew the decision he must make was too great and the potential mistakes too costly for him to do it alone. This is the creative anxiety of seeking first the kingdom of God—His will and rule.

How about you and me? What have our anxieties driven us to: despair or discovery, frustration or fellowship?

Today's Thought: Living in God's will is not like flying on automatic pilot where you turn on the flight pattern and forget about it. Instead, it is a sensitive relationship with the Lord in which He uses everything to communicate His guidance. Communication from the Lord comes in communion with the Lord.

O My Father, if it is possible, let this cup pass from Me; nevertheless, not as I will, but as You will (Matthew 26:39).

Nevertheless

The Scriptures are very honest about the agony of will that Jesus went through both before and during His death on the cross. Don't forget His humanity as well as His divinity. As representative man, He sweated blood in the exercising of His will. We are told that in Gethsemane He fell on His face and prayed, "O My Father, if it is possible, let this cup pass from me; nevertheless, not as I will but as You will" (Matthew 26:39). This shows us the startling and ultimately comforting truth that Jesus as Son of man had taken on Himself the burden of the release of our crippled wills. He knew He had to go to Calvary, but if there could have been a different way than the anguish of the cross, He humanly desired it. The key word on which the redemption of the world was held in balance was "nevertheless." Now the Son of God made the choice: "Not as I will, but as You will." He went on to be the ransom for our sins, the One who took our sentence and paid the price for man's sin and rebellion before that awesome cross and ever since. He fulfilled the judgment of God for our sin and established in history the eternal basis of our knowledge and experience of God's grace.

Suddenly we are possessed with an entirely new thought about His purpose and our plans; we want to live for the One who gave Himself for us. Praise and thanksgiving result in a capacity we never knew before: willingness. We want to follow our Savior and do what He commands.

The risen Christ shows us that His will is not against ours; it is infinitely better than ours. With that we are able to say, "Not my will based on my limited perception, but Your will enabled by Your unlimited power!"

Today's Thought: Nevertheless, Lord, Your will be done in my life and in all my concerns.

He who does the will of God abides forever (1 John 2:17).

Twelve Questions to Ask to Know God's Will

Here are 12 questions to ask and answer in a practical inventory for making a maximum decision under the Lord's guidance:

1. Is it consistent with the Ten Commandments?
2. Will it deepen my relationship with Christ?
3. Is it an extension of Christ's life, message, and kingdom?
4. If I do it, will it glorify Him and enable me to grow as His disciple?
5. Is there a scriptural basis for it?
6. Is it adventuresome enough to need the Lord's presence and power to accomplish it?
7. Has prolonged prayer and thought produced an inner feeling of "rightness" about it?
8. Is it something for which I can praise Him in advance of doing or receiving it?
9. Is it an expression of authentic love, and will it bring ultimate good in the lives of the people involved?
10. Will it be consistent with my basic purpose to love the Lord and be a communicator of His love to others?
11. Will it enable me to grow in the talents and gifts the Lord has given me?
12. Will my expenditures still allow tithing plus generous giving of my money for the Lord's work and the needs of others?

These are questions I ask. There are many things I have not done because I could not say yes to all 12 of these. Of course, when I look back, the poorest choices and decisions have been made when I didn't ask and answer all of them. But the Lord gives forgiveness and the challenge, "Tomorrow's another day, another chance, and a new beginning!"

Today's Thought: Doing the will of God is the primary calling of a disciple.

It is enough for a disciple to be like his teacher and a servant like his master (Matthew 10:25).

The Gift of Christlikeness

The sublime example of the beauty of sharing is Jesus Christ. He came to reveal what God is like and what we were meant to be. As the Son of God, He reveals God's nature; as the Son of Man, He makes known the potential person each of us is called to become. But the new persons you and I are to be cannot be realized by our trying harder or striving for perfection. Paul gave us the secret when he said, "Christ in you, the hope of glory" (Colossians 1:27).

When Christ takes up residence in us, He makes us like Himself. It does no good to say to ourselves, "I should be a less selfish, more generous, sharing person. I must make an effort to do better in giving myself away." This usually results in continued failure and self-incrimination.

What the Lord wants is an invitation like this: "Dear Lord, I've tried to think of myself less and of others more; I've made repeated attempts to be a sharing person, really caring for others; but I've failed miserably. Come into my heart, Lord Jesus. Transform my self-concern. I ask You to share Your love through my words, actions, and involvements. Take over, Lord. Give me a new heart, a new will to serve You by serving others. You are my only hope of glory." The inadvertent result will be the gift of Christlikeness.

Today's Thought: "To become Christlike is the only thing in the whole world worth caring for, the thing before which every ambition of man is folly and all lower achievements vain" —Henry Drummond.

Take care of him (Luke 10:35).

Spontaneous Caring

The parable of the Good Samaritan calls us to spontaneous caring. The key phrase is "now by chance." The Greek word translated by the word "chance" means "coincidence." But not even that word gets at the core of the meaning of the Greek word. Actually, it means a confluence of circumstances which seem to happen by chance but are really events interwoven by divine providence for the accomplishment of a greater purpose.

None of the three men who came upon the wounded traveler planned ahead for the opportunity of caring. The two religious leaders passed by the beaten man because of rules and regulations. Perhaps they supposed him dead. To touch a dead body would have made them ceremonially unclean for 24 hours.

But didn't the man groan in pain? Try as we will, our efforts to excuse the priest and the Levite do not hold true to the caring God whom they would worship in the temple. Their problem was that they lacked spontaneous caring—an immediate response to unexpected need.

The Samaritans were hated by the Jews, and yet it was a Samaritan whom Jesus exemplified as a caring neighbor. His plans, schedule, privacy, and the danger of being attacked by the very robbers who had beaten the wounded man did not dissuade the Samaritan. He cared for him personally and then paid the innkeeper to care for him until he returned.

God does not cause the tragedies of human needs, but He does use them as opportunities for us to cooperate with Him. Stop praying, and the coincidences stop happening. Our task is to be prepared for what life prepares. Jesus was sublimely interruptable and ready to respond. He expects nothing less from us.

Today's Thought: Our lack of caring in the past haunts us. Confession of our "care-lessness" can open us up to the healing of the past. We can become caring persons!

Be kindly affectionate to one another with brotherly love, in honor giving preference to one another; not lagging in diligence, fervent in spirit serving the Lord; rejoicing in hope, patient in tribulation, continuing steadfastly in prayer; distributing to the needs of the saints, given to hospitality (Romans 12:10-13).

Caring Is Everything

When the great mystic, philosopher, and saint, Von Hugel, lay dying, his niece noticed his lips were moving. She could not hear what he was trying to say, so she put her ear close to his mouth. What she heard was this: "Caring is everything; nothing matters but caring." Caring is friendship in action. A caring friend is a precious gift.

At the close of a retreat some time ago, we sang the refrain, "He careth for you. He careth for you. Through sunshine or shadow, He careth for you." Then we turned to the people around us and sang it again, changing the pronoun from "He" to "I." Tears streamed down many faces as people sang what they felt so deeply: "I care for you."

But the real test of that moving expression of friendship was in what happened in the weeks and months that followed. We made prayer lists of one another's names. Caring was expressed in daily prayer. The people kept in touch with one another and were available to one another in time of need. Time, involvement and resources were shared unselfishly. Barriers were broken down as people opened their hearts and homes. The motto of the group became "God cares, and so do I!"

Today's Thought: Call, write, speak—make today a day of caring. And then spend the rest of your life duplicating today.

August 4 Romans 12:9-12

Let love be without hypocrisy. Abhor what is evil. Cling to what is good. Be kindly affectionate to one another with brotherly love, in honor giving preference to one another (Romans 12:9,10).

Love Is Its Own Reward

To love is to will the ultimate good of another. The key is the word "ultimate." When we love God with all our minds and hearts and ask Him to guide us in our loving, He will reveal the best among the good alternatives. There are times that love requires firmness and honesty, directness and decisiveness.

Temporary pain is better than an easy way that leads to ruin. If we discern the word or action that will enable a person to grow and experience full potential, the Lord will take care of the rest. Love without honesty is sentimentality; honesty without love is severity. The Lord wills and enables an ultimate good and trains us in loving others as He has loved us.

When we allow God to love us, we can open all the hidden resources of our personality to Him. He knows all about us, anyway. Real love replaces self-generated efforts of adequacy with intimacy. This means opening our innermost being so our intrinsic self may be known in a profound, personal friendship with the Lord.

He has shown us His essential nature in the incarnation. We are given the freedom to remain open or closed to Him. Though He knows all about our innermost thoughts, He will not invade our privacy without our invitation. But He will persist until we say, "Lord, You know all about me and love me just as I am. Now I want You to not only love me but make me the lover of others." Life really begins when we allow God to love us. The abundant life is not straining to love God, but opening ourselves to His love. Then we will love because we are loved.

Today's Thought: "Love seeks one thing only: the good of the one loved. It leaves all other secondary effects to take care of themselves. Love, therefore, is its own reward" —Thomas Merton.

Do not quench the Spirit (1 Thessalonians 5:19).

Contagious Love

One of the finest things I have ever heard said about a person was, "He has the fire of God's love burning inside him. You can't be with him for very long until you feel the icy fingers of fear and doubt melt from around your own heart."

The man is one of my best friends. The fire of the Holy Spirit burns in him. He has a gracious warmth that communicates acceptance and confidence to others. The remarkable thing is that a few years ago he was hostile and negative. He believed in Christ but had not allowed His Spirit to heal him with love.

A painful tragedy in his family forced him to see how little emotional warmth had been communicated by him. He asked for the Lord's forgiveness and for the infilling of His Spirit. The dry kindling of his heart was set ablaze. You cannot be with him without the flames leaping from his heart to yours.

Here is a prayer to claim the same contagious love:

> Living Lord Jesus, I want to know You and Your unqualified love. Thank You for dying for me. Your love for me right now melts the cold resistance of my heart. By faith I accept Your forgiveness for the sin of running my own life and limiting the immense possibilities of the love You offer to communicate through me. I want to know You and experience life through the power of Your Spirit. I surrender myself and all my relationships to You. Here is my mind—think through it to show me what love demands; here is my will—guide and direct all my words and actions; here is my heart—come and live in me to make me warm, affirming, and accepting. Make me a miracle of love now. I want to be to others what You have been to me. Thank You, Lord, that with this commitment I have died to myself and am alive forever. Amen.

Today's Thought: All things are possible now!

I appeal to you for my son Onesimus. . . . I am sending him back . . . for perhaps he departed for a while for this purpose, that you might receive him forever, no longer as a slave but much more than a slave, as a beloved brother (Philemon 10,12,15,16).

People Become What We Imagine

One of the great uses, and potential misuses, of the gift of imagination is in our relationships. Just as we are in the process of becoming the persons we envision ourselves to be, so too the people around us are encouraged or discouraged by the image we hold of them. They rise to the best we picture prayerfully and are often kept down by the worst we categorize them to be.

A sure evidence that we have a Christ-filled imagination is that we have His magnanimous attitude toward the people in our lives. He has encouraged us when we least deserved it; He asks for nothing less in our own relationships.

Once we form an opinion of a person and fortify that with our lack of expectation of change or growth, our imagination continues to hold this image. But the good news of the gospel is that our imagination can be transformed. The New Testament is filled with the accounts of people who have been changed by Christ.

A great example is in the transformation of the runaway slave Onesimus. In the brief book of Philemon, the apostle Paul writes to Philemon, Onesimus' owner, asking him to receive him back not as a slave but as a beloved brother in Christ. Surely Onesimus heard Paul when he dictated the letter and was uplifted by the affirmation and encouragement of the apostle. But he knew Paul believed in him long before that. In fact, Paul's love, encouragement, and affirmation had enabled him to become a new man in Christ. Now Paul asked Philemon to change his mind about Onesimus. We are thankful Philemon did and helped the church at Colosse to do the same. History records that Onesimus became a great leader of the early church.

Today's Thought: Who is your Onesimus?

That the sharing of your faith may become effective by the acknowledgement of every good thing which is in you in Christ Jesus. . . . Yes . . . let me have joy from you in the Lord; refresh my heart in the Lord (Philemon 6,20).

Pass It On!

There's an old saying, "You can't take it with you!" Not true. What is implied is that we can't take our possessions with us when we die. But we will take our soul—the inner person made up of mind, intellect, and will. That indestructible portion of us which exists beyond death's door will be eternally affected by what we believe and what we have shared because of what we believe.

When Christ is the Lord of our lives, we will want to share Him, His love, and the material resources we have received from Him. We grow as healthy, mature people as we share. Heaven is a glorious eternal life of sharing with God and the whole company of heaven. Helping the living on earth, we become angels with a ministry of intervention. Sharing what we are and have is the best preparation for heavenly life. We will take with us the person who has been prepared to enjoy what God has prepared.

We will be uncomfortable when we meet the sharing heart of God if we have refused to share here and now. If you died today, would you be ready? You know you are when the passion of your life is to pass on to others the joy and hope of the Lord. My friend Kurt Kaiser has expressed this in a lovely song:

> It only takes a spark to get a fire going,
> And soon all those around can warm up
> in its glowing.
> That's how it is with God's love;
> Once you've experienced it,
> You spread His love to everyone;
> You want to pass it on.
> (Taken from "Pass It On.")

Today's Thought: "You can give without loving, but you cannot love without giving" —Amy Carmichael.

Then He will answer them, saying, "Assuredly, I say to you, inasmuch as you did not do it to one of the least of these, you did not do it to Me." And these will go away into everlasting punishment, but the righteous into eternal life (Matthew 25:45,46).

Taken By Surprise

Some people enjoy surprise visits. Others are disturbed by them. They would rather be prepared and have planned ahead. There are some who don't even like surprise birthday parties because they are thrown off balance before they can prepare themselves for how they will respond. They feel the privacy of how they would like to celebrate their special day has been invaded and taken out of their control.

There are lots of surprises in the Christian life. Christ surprises us all the time with what He can do with the problems we surrender to Him. But He has another way of surprising us. It's when He comes to us in people who are in need. How we respond to them is our response to Him. Intentional discipleship is spelled out in how we minister to people.

We wish we could manage our benevolence or concern for people on our time schedule and our perception of what are legitimate needs. It's not easy to relate to needy people as if relating to Christ. Often He comes to us to meet our own deeper need: to be partners with Him in ministering to people. When we give for the care of the needy in our offerings at church, we wish that would be the end of it. Then on Monday morning, or during some inconvenient moment of a busy week, someone at home, work, or in the community comes to us with one of the manifold needs of life. "Surprise!" Christ says. "You didn't expect Me right now, did you? Well, how you respond to this person will be your response to Me!"

Today's Thought: None of us can do everything. But once we belong to Christ we are no longer our own. He will guide us to know what we are to do and for whom.

You are manifestly an epistle of Christ (2 Corinthians 3:3).

How Do You Want to Be Introduced?

Often when I give a talk to an audience I have not spoken to before, I begin by telling about an introduction I was given in Darian, Connecticut, where I was to speak to a women's luncheon. The introducer said, "We have someone with us who is going to change our lives. He is going to give you hope, self-esteem, and vision of the future and authentic power."

That made me nervous. The woman went on. "As a matter of fact," she said, "it will be as if the rivers of your life were flowing in one direction and stopped and went in the opposite direction." Panic seized my heart and my palms began to sweat. I wanted to crawl under the table because of what seemed to be a very egregious introduction. Who could live up to that?

Then the introducer stopped abruptly with the words, "This person's name is Jesus Christ, and here's Lloyd Ogilvie to tell you about Him!" The surprise was electric—on both me and the audience. It was the finest introduction I've ever had. It declared my real purpose in any talk I give or book I write—to tell about Christ and the abundant life in Him. And He is able to do all and more than the woman said He could.

The purpose of all of our lives is to communicate Christ. We don't need to draw attention to ourselves but to Him. And more people are ready to hear about what He means to us if we live our faith and share honestly what He's done with our problems and needs. So wherever you go today, remember that introduction and say to yourself, "Here I am to tell you about *Him*!"

Today's Thought: If our lives were the only means people had to know about Christ, what would they say about Him?

August 10 1 Corinthians 16:9-24

Share each other's troubles and problems, and so obey our Lord's command (Galatians 6:2 TLB).

Better Than Our Best

Friendship is sharing life in all its difficulties and delights. A friend is one to whom you can open your heart completely and unburden what's happening to and around you. He or she will try to understand and then draw from experience to give insight or advice.

But our human resources are limited. Our counsel is often confused by our own perspective and preconceptions. More than advice, we all need God. An honest friend is able to admit his limitations, pray with us, and then pray at length for us. Wisdom is much better than sagacity. Wisdom comes only as we pray.

The other day, a friend shared a problem. None of the alternatives was attractive. The dangers were alarming. My temptation was to tell him what I thought. Then I overcame my desire to be his "answer man." I told him that I wanted to spend as much time talking to God about the problem as we had spent talking about it. The result was guidance from the Lord that revealed a direction I could never have envisioned. My friend was blessed—and so was I!

Today's Thought: "It is more effective to spend time talking to Christ about a man than talking to a man about Christ, because if you are talking to Christ about a man earnestly, trustingly, in the course of time you cannot help talking to the man effectively about Christ" —Robert Boyd Munger.

And one standing alone can be attacked and defeated, but two can stand back-to-back and conquer; three is even better, for a triple-braided cord is not easily broken (Ecclesiastes 4:12).

The Triple-Braided Cord

Christian friendship is a triple-braided cord. One friend, plus another, plus Christ, makes the cord not easily broken. Bonhoeffer said that there are no direct Christian relationships. We go through Christ to each other. The Christ in a friend is stronger than the Christ in us and strengthens the Christ in us. When Christ is the third strand of the triple-braided cord, we are able to love and forgive each other with His power.

Our commitment to Christ binds us irrevocably to each other. We find our oneness in Him. We begin to think, feel, hope, and work with unity of purpose and direction. When Christ is the source and center of a friendship, forces to pull us apart are impotent. There is the buffer of Christ's grace when we fail or disappoint each other. We belong to Him and to each other in spite of what happens around us. Pressures may strain the cord but cannot break it. We will experience the fulfillment of Christ's prayer that we considered on April 1. The prayer for oneness He prayed in the upper room is His constant prayer for us. He's praying for you and me today. He longs for us to know the same oneness with one another that He has with the Father. And to implement the answer to His own prayer for us, He engenders in us love, forgiveness, and patience for one another. When Christ is the unbreakable strand of the triple-braided cord, it will not be severed. Praise Him for truly great friendships in which He is the strength of the relationship.

Today's Thought: "One, plus one, plus one, equals one"—Louis H. Evans, Sr.

Therefore, whatever you want men to do to you, do also to them, for this is the Law and the Prophets (Matthew 7:12).

Be That Kind of Friend

A college student complained that she had few real friends. "What kind of friends would you like?" asked a wise Christian counselor. The young woman listed the qualities she wanted in friends. She wanted them to be faithful, loyal, caring, and share her commitment to Christ. "Then be that kind of friend to others, and you will never lack true friends again," the counselor suggested. The advice was simple, yet is the secret of developing enriching friendships.

In a lonely world, it's tragic to be alone. Everyone longs for the same kind of friendships. A Christian is an imitator. Having been loved by Christ, we are set free to reach out to others. Life will never be boring or lonely. We will have more friends than we ever dreamed possible.

Jesus' Golden Rule encourages us to do to others what we want them to do to us. Our difficulty is in picturing what we need others to do for us. We expect little and are not disappointed. When we experience the Lord's unlimited generosity, we begin to appreciate what a loving friend is like. A friendship revolution is started when we dare to be to others what He has been to us.

Make a list of ten qualities of Christ as a friend. Then place a number from one to ten beside each of these qualities, with ten for the quality you emulate the best and one for the quality you find most difficult to express. Rank the others in between. Then thank Christ for your strengths and ask Him for His power to grow in the qualities where you are weakest. Christ wants to make you capable of being a friend like Him.

Today's Thought: "The only way to have a friend is to be one" —Emerson.

If you love someone you will be loyal to him no matter what the cost. You will always believe in him, always expect the best of him, and always stand your ground in defending him (1 Corinthians 13:7 TLB).

A Six-Way Test of Friendship

Over the years, my understanding of what it means to be a friend and have friends has deepened profoundly. The more I experience friendship with Christ, the more I realize that there are six words, all beginning with an "L," that spell friendship. They provide a helpful six-way test of the kind of friend we are or can be. Compare them with the list of Christ's friendship qualities you wrote yesterday.

LOVE—A friend loves unconditionally. Friendship is not dependent upon performance or perfection. We are a friend not for what we can get but for what we can give.

LOYALTY—True friends can count on each other to be for them, defend each other when others criticize or misunderstand, and remain steadfast in difficulties and discouragements.

LISTENING—We all long to have someone hear what we are saying and what we mean beneath the levels of words.

LAUGHTER—We all get grim when we take ourselves too seriously and fail to take God seriously enough. Without ever laughing at us, a friend helps us to laugh at ourselves.

LONG-SUFFERING—Any real friendship endures the test of our failures and foibles. Patience takes the long view and claims what we will be, not what we've been.

Today's Thought: Make a list of the six-way test. Throughout the day, keep a record of ways you expressed these six qualities. Then review what were your strongest points and what were your weakest. Then pray for strength to put into action tomorrow what you learned today.

Whatever your hand finds to do, do it with your might (Ecclesiastes 9:10).

A Lovely Thing

A man stood beside me at the open grave of his wife. He grasped my arm and said, "How I wish I had her back—there were so many lovely things I'd planned to do for her!" We all know the feeling of remorse over things unsaid and undone. We think of all the kind and gracious things we should do, but the days slip by in the busy rush of responsibilities. When we are too busy to enact the lovely thoughts, we are simply too busy.

Christ Himself is the author of the good feelings which need to be enacted. Action on the basis of those feelings is obedience to Him. He has entrusted sharing His love to us. When we resist putting our thoughts into action, we cripple our relationship to Him.

Start today by acting on your lovely thoughts. Start a new past. Today can be the first day of a new life! Here's a prayer with which to begin:

> Lord, thank You for placing in my mind loving thoughts and feelings for the people in my life. You gently suggest lovely things we can do to enact what's in our hearts. Starting right now, I am going to do what You direct in the specific acts of sharing what You motivate in my heart. Don't let me forget, Lord. Give me the will to act! Amen.

Today's Thought: "Every man feels instinctively that all the beautiful sentiments in the world weigh less than a simple lovely action" —James Russell Lowell.

Who touched Me? (Luke 8:45).

The Linus Limit

The "Linus Limit" is wrong: "I love humanity; it's people I can't stand." Jesus Christ came to save humanity, but His love was always personal. He had time for people. In a crowd, His attention was always focused on the person in greatest need. He consistently lived the love He preached.

I am leery of people who say more than their love bears out. Often those who make the loudest noise about human need and wring their hands over human suffering are the least involved in caring for individuals. We have no right to organize movements, start great causes, and lead others unless we are living out what we say in specific circumstances and with specific people. It is easier to love humanity in general than people in particular.

When Jesus was moving through a crowd, a woman who had been ill for years pressed through the crowd, seeking to touch the hem of His garment. She kept saying, "If I can only touch Him!" When she did, He stopped immediately. "Who touched Me?" He asked. The disciples were astonished. How could the Master ask that with thousands of people thronging around Him? Yet He was God particularized, caring and sharing, incarnate.

The story tells us that He knows and cares whenever we seek to touch His healing power. Christ is the sharing heart of God not only for humanity, but for people—people like you and me! The litmus test to determine our level of personal commitment beyond the "Linus Limit" is to honestly ask ourselves how actively involved we are in specific sharing of our lives with individuals.

Today's Thought: Christ has healed us so we can be healers of the hurts of people. He has time for us; do we have time for others? He has met our needs; are we touched by the needs of others?

And whoever compels you to go one mile, go with him two (Matthew 5:41).

Millionth-Mile Living

Really caring means millionth-mile living. In the Sermon on the Mount, Jesus gives us a radical challenge for remedial caring. His people were very proud of their distinctive application of the Lex Talionis, the practice of exact tit-for-tat retribution which appeared in the Code of Hammurabi. It brought sanity into the measurement of what a person could do to someone who had harmed or hurt him. Jesus outdistanced that practice by a million miles; He called for no retribution at all! No longer was there to be eye-for-an-eye, tooth-for-a-tooth retaliation.

The Master went way beyond the quid pro quo of equal expression of anger and resentment. He drives this home with three very pointed illustrations: turning your right cheek toward your assailant after the left one has been given a blow by the palm of his right hand, giving a person who sues you for your tunic your only cloak, and going the second mile for someone who compels you to go one. The Romans flaunted their authority to conscript a citizen of a captured territory to carry a load. Imagine a follower of the Master saying to a Roman soldier, "I've finished my mile. Can't I help you by going on farther?"

The Lord exemplified going not one extra mile but limitless miles of caring, concern, forgiveness, and willingness to help others. His cross is our mandate and motivation for that. The only way to live millionth-mile caring is by His power. The life He challenges us to live can be accomplished only when He lives in us. As we assume the burden of caring for others, He says, "Come to me, all you who labor and are heavy laden, and I will give you rest" (Matthew 11:28).

Today's Thought: We will never be free to be truly caring persons until we accept interruptions as gifts from God. We will fret and fume until we welcome the intrusions as the Lord Himself coming to us in people's needs.

So don't criticize each other anymore. Try instead to live in such a way that you will never make your brother stumble by letting him see you doing something he thinks is wrong (Romans 14:13 TLB).

The Blight of Gossip

Nothing blights the beauty of a friendship more quickly than gossip. When a friend gossips to you about another person, there is always the lingering suspicion that he or she will do the same about you.

Friendship is based on mutual acceptance. We entrust ourselves to friends whom we know will keep our confidences. A budding friendship is often withered when a person draws us into destructive analysis of someone else. We begin to feel uneasy, guarded, defensive. Our concern is to say or do nothing which could be used against us. The friendship soon is strained and reserved. The Spanish proverb is right: "Whoever gossips to you will gossip of you."

A sure cure for gossip is to never say anything about another we have not said to that person or are willing to say within 24 hours. Often we need a friend with whom to talk out our feelings about another person. But that can never be a substitute for honest and loving confrontation with the person. A helpful friend is one who can listen, enable us to clarify our feelings, and then press us to discern what we can do to be creative instead of critical.

Today's Thought: "To speak ill of others is a dishonest way of praising ourselves" —Will Durant.

"Insinuations are the rhetoric of the devil" —Johann Wolfgang von Goethe.

"Avoid gossip lest you come to be regarded as its originator" —Cato.

August 18 Proverbs 26:20

Where there is no wood, the fire goes out; and where there is no talebearer, strife ceases (Proverbs 26:20).

"Concerned" Gossip

Years ago, I had a friend who, rather than claiming his own immense gifts, was in competition with me. I could handle this in our personal relationship, but when he decided to attack me by gossiping to others, it was difficult to handle.

The problem was that he was a "concerned" gossip. He couched the things he said about me in the guise of being deeply worried about my welfare and what I might be doing to my ministry.

Friends started calling me wondering if I was all right. They said they were worried about me. Finally I began asking why they were alarmed. "Well," they said, "a friend of yours came to see me about you and asked me to pray for you. He shared some insights about you and your leadership. Now, mind you, he was just doing that as a concerned friend." Problem was this friend had talked to dozens of people! He had mounted a prayer crusade for me—or was it that?

At long last I was able to confront the man with what he had done and tell him that if he had concerns to share them with me directly and not with other people. Then we got to the bottom of the problem: his own lack of self-esteem and sense of failure. When God healed that, my friend was liberated from putting others down to lift himself up. The experience made me all the more sensitive to how I too might fall into the beguiling, divisive pattern of "concerned" gossip.

Today's Thought: Rule One: Spend more time talking to God about a person than you do talking about him or her.

Rule Two: If you need to talk over your feelings about a person, limit it to one person who doesn't know the person you're concerned about.

Rule Three: Talk to the person himself or herself and leave it to God to impress whatever truth you've shared. After that, there's no need to talk with anyone else.

If someone who is supposed to be a Christian has money enough to live well, and sees a brother in need, and won't help him—how can God's love be within him? (1 John 3:17 TLB).

I Know How You Feel

William Cowper said, "Man may dismiss compassion from his heart, but God will never." Caring and compassion are inseparable. The Latin word for "compassion" is a combination of *com*, "together," and *pati*, "to feel or suffer." It means to feel together with, as well as for, another person.

The conversation of our feelings is a vital part of becoming dynamic Christians. Life, with its disappointments and hurts, can harden our feelings. We learn how to protect, guard, even hide our true feelings. When Christ begins His transforming work in us, He not only reorients our minds around His lordship, but makes us feeling persons again. He helps us to get in touch with our feelings.

The fact of the gospel engenders faith, and faith releases our feelings. The result is that we are able to feel what's happening to the people around us. Compassion is caring in action. Our care about how people feel must be expressed in some action—a giving of ourselves and our resources—as a tangible expression of our feelings. The words "I know how you feel" communicate comfort and oneness. Then proof that we really know comes when we step into action to actually help lift the burden. Who needs this from you today?

Today's Thought: "I prayed to God that He would baptize my heart into the sense of all conditions, so that I might be able to enter into the needs and sorrows of all" —George Fox.

Do everything for the glory of God (1 Corinthians 10:31 TLB).

Who Can Share the Joy?

Who is the first person you think of calling or going to see when you've had a great success or victory? A good determinant of a great friend is that you can share your joys as easily as your sorrows. Everyone needs a cheering section. Genuine friends can enter into our celebration with as much or more enthusiasm as they would have if the fortuitous serendipity happened to them. A true friend is a maximizer, rejoicing and giving God the glory for the great things He has done in our lives.

It takes a lot of confidence to trust our friends with our accomplishments. We assume they are for us and will not confuse our praise with pride. They know that all we have and are is God's gift, and they can join us in thanksgiving. There is no envy or competition. They are so secure in their own gifts that they can celebrate with us.

Questions linger and demand answers: Am I this kind of friend? Do people know I am pulling for them? What keeps me from being enthusiastic when others succeed? Can I give God glory and not worry about getting the glory? Then we can say, "Isn't that wonderful!" when friends succeed and God's glory is revealed in their lives. Our calling is to be a boost and not a burden.

Today's Thought: "To God be the glory, great things He hath done" —Fanny Crosby.

Blessed be the God and Father of our Lord Jesus Christ, the Father of mercies and God of all comfort, who comforts us in all our tribulation, that we may be able to comfort those who are in any trouble, by the comfort with which we ourselves are comforted by God (2 Corinthians 1:3,4).

Sharing Life's Grief

Grief is a many-sided sadness. It is caused by loss—the death of a loved one, a diminished or shattered hope, a broken relationship, an anguishing disappointment. In such times we need a friend who can share the heartaches. We need someone who will allow us to feel through our grief without offering glib jargon.

Grief is like pus in a sore; it needs a poultice to draw out the pain. Our task is to be that poultice to others when life falls apart for them. We are called to comfort by listening with love before we speak gentle words of encouragement. People need to know it's all right to express their grief, to get it out, and then to hear assurance that the Lord is there with them and will not forsake or forget them.

After someone has ached through the grief, there is a right time to help the person talk to God about the hurt in prayer. He will give us the right words—perfectly timed—for a communication of His comfort. The most important thing is to help the person surrender the grief to Him, the Healer of the hurts of life. Any grief we have gone through ourselves and given over to the Lord's healing is a preparation for comforting others.

Today's Thought: As one who has received comfort from Christ, I will think of myself as a communicator of comfort. I will seek to be aware, sensitive, and empathetic. Today I will say "I understand," with greater tenderness and willingness to listen, and pray with and for the people Christ brings into my life.

August 22 2 Corinthians 5:11-16

The love of Christ constrains us (2 Corinthians 5:14).

I Couldn't Care More

Interesting people are those who communicate to others that they are interested in them. The servants of Christ are called to be this quality of interesting people. The result will be a new interest in the Christ they love and seek to communicate.

A servant of people asks the Lord for guidance about the particular people He has placed on his or her agenda. No one can care profoundly for everybody. Our task is to allow the Lord to give us the particular people who are to be the focus of our concentrated, deep caring. The group will change as some are helped and others take their place. Who are these people for you?

Caring means getting into other people's skin. It demands seeing things from their point of view, being available to help lift their burdens, and giving our time, energy, and money when it's needed.

A while ago I was sitting in a restaurant having lunch. I overheard a woman in the next booth exclaim, "Listen, I couldn't care less!" I turned around and said, "About what?" Her embarrassed reply was "It's none of your business!" Afterward, I reflected on those oft-repeated words, "I couldn't care less." I suspect the woman really meant, "I wish I didn't care so much." But her own need to be free of caring and to be cared about were blocking her own calling to be a caring person.

From the foot of the cross as we look into the face of the Savior, our real question becomes, "How can I care more about people?"

Today's Thought: What would we do today if our goal were to hear the Lord say, "Well done, you could not have cared more today?"

To establish you and encourage you concerning your faith (1 Thessalonians 3:2).

Make That Call!

The phone rang early on a Saturday morning. My wife, Mary Jane, answered. "Is Lloyd all right?" the woman asked. "I've had him on my mind all through the night. I didn't have your phone number so I couldn't call to express my concern. This morning the number popped into my mind and I dialed it immediately. All I want Lloyd to know is that I will be praying for whatever the need is. The Lord seemed to be telling me to call and say that He has an answer on the way."

Indeed, I had been going through a tough time. The scandals about televangelists had radically affected the giving to all ministries, including my own radio and television outreach. I needed an intervention from the Lord and an outpouring of funds to go on. I had prayed for a definite sign, and it came in this dramatic phone call. The Lord was faithful; we ended that year of the ministry in the black.

Both my wife and the woman who was miraculously given our unlisted home number are willing to document that Saturday morning call of encouragement. But that's not the point. How about all the people the Lord puts on our minds whose phone numbers we have? It only takes a few moments to call and tell a person he or she has been on our hearts and in our prayers. What a lift that will be!

The Lord wants to use us as agents of encouragement. To get started, ask the Lord whom He wants you to call today with a word of hope and love. Make that call!

Today's Thought: It's the little things we do that encourage people with their big problems.

August 24 — 1 Thessalonians 2:1-8

So, affectionately longing for you, we were well pleased to impart to you not only the gospel of God, but also our own lives, because you had become dear to us (1 Thessalonians 2:8).

A Finger on the Shoulder

When we are motivated by an inner urge to share ourselves and what we have with others, we can be God's tap on a person's shoulder.

The other day I felt compelled to go see a friend. "How did you know I needed you?" he asked. "I had prayed for guidance in a problem I'm facing and really needed a friend to talk to. I guess I need to talk until I know what I want to say. God told me He would send someone, and here you are!" Imagine the joy I felt. What if I had neglected the nudging?

It is awesome to realize that God can use us as His messengers, healers, and helpers. He's up to exciting things, and all He needs is a willing, receptive, and obedient spirit.

Amy Carmichael's poem "Make Me Thy Fuel" is a daring daily prayer for our life of sharing. When we truly believe that the joy of life is sharing, this prayer of commitment is the charter for our caring.

From prayer that asks that I may be
Sheltered from winds that beat on Thee,
From fearing when I should aspire,
From faltering when I should climb higher,
From silken self, O Captain, free
Thy soldier who would follow Thee.
From subtle love of softening things,
From easy choices, weakenings,
Not thus are spirits fortified,
Not this way went the Crucified,
From all that dims Thy Calvary,
O Lamb of God, deliver me.

Today's Thought: Follow God's nudge today.

Do not let the sun go down on your wrath (Ephesians 4:26).

Don't Turn Me Off!

There was a strange note stuck on the dashboard of a friend's car: "Dear Roger: What do you turn off before you turn off the ignition?" I asked my friend what it meant. He explained that he had a bad habit of turning the ignition off before he had turned off the heater, radio, and lights. Later, when he would turn the ignition on again, it would drain the battery. His wife had attached the question as a reminder.

The question lingered in my mind long afterward. It gave me a living parable. We turn people off, little by little, before we get turned off by them. What do you turn off before you turn your friends off? The things people do and say often distress us. We become inwardly impatient. One thing is added to another until we have a pile of resentments. Before we know it, we have cut off any deep communication.

It is impossible not to be distressed by the things our friends do. Great friends keep short accounts. They deal with their feelings day by day rather than building up a resentment reservoir. Just as God's grace for us is fresh every morning, so we need to couple the expression of our feelings with forgiveness. Love and honesty are inseparable in an ever-deepening friendship. Get it out; get it healed; get it over!

Today's Thought: "The continuance of anger is hatred" —Frances Quarles.

August 26 Romans 8:1-11

But if the Spirit of Him who raised Jesus from the dead dwells in you, He who raised Christ from the dead will also give life to your mortal bodies through His Spirit who dwells in you (Romans 8:11).

Take the Opposite

Dr. F. B. Meyer described an experience in his life which helps us discover how to take the opposite. When he was a young man he was very irritable. An old man told him a secret of overcoming the proclivity. The man found freedom from irritability by turning to the Lord the moment he felt it coming on and saying, "Thy sweetness, Lord."

Amy Carmichael comments on Dr. Meyer's discovery in a very helpful way: "Take the opposite of your temptation and look upwardly, naming the opposite; Untruth—Thy truth, Lord; Unkindness—Thy kindness, Lord; Impatience—Thy patience, Lord; Selfishness—Thy unselfishness, Lord; Roughness—Thy gentleness, Lord; Discourtesy—Thy courtesy, Lord; Resentment, inward heat, fuss—Thy sweetness, Lord, Thy calmness, Thy peacefulness." I think no one who tries this very simple plan will ever give it up. It takes for granted, of course, that all is yielded—the "I" dethroned.

Responding to the opportunity to follow Christ is to adopt His purposes as our purposes. We discover the joy of serving rather than being served. Focusing on the self shrivels the growth of the self. Centering our attention on Christ and the people He puts in our lives develops the self into a composite of new characteristics: love, forgiveness, compassion, and sacrificial service. Our attitudes change. We are not enervated by constant efforts to defend our turf. We are freed from aggressive competition, jealousy, and envious hostility. We become much less sensitive to what people do to us and far more sensitive to their needs and what the Lord wants to do for them.

Today's Thought: I will name the opposite of what I'm tempted to be and thank the Lord that He will make it possible.

For with God nothing will be impossible (Luke 1:37).

I thank God there is a way out through Jesus Christ our Lord. (Romans 7:25 PHILLIPS).

Sharing the Impossibility of Impossibilities

There is a famous painting in which the artist depicts the great encounter between Faust and Satan. Faust gambled for his soul. The painting pictures the two sitting at a chessboard, the devil leering because he has checkmated Faust's king and knight.

One day a famous master of chess went to the gallery in London to study the picture. He spent hours meditating on the seemingly impossible situation it depicted. He paced back and forth. Then, to the utter amazement of the other art viewers in the gallery, he shouted his discovery. "It's a lie!" he blurted. "It's a lie! The king and the knight have another move!"

There's always another move for God. However black and grim things seem, He has a next move we could never have imagined. Whenever we are tempted to say, "I'm done in, I'm beaten, there's no hope left," the Lord is ready for His big move.

Once we've experienced God's way out when we've found ourselves in a cul-de-sac of impossibility, we become people who can go to people who are worried and boxed in and say, "Be sure of this: God always has one more move!"

Faith is risky. It isn't real faith without risk. A willingness to risk is all that God asks of us. The greater the risk, the greater the power of faith that is given to us. We all face what we perceive to be impossibilities. We say, "That's impossible!" Then we need to remember the bracing words of the angel to Mary: "With God, nothing is impossible." In the incarnation Jesus did the impossible all through His ministry. He is our impossibility-defying Lord. He knows what is best for our lives, and when we trust Him, He surprises us with solutions beyond our expectations.

Today's Thought: "The things which are impossible with men are possible with God" (Luke 18:27).

For this reason I also suffer these things; nevertheless I am not ashamed, for I know whom I have believed and am persuaded that He is able to keep what I have committed to Him until that Day (2 Timothy 1:12).

A Commitment to Share

Commitment is a crucial part of becoming a Christian and growing in Christ. We begin the Christian life with a response of faith to Christ's amazing love by giving as much as we know of ourselves to as much as we know of Him. Commitment is our part in realizing all that the Lord offers to us. It is an act of the will in which we yield total control of our lives and turn all of our relationships and responsibilities, problems and potentials, completely over to the Lord. The act of commitment opens the floodgates of the Lord's power in our lives.

There is no growth in this initial commitment without a commitment to share what Christ has done for us and given to us. When we commit our lives to share in Christ's name, He can use us in healing the hurts of others. Paul discovered that Christ is able! The words "He is able to keep what I have committed to Him" can also be rendered "He is able to keep what He has committed to me." Both are correct translations of the Greek. The dynamic Christian life is being committed to what He's committed to us.

Have you ever made an unreserved commitment to be a sharing person? Exciting opportunities will happen when you do, and with each challenge Christ will be more than able to give you what you need!

Today's Thought: "Commitment to Christ must involve commitment to our neighbor and our world, for Christ's sake" —Leighton Ford.

For I know the thoughts that I think toward you, says the Lord, thoughts of peace and not of evil, to give you a future and a hope (Jeremiah 29:11).

Sharing the Future

People need us to believe in their futures. A sharing person is one who can infuse expectation about their tomorrows. When Christ lives in us, we believe in the future more than in the past. A Christ-filled person is one who knows that however great the past has been, it is pale in comparison to what God has planned for the future. Yesterday is past; tomorrow is wide open with possibilities!

The world needs people to share the excitement that Joshua communicated to the people of Israel when they were more concerned about what God had done than about what He was about to do. "Consecrate yourselves, for tomorrow the Lord will do wonders among you" (Joshua 3:5, AMERICAN STANDARD VERSION).

One of the most creative ways of sharing hope for the future is to help people picture their dreams. There are so few people with whom we can unashamedly throw off our reservations and dream a bold dream. God has plans for us, and we need fellow visionaries to share the conviction that the best is still to be!

The other day I talked to a friend who had been through tough times. She needed an opportunity to talk out all she had been through. It had drained her of expectancy for the future. At the right moment, I quoted our verse for today from Jeremiah 29:11. I shared what that promise had meant to me through the years and especially during a long recovery from a crushed leg when I wondered if I would ever be able to resume a normal life. "I have plans for you . . ." the Lord had reminded me. With the authority of personal experience, I said to my friend, "And the Lord has plans for you too, to give you a future and a hope." She put the past behind her and accepted the promise. Who needs you to be a communicator of hope today?

Today's Thought: "There are better things ahead than any we leave behind" —C.S. Lewis.

Now we exhort you, brethren, warn those who are unruly, comfort the fainthearted, uphold the weak, be patient with all. See that no one renders evil for evil to anyone, but always pursue what is good both for yourselves and for all (1 Thessalonians 5:14,15).

Knowing Where to Land

People are like islands. Sometimes you have to row around them before you know where to land. Each person's needs are different. In the Christian fellowship, we are responsible for one another. When we listen attentively and care deeply, we are able to love profoundly. Paul reminds us that some need a warning, others comfort, some uplifting, and all require patience. Christ in us guides us in what to say and how to say it.

We are to talk to Him about people as much as we talk to people about their needs. He will give us X-ray vision of the unique and special needs of each person. But we cannot give what we do not have, nor can we communicate what we are not receiving. As we allow Christ to deal with us, we learn how to communicate with people. Paul describes gracious Christlikeness. This quality can be ours in our dealings with people today.

Think of the people in your life who fit into the various categories that Paul lists in these verses. We are given the awesome opportunity to lift burdens today. A pastor friend made a call at a home where tragedy had struck. The little son of the family met him at the door, then ran to his mother exclaiming, "Mommy, our friend is here, and he has brought Jesus with him!" Ah, I would that this may be said of you and me today!

Today's Thought: When we get involved in the needs of people we can be sure that Christ will give us exactly what we need for each person. He will guide us in what to say and how to say it. We are never left alone. We bring Jesus with us!

And let us not grow weary while doing good, for in due season we shall reap if we do not lose heart. Therefore, as we have opportunity, let us do good to all . . . (Galatians 6:9,10).

Ring the Bell!

Mary Martin was facing a difficult time physically and emotionally. She needed courage and fortitude. One night, at curtain-time, she was not sure that she could go on stage for one more performance.

There was a knock at her dressing-room door. A messenger handed her a note. It was from her friend Oscar Hammerstein. It communicated love and encouragement and included these words: "A bell is a bell if you ring it, and love is love when you give it."

Miss Martin went on stage to give one of her finest performances. She gave herself away. She never forgot the challenge to ring the bell! Love is entrusted to us by God to give away.

Today's Thought: "He who loves not, lives not" —Ramon Lull.

September 1 Hebrews 13:1-6

For He Himself has said, "I will never leave you nor forsake you." So that we may boldly say: "The Lord is my helper; I will not fear" (Hebrews 13:5,6).

A Friend Who Won't Go Away

How many friends do you have who would never go away? How many people could count on you to be that kind of friend? So many people are afraid of others knowing them because they suspect that if the truth were known, the friendship would end or, what's worse, become superficial. We keep our thoughts and feelings hidden in fear of censorious judgment. The tragedy is that most people have the same inner secrets. A friend is a person who can dare to be vulnerable about himself so that we feel free to be honest about ourselves. When we spend our energies putting up fronts of pretense, we close out our friends and keep them from being authentic with us.

Something . . . someone must break the syndrome. His name is Jesus Christ. He knows all about us and will never go away. The more we know Him in intimate friendship, the more free we become to be open about our needs and inadequacies with others. They begin to feel at ease with us. When we feel sure of Christ, we can dare to communicate indefatigable acceptance of others. They will be able to say, "There's one person whom I can trust. His friendship is so profound that there is nothing that would make him go away!"

A friend is a fellow adventurer who can help us throw caution and reserve to the wind and discover what we were like in the mind of God when He first thought of us. In times of indecision, we need friends who can help us get the vision of God's maximum into focus. An adventuresome friend will help us do more than solve problems. He or she will enable us to grasp the potential of God's dream. Most of us plan our lives around our strengths and abilities. What are you attempting that you couldn't do without the energizing power of the Holy Spirit?

Today's Thought: A friend is one who knows all about you and won't go away.

You are the salt of the earth. . . . You are the light of the world (Matthew 5:13,14).

Someone Believes in You

I will never forget when I first heard the four most powerful words a person can say to another. They changed my life. I can remember the occasion as if it happened yesterday.

I was a frightened 17-year-old speech student, waiting in the wings of an auditorium to compete in the finals of a national oratorical contest. My future education and development hung on the results. I shook inside with anxiety. Pacing back and forth, I rehearsed in my mind the lines of my carefully prepared oration.

Then suddenly there was someone standing beside me. It was John Davies, my coach and inspiring teacher who had helped me find courage and confidence so often in my high school years. He turned me around, put his hands on my shoulders, looked me in the eye, and said the four esteem-building words, "I believe in you!" With that ringing in my heart, I went out to win the contest and an opportunity to go to college.

Through the years, these four words have been spoken when I needed them most. In times of challenge, of self-doubt, of opportunity, the Lord has given me friends who have dared to say, "I believe in you!" The words have turned fear into hope, uncertainty into courage, and anxiety into confidence.

It's one thing to have a friend say this, but it's all the more liberating to hear the Lord tell us that He believes in us. When the Savior of the world looks us in the eye and says, "I believe in you!" we know anything is possible.

Today's Thought: Christ has trifocal vision. He sees what we've been, and knows what we are, but also has a vision of what we will become.

September 3 Galatians 6:8-10

And let us not grow weary while doing good, for in due season we shall reap if we do not lose heart (Galatians 6:9).

"Do-It-Now Day"

The other day, I called a friend to find out how he was doing. "Just great!" he responded exuberantly. I inquired about the cause of his delight. He told me that he had just finished a "Do-it-now day."

"A what?" I exclaimed.

"Well," he explained, "I'm a procrastinator, and after awhile all the unfinished and neglected things I need to do get at me. Then I must set aside a day to clean up what I've put off. I feel great now that I'm back on the track." Great friendships require "Do-it-now" days. Action is the final step of learning—and loving. It is easy to put off expressing our affection and concern. Friends begin to wonder if we care. No one wants to be taken for granted. A phone call, a letter, or a specific expression of love in action is to a friendship what oxygen is to the lungs, or food to the body.

There is a special moment when a thought about and feeling for a friend converge and, unless we act, we may never have another chance.

Today's Thought: "I will pass through this world but once. If therefore, there be any kindness I can show or any good thing I can do, let me do it now; let me not defer it or neglect it, for I shall not pass this way again" —Etienne De Grellet.

Also I heard the voice of the Lord, saying: "Whom shall I send, and who will go for Us?" Then I said, "Here am I! Send me" (Isaiah 6:8).

Here Am I, Send Me!

Isaiah's vision of the Lord resulted in an undeniable call. Life really begins when our experiences of the Lord's glory, love, and forgiveness open us to hear the "Whom shall I send?" The world is filled with lonely, worried, anxious, troubled people. Say, "Here am I, send me!" and He will.

The sense of being sent, of being a person under orders, under new management, changes everything. We can work, give ourselves away, become involved in caring, with a winsome freedom. The *must* becomes a joyous *may*. When we are called, there is no grim compulsion. The "have-to's" become delights because we are working for the Lord. Then there is no limit to what we are willing to attempt in caring for people and their needs.

Have you been called? Focus your attention on the Lord, the cross, the abundant life He has given you now, and the eternal life which death cannot end. Then listen for His call. Say the words in your own soul. "Here am I, Lord—my time, my schedule, my influence, my money, my talents, and gifts. Send me!"

Rebirth is a recall to caring. When the stone of indifference is rolled away and we are raised to new life with Christ, our urgent desire is to brother and sister all the souls on earth. A sure sign that we have accepted Christ's resurrection is that we have experienced our own, and the authentic test of this is in ascertaining whether or not we have Christ's indwelling Spirit of caring.

Today's Thought: "My mind is absorbed with the sufferings of man. Since I was twenty-four, there never has been any vagueness in my plans or ideas as to what God's work was for me" —Florence Nightingale.

September 5 Isaiah 43:18-21

Do not remember the former things, nor consider the things of old. Behold, I will do a new thing, now it shall spring forth. . . . I will even make a road in the wilderness and rivers in the desert (Isaiah 43:18,19).

A Good Forgettery

I have a friend who has what he calls a highly trained "forgettery." The word is not in the dictionaries, but it should be. My friend makes a conscious effort to forget the slights and oversights done to him. He feels it's a qualification of friendship. I've tested him several times to see if he can recall the hurt of some harm done to him. All he will say is, "I don't remember anything about that except when I decided to forget it."

Henri Bergson, the French philosopher, once said, "It is the function of the brain to enable us not to remember, but to forget." We laugh at that and say, "I must have a spectacular brain. I'm very forgetful." But there's a real difference between being forgetful and being able to forget painful memories. A good forgettery is developed by a gracious capacity to forgive. God is the only reliable guide to healthy forgetting and creative remembering. He tells us that when we seek His forgiveness, He will not remember our sins and failures. When we know God has forgotten, we can forget. Then we will be tender in forgetting what others have said or done to us. We will be able to say with Joseph, "God has made me forget" (Genesis 41:51). God will help us erase from our minds what will destroy a friendship and will bring to our remembrance the motivating power of His love.

Immanuel Kant, the great philosopher, had a trusted servant named Lampe. One day Kant discovered that Lampe consistently robbed him. The servant had to be dismissed but Kant was deeply troubled by the memory of what Lampe did. The philosopher entered one brief line into his journal: "Remember to forget Lampe." This line should have read: "Remember to forgive Lampe." Only forgiveness frees us to forget the hurts of the past.

Today's Thought: Today I will remember to forgive and forget.

Likewise you also, reckon yourselves to be dead indeed to sin, but alive to God in Christ Jesus our Lord (Romans 6:11).

The Wonderful Button

I have a miniature hand computer on which I figure my finances and store personal data for ready reference. Even though it is only six inches long and an inch and a half high, it's amazing how much information can be typed into the memory factors of this mechanical brain.

On the left side of the tiny keyboard is a magnificent and powerful button. It is called the clear button. When I make a mistake in typing an entry, a touch on the clear button eliminates it immediately. Also, any information I have stored which is incorrect or no longer useful can be brought up out of the little computer's trusty memory and wiped out forever. It is as if it had never been entered.

Each time I use this handy computer, I am reminded of how much it's like the brain. It has the capacity to store good and bad memories. How often I wish I had a clear button to press to immediately correct my mistakes, or that I had the capacity to bring up old memories that disturb me and have them taken away, never to be thought about again.

Then, as I contemplate how wonderful that would be, I am reminded how the Lord has built into us a "clear" button. It's called forgiveness. When we accept His forgiveness, we can forgive ourselves, and then out of the assurance of that grace, forgive others.

Today's Thought: Press the forgiveness button—now!

September 7

Matthew 6:12
Ephesians 4:32

Forgive us our debts, as we forgive are debtors (Matthew 6:12).

Be kind to one another, tenderhearted, forgiving one another, just as God in Christ also forgave you (Ephesians 4:32).

When Love Is Blocked

"I just don't love him anymore. Something has happened; I don't feel the way I did. Is it possible to fall out of love?" The woman's earnest question explained her broken relationship with her husband.

The same question could be asked about friends. Have you ever experienced a time when your love for a person has grown dull and dim? Often, it's not just what a person has done but our lack of honesty about our feelings. We think of ourselves as magnanimous people who are all-accepting. Yet the actions of others distress us.

No one thing destroys a love relationship. Little things pile up. Soon our feelings are blocked. Then it's time to talk to God and eventually to the person. God will give us the graciousness to share our frustrations and misunderstandings in a way that will not make the person defensive.

Eventually, every relationship is tested by the necessity to forgive. When we say we forgive but brood over the memory of the hurt or failure, we have not forgiven. The Lord's forgiveness is so complete that He relates to us as if we had never sinned. This is the awesome message of the cross. "Father, forgive them" is the constant, eternal expression of love that forgives even before we ask.

Arthur's magnanimous word to Guinevere in *The Idylls of the King* portrays the depth of true love and forgiveness: "And all is past, the sin is sinned, and lo, I forgive thee as Eternal God forgives." Love and forgiveness are inseparable.

Today's Thought: "Everything can be taken from us but one thing—the last of the human freedoms—to choose one's attitude in any given circumstance" —Victor Frankl.

If someone says, "I love God," and hates his brother, he is a liar (1 John 4:20).

Loving Impossible People

We can with the same breath say, "I love that place!" and "I love you!" and mean something very different. To some, love means a feeling, to others conviction, to still others a loyalty.

Love is the one capacity which is experienced and expressed by every facet of our being. It is mental, emotional, volitional, and physical. The reason is that we were created for love and to love. God is love. The sublime fulfillment of our destiny is to receive His love and love people as He has loved us. God's love revealed in Christ is free, giving, forgiving, and totally unconditional. The love-shaped vacuum in all of us is God's gift. It makes us capable of believing and feeling that we are loved by Him.

A woman shared her ambivalent heart: "I love him but I don't like him!" Can we love without liking? Isn't "liking" the expression of love? We can all empathize with the woman. There are people we dislike because of what they do and say.

What can we do with negative feelings about certain people? How can we overcome our critical judgments which block the flow of love? People desperately need to be liked as part of our loving. They need to know we are delighted in them.

The only way I've ever conquered my dislikes is by daring to care. Distressing people drive us to our knees where we plead for the power to love profoundly enough to be able to help them.

It is in prayer that the Lord allows us to see ourselves and all He has endured in us. Then He helps us to truly see the persons we dislike in their need and what has made them what they are. Then He says, "This task is too big for you alone. Let Me love them through you. Trust Me. I will surprise you with the power to love and like."

Today's Thought: Nothing is impossible when we trust God—not even "impossible people"!

Judge not, and you shall not be judged. Condemn not, and you shall not be condemned. Forgive, and you will be forgiven (Luke 6:37).

A Forgiveness Inventory

Every day I meet Christians who are not free because of unclaimed forgiveness of sin—their own and other people's against them. It shrivels their joy and makes them negative people. G. K. Chesterton admonished, "Let your faith be less a theory and more a love affair!" When it is, we grow more in love with the Savior each day. This love frees us to tell Him about our failures, with the assurance that nothing can ever separate us from Him.

A friend of mine took these forgiveness principles seriously and wanted to be completely free of any impediment in the way of her experience of the Savior's love. She did an inventory of people in her life whose forgiveness she needed to ask and those to whom she needed to express forgiveness. It was a liberating experience. We all need to do this. Freedom is living in the flow of Christ into us, and through us to others. When we think of freedom, rooted in our justification through faith in Christ's atonement, we will feel freely His forgiveness and communicate it to others with accepting love. Make an inventory of the people you need to forgive. Forgive them and burn the list. We are free only when we forgive.

Today's Thought: Here's the motivation for a forgiving person:

I sometimes think about the cross
And close my eyes to see
The cruel nails and crown of thorns
And Jesus, crucified for me.
But even could I see Him die
I could but see a little part
Of that great love which like a fire
Is always burning in His heart.

In Him we have redemption through His blood, the forgiveness of sins, according to the riches of His grace (Ephesians 1:7).

Forgive Yourself—in Jesus' Name

Do you still harbor memories of past sins and failures? Does the recall of them make you feel fresh guilt or fresh grace? Do you ever think you have no right to give yourself permission to feel freed and released? Is there anything you have done or said that is too big for God to justify? Are you nursing any feelings of guilt right now for unconfessed or unrelinquished sins? Then think about this:

Down beneath the shame or loss
Sinks the plummet of the cross
Never yet abyss was found
Deeper than His love can sound.

Repeat this over and over again until you know it's true for those past sins or hidden sins which you've kept guarded from the love of the Savior. His judgment has already dealt with those festering memories. His forgiveness, bought at so high a price, has taken them from His memory. We are not free, cannot feel free, until the conviction of forgiveness is the controlling condition of our minds. Jesus' words give us the content of our own words to ourselves: "Neither do I condemn you; go and sin no more" (John 8:3). List any unrelinquished failures, mistakes, or sins. Hear the Savior pronounce you "Not guilty!" Then, using your own name, say to yourself the assurance of pardon: "Neither do I condemn you!" We are called to be priests to our own souls, mediating the pardon of Calvary. A priest is the one who goes to the Lord on behalf of another and brings the Lord's love and forgiveness to another. Do this for yourself!

Today's Thought: Today, I will not withhold forgiveness for myself.

September 11 Matthew 5:23-26

Therefore if you bring your gift to the altar, and there remember that your brother has something against you, leave your gift there before the altar, and go your way. First be reconciled to your brother, and then come and offer your gift (Matthew 5:23,24).

Love Yourself Enough to Forgive

I overheard a conversation between two of my friends. One had forgiven the other. The man who had deeply hurt him said, "How can you forgive me after what I've done to you?" The other said an astounding thing: "I cherish my freedom and treasure my experience of God's forgiveness too much not to!" What he meant was that unforgiven memories would hurt him more than the offender. He had come to love himself as loved by the Lord. He did not want to harbor resentment and anger because of what it would do to him. Further, he valued so much the Lord's forgiveness of him for his own sins and mistakes, that he did not want a refusal to give forgiveness to block the free flow of the Lord's forgiveness of him.

"Forgive" is an active and initiative verb. We do not wait for people to measure up or even ask for the forgiveness. Our challenge is to forgive, and then relate to the person as totally forgiven. Often this creates the desire in the other person to ask for forgiveness. But remember, God's forgiveness is not given because we ask, but given so that we can ask. Our unqualified love for a person will usually bring a request for our forgiveness. But our forgiveness is not to be measured by the other person's contrition. We can share our perception of what happened and how we felt without an "almighty" attitude. What's important is removing the barrier by expressing our forgiveness to the person.

Today's Thought: Our calling is to be people who set others free. This means forgiving, asking to be forgiven, and working tirelessly to establish reconciliation. But we are not alone in the challenge. The Lord is with us.

And He has taken it out of the way, having nailed it to the cross (Colossians 2:14).

Nail It to the Cross!

Paul uses two vivid metaphors to communicate the power of the cross for our forgiveness. Both have to do with the custom in his time of writing a charge list against a person. The list could be of wrongs committed or debts owed. The charge list was often displayed in a city square or near the town hall where everyone could read it. The offending person was disgraced.

On a deeper level, God had a charge list against humankind. There was no way men and women could pay the debt of sin. In search for images to communicate the grace of Calvary, Paul told the Colossians that the redemption through Christ was like wiping clean the charge list and nailing it to the cross.

In Paul's day writing paper and ink were very different from what they are today. There was no indelible ink, and parchment was often smooth. Writing could be wiped off with a damp sponge. In Christ's death all our trespasses were wiped from our charge list.

Now the metaphor shifts slightly. Not only is the charge list wiped clean, it's nailed to the cross. When a nail was driven through a displayed charge list, it was proof that the charges had been paid or canceled. When the nails were driven through Christ's hands, our debts were canceled. So whenever we sin, we need to claim that our failure has been nailed—paid in full. But this is not all. We nail it to the cross.

We also have charge lists against others. There are the painful memories of past hurts from what people have said or done to us or to the cause of Christ. It's liberating to write our own charge list now and then of those against whom we hold justified grievances. Now, when the lists are finished, nail them to the cross!

Today's Thought: I will no longer brood over what Christ has nailed to the cross.

September 13 Luke 7:36-50

But to whom little is forgiven, the same loves little (Luke 7:47).

Stingy Receivers

We cannot share what we do not have! Therefore, the first step is to become an open receiver. The more we allow God to give us, the more we will have to give away. We often talk about stingy givers. The reason they give grudgingly is that they have been stingy receivers. The root of the problem is our pride, self-sufficiency, and arrogance. God wants to give us Himself: His gifts of intervention in our problems, His abundant mercy in our failures.

When Jesus visited the home of Simon the Pharisee, the banquet was interrupted by a woman who washed Jesus' feet with her tears of gratitude. The Pharisee was enraged. What Jesus said to him is for all stingy receivers in every age. He told Simon the parable of the two debtors. One owed 500 denarii, and the other 50. (A denarii was worth about 20 cents.) The creditor forgave them both. "Tell me," Jesus asked, "which of them will love him more?" Simon responded with the obvious, "I suppose the one whom he forgave more."

Then Jesus drove the point home. When He had entered Simon's house, no one had washed His feet, a kiss of peace had not been given to Him, and no one had anointed His head. All of these were customs of hospitality and blessings. But the woman, out of gratitude for the forgiveness Christ had previously offered her, had invaded the propriety of the banquet because she had to express her love. "Therefore," the Master said, "I say to you, her sins, which are many, are forgiven, for she loved much. But to whom little is forgiven, the same loves little."

Simon's pride needed forgiveness as much as the woman's sins. If he had received the love Christ freely offered, he would have been able to share his gratitude with Christ and other people.

Today's Thought: Today I will displace pride with praise.

For I say to you, that to everyone who has will be given; and from him who does not have, even what he has will be taken away from him (Luke 19:26).

The Danger of Hoarding

The parable of the ten minas focuses on the fear of false assumptions. A nobleman went into a far country to receive a kingdom and return. He called ten of his servants and gave them ten minas (about $3,640 in our money) to invest and multiply. When he returned he called for an accounting from his servants. One used his mina to earn ten for the nobleman's investment. The next earned five more minas with his investment. The third, however, said "Master, here is your mina, which I have kept put away in a handkerchief for I feared you . . ." The servant did not really know his master.

Christ's commentary makes the point of the parable inescapable. "For I say to you, that to everyone who has will be given; and from him who does not have, even what he has will be taken away from him."

The salient issue of the whole parable is given us in the parenthesis of verse 25. (But they said to him, "Master, he has ten minas.") One of two things must have happened. The servant must have kept back nine minas in reporting to the master or he had ten minas before the master left him with an additional mina to invest. If this was the case, then the message of the parable was intended for the Jews who were hoarding their religious heritage and would not receive or appropriate Jesus' message and ministry. They could not accept his authority.

The fear of losing control of our lives and completely trusting Christ's control is a present, persistent problem. And to those who trust Him in faith, more faith and more of His Spirit will be given. But to those who refuse? What little they have hoarded will be taken away. Now there's a reason for fear!

Today's Thought: The fear of losing control keeps us from realizing Christ's power.

September 15 Romans 16:3-5

Greet Priscilla and Aquila, my fellow workers in Christ Jesus, who risked their own necks for my life, to whom not only I give thanks, but also all the churches of the Gentiles. Likewise greet the church that is in their house (Romans 16:3-5).

Risking Our Necks

A mark of greatness is being a true friend and having trusted friends. The subject of friendship has been talked and written about so much in secular literature, but too seldom do we discuss it as a part of our faith. And yet, what would we do without Christian friends? The basis of our relationship with others is that we have been called Christ's friends (John 15:12-17). He has told us that the crucial ingredient in friendship with Him is doing His commandments. We are called to keep His commandments in our relationships with one another. This means needing Him more than our friends and never substituting time with them for quality time with Him. But it also means living His commandment to love another as He has loved us. As I've expressed it often, "Christ is a friend who won't go away. Once we've experienced His quality of friendship, we can be that kind of friend to others."

This concept of friendship leads us to consider two unsung heroes of our faith—a couple named Priscilla and Aquila. They were fellow workers who risked their necks in Paul's defense. Also, they were distinguished for the church in their home.

Whenever we meet this stellar couple on the pages of the New Testament, they are ministering to others. They not only helped Paul but led Apollos into the power of a Spirit-filled life. But the question lingers: Is there anyone who would say about us what Paul said about them? For whom are we risking our necks in the name of Jesus?

Today's Thought: Risk something for a friend today!

God, who gives us richly all things to enjoy (1 Timothy 6:17).

Just Enjoying Now

Actress Helen Hayes, in her book *Our Best Years*, says, "I'm having the best time, now! The advantage of being at this point in my life is that I neither look back nor forward—more than a few days at a time. I just enjoy now," she wrote.

A Christian can focus on now because the future is settled. He knows where he will spend eternity, so he can invest himself in the present moment. Henry Drummond called this a mirror set at right angle: "The eternal life, a life of faith, is simply a life of higher vision. Faith is an attitude—like a mirror set at right angle. To become like Christ is the only thing in the world worth caring for, the thing before which every ambition in the world is folly, and all lower achievement is vain."

I have a wooden plaque in my office that has the words "Yes Lord" carved on it. The words remind me of the secret of grasping every moment with gusto.

We all have 168 hours each week. If we spend eight hours sleeping each night, that leaves 112 precious hours to live to the fullest—even during the tough times. They bring us closer to the Lord. And what else is really important?

Today's Thought: The time to be happy is now; the place to be happy is here; the way to be happy is to make others happy.

September 17 — 1 John 3:1-3

Behold what manner of love the Father has bestowed on us, that we should be called children of God (1 John 3:1).

We Are Loved

The other day I visited with a friend who is usually very grim and negative. Talking with him is usually a down time. But this time he was completely different. His face was radiant, his voice had a lilt to it, and he was full of fun. "What happened to you?" I asked. He burst out the good news, "She loves me!" The man had been dating a woman for years. She had been reluctant to express her love and commit herself to marriage. When she did, it transformed the man's thinking about his life and his future. "It's amazing! Being loved, really knowing you're loved, gives me a wonderful feeling of freedom." Love had given him self-esteem, relaxed his inner tension, and lifted the grimness of his attitudes.

Now multiply the finest expression of human love ten million times and you have just begun to experience the unlimited love the Lord has for us. Thinking about this love, building our whole lives around it, makes us joyous people who are free to enjoy life. It makes us free to give ourselves away, free to care, free to dare.

Whatever keeps us from receiving and enjoying this love is sin. Sin is separation, missing the mark. We were created to live in intimate oneness with the Lord. We lose our freedom whenever anything blocks the free flow of His Spirit in us.

Jesus clarified this with a very pointed illustration of the difference between being a slave and a son. "Most assuredly, I say to you, whoever commits sin is a slave of sin. And a slave does not abide in the house forever, but a son abides forever. Therefore, if the Son makes you free, you shall be free indeed" (John 8:34-36).

Today's Thought: Once we have known the Lord's unqualified love and felt the power of His presence, we are given an unquenchable thirst to know more of Him.

No one, having put his hand to the plow, and looking back, is fit for the kingdom of God (Luke 9:62).

Too Young to Retire

Some time ago, a full-page ad appeared in the *Wall Street Journal* entitled "How to Retire at 35."

I read the advertisement immediately. Though I had long passed 35, I wanted to know what I had missed. This is what it said:

> It's so easy. Thousands of men do it every year. In all walks of life. And it sets our economy, our country, and the world back thousands of years in terms of wasted human resources. But worst of all, it is the personal tragedy that almost always results from "early retirement."
>
> It usually begins with a tinge of boredom. Gradually a man's work begins to seem endlessly repetitious. The rat race hardly seems worth it any more.
>
> It is at this point that many a 35-year-old boy wonder retires. There are no testimonial dinners or gold watches. He goes to work every day, puts in his forty hours, and even draws a pay check. He's retired, but nobody knows it. Not at first, anyhow.
>
> The lucky ones get fired in time to make a fresh start. Those less fortunate hang on for a while—even decades—waiting and wondering; waiting for a raise or promotion that never comes, and wondering why. With the life expectancy approaching the century mark, 65 years is a long time to spend in a rocking chair.

I began to think of people I knew like that—not just in their work, but in their discipleship. Christ never allows us to take an early retirement. In fact, He recalls us today into active service.

Today's Thought: Find someone today who needs Christ and share your faith. Seek out a specific area of human need and get involved whether you're 20, 35, or 85. You're too young to retire!

September 19 Matthew 23:1-12

And whoever exalts himself will be abased, and he who humbles himself will be exalted (Matthew 23:12).

Taking the Punch Out of Pride

Pride takes the place of praise in our hearts. It's the desire to be adequate in our own strength, to be loved by God because we are good enough, and to be admired by people because of our superior performance. The snake is not in the grass—it's in our souls.

Pride pollutes everything it touches. It keeps us from growing spiritually, creates tension in our relationships, and makes us a person difficult for the Lord to bless. It is the basic sin causing separation from God, from our real selves, from others, and from the splendor of living as a spectator of the blessings of God in people and events.

Spiritual pride is the root of all other manifestations of pride. It is Satan's most powerful tool. With it we can miss meeting the Lord, and because of it we can be kept from spiritual growth after we have begun a relationship with Him.

Christ's words state the case flatly. When we exalt ourselves (in subtle and not-so-subtle ways), we must be abased. Problems can do that to us. When they do, they are angels of light and not darkness. We are brought low and to a place where the Lord can get through to us again. The question that needs careful consideration is how to respond to Christ's promise that those who humble themselves will be exalted. How do we humble ourselves? The way we handle problems is a way to begin. Rather than thinking that given time and our own cleverness we can solve them, we are to admit our inadequacy to find the creative solution. The Lord delights to bless a person like that.

Today's Thought: When we do become proud and then problems hit us, we can rediscover two humble qualities: laughing at ourselves that we thought we could make it on our own, and surrendering ourselves to the Lord for His guidance and intervention.

Then our mouth was filled with laughter, and our tongue with singing. Then they said among the nations, "The Lord has done great things for them" (Psalm 126:2).

Laugh at Yourself

People who can laugh at themselves are fun to be with. Their freedom is contagious. A person who is free to laugh at herself or himself gets a lot less criticism. Why point out faults of a person who is usually aware of his or her goofs and laughingly tells us about them? We really break the bond of uptight perfectionism when we can laugh at the absurd things we do and say.

An Episcopal priest was ready to begin a prayer service in a large sanctuary with the customary words, "The Lord be with you," to which the people were expected to respond, "And with your spirit!" As the priest spoke into the microphone, he realized it wasn't working and he tapped and jiggled it. Thinking it still was not operating, he shouted, "There's something wrong with this microphone!" As he exclaimed those words, the microphone clicked on. And out of habit, the people responded, "And with your spirit!" The priest laughed uproariously and the congregation joined in, enjoying the clergyman's ability to laugh at himself. Then he said, "Indeed, there is something wrong with my spirit and with yours. And that's why we've come to pray. We all need the Lord's power and guidance—priest and people. It's great to know that the Lord is probably laughing with us about what just happened. I'd like to join with you in praying to that kind of God. Let us pray. . . ."

Laughter loosens us up, is a healing agent, and frees us to take ourselves less seriously.

Today's Thought: Start laughing at yourself and begin living care-freely.

September 21 — 2 Corinthians 4:1-7

But we have this treasure in earthen vessels, that the excellence of the power may be of God and not of us (2 Corinthians 4:7).

"I Enjoy You!"

The other day, I visited a fellow pastor who is one of our nation's most able communicators. He has a receding hairline. I seldom notice it because of the radiance of his face. On the wall in his private restroom is an embroidered plaque that says: "God made a few perfect heads. Others He covered with hair."

I am amazed at how few people enjoy themselves. Their freedom to be themselves is frustrated when they focus on their earthen vessel rather than on the power of the Lord. They become concerned about how they look instead of allowing Christ to shine through them.

The same thing can happen to us because of our remorse over mistakes and failures. "How can the Lord love and use a person who did or said that?" we demand of ourselves in self-incrimination. But He does. None of us is perfect. Good thing—our pride over our self-generated purity would make us unusable. The Lord delights in surprising the world around us with what He can do with imperfect people like us.

When we acknowledge that, we can give the Lord the glory. Our enjoyment of being used in spite of our limitations will spill over to other people. Our task is not to convince people of how bad they are, but of how powerful God is.

A conversation with a friend drifted into concern about a mutual friend. He is a very gifted man who is plagued with lack of self-esteem. My friend said, "I wish that guy enjoyed himself more!" My response was, "Perhaps the place for us to begin to help him is to tell him how much we enjoy him. There's a lot about him I do enjoy." After that conversation I thought long and hard about the people in my life who need to know that I enjoy them. I decided to express my feelings so they would know.

Today's Thought: Who can I tell today that I enjoy them?

Now if God so clothes the grass of the field, which today is, and tomorrow is thrown into the oven, will He not much more clothe you, O you of little faith? Therefore do not worry, saying, "What shall we eat?" or "What shall we drink?" or "What shall we wear?" (Matthew 6:30,31).

Living Care-Freely

Jesus had a rich sense of humor. Nowhere in the New Testament is it more vividly exposed than when He tried to help His followers laugh at some of their freedom-sapping cares. In the Sermon on the Mount, in the section on worry and care (Matthew 6:25-34), He enables us to poke fun at our own furtive concerns over material things, the length of our lives, and what the future holds. Careful exposition of the passage makes us laugh at ourselves. Then as the laughter releases us from taking ourselves so seriously, the deeper point the Master is making penetrates our thinking and enables greater freedom. Freedom in the Spirit means living "care-freely."

It's helpful to note the Greek word used for "care" in this section of the Sermon on the Mount. It is also translated as "worry" or "anxiety" in other versions. The noun is *merimna* and the verb *merimnao*, from *merizo*, "to draw in different directions, distract, or pull apart." Building on this, inordinate care is a distraction from trusting the Lord; care pulls us apart from confident trust in His provision, power, and plan. Worrisome care comes from thinking we have to handle life on our own, with our inadequate human resources. This kind of anxiety is living horizontally, depending on our own potential. This is rather laughable, isn't it?

Today's Thought: I will accept the gift of the Lord's care and live care-freely. It's absurd for both of us to carry the burden, and He's the expert.

September 23 2 Corinthians 1:20,21

Amen (Matthew 6:13).

The Amen Corner

The "Amen Corner" years ago was the section of the sanctuary usually occupied by those who punctuated a pastor's sermon with "amens" of approval. Sometimes the amens became a thoughtless repeated response and were distracting to other worshipers who were still thinking about whether they could say *and live* an "amen" to what was being preached.

Some preachers deliberately seek a response to what they are saying by asking, "Amen?" That, too, can become a habit, and often people respond with their amens without counting the cost of what they are agreeing to.

The word "amen" means "truth." Jesus often said, "Truly, truly, I say to you." When we say "amen," we mean that we have accepted the truth our Lord has spoken to us.

So "amen" is a word of commitment. It means "so be it." At the end of prayers, it means that we really want and expect that for which we have prayed. Whenever we say "amen" about any of the affirmations and promises of Scripture, we are declaring our belief in what is assured and claiming it for our lives.

There's another kind of "amen corner." It's in all of us. It's the compartment of our lives in which we attest to our faith and convictions. But just as an "amen corner" of a sanctuary may not reflect the discipleship of the whole church, so too most of us talk beyond where we are living.

Today, let's experiment with getting the "amen corner" of our lives expanded to an "amen life." Christ is the Amen of God (2 Corinthians 1:20; Revelation 3:14). The company of heaven sings, "Amen! Alleluia!" (Revelation 19:4). We can join that company as we praise the Lord for His kingdom, power, and glory. Say "amen"?

Today's Thought: Today I will live an "amen" life.

Judge not, that you be not judged. For with what judgment you judge, you will be judged; and with the same measure you use, it will be measured back to you (Matthew 7:1,2).

The Boomerang

The icy body language between the husband and wife spoke volumes. They had come to see me about the lack of communication in their marriage. They sat at opposite ends of the couch in my study. I asked each of them what was happening to their marriage. The husband went first. "Criticize, criticize, criticize!" he blurted out. "All she does is criticize!" I looked over at the wife, inviting her analysis. "Judge, judge, judge!" she said angrily. "All he ever does is judge!" Then she went on to say, "My criticisms are not half as bad as his judgments!"

Which would you say is the worst? Cankerous criticism or jaundiced judgment? Actually, neither was in any position to judge or criticize. They were both insecure, loveless people, who were stabilizing the frustration inside them by lambasting each other. Nothing can destroy a marriage or a friendship more quickly than judgmentalism or constant criticism. Most of us have "plankated" vision. We have a plank in our own eye and judge the speck in another's eye. Jesus tells us to take the plank out of our own eye and then we will be able to help a friend with the speck in his eye. Once we allow the Lord to help us with our planks, we will be enabled to tenderly and graciously help people with their problems, rather than being censorious sources of problems.

Today's Thought: Think about the planks in your own eye that need to be removed.

September 25 1 Corinthians 2:6-16

For what man knows the things of a man except the spirit of the man which is in him? Even so no one knows the things of God except the Spirit of God. Now we have received, not the spirit of the world, but the Spirit who is from God, that we might know the things that have been freely given to us by God (1 Corinthians 2:11,12).

Theotelepathy

Evelyn Underhill said, "One human spirit can, by its power and love, touch another human spirit. It can take the soul and lift it into the atmosphere of God.... Those in need of help will find that the praying person is a transmitter of the redeeming power of God. There is actually a mysterious interpenetration of all living souls." On the basis of that thought, I want to establish a new word for the beauty of friendship: "theotelepathy." It's a combination of telepathy and theopathy.

Telepathy is the communication of one mind with another at a distance by other than sensory means; i.e., contact beyond the physical senses of sight, touch, and hearing of proximity. "Tele" means "distance." "Pathy," from the root of the Greek *paschein*, "passion," means "to suffer or feel deeply for, or on behalf of, another." Sympathy and empathy come from this stem.

Theopathy, on the other hand, is spiritual emotion aroused by meditation on God. In prayer we feel the pathy of God—His love, passion, and suffering concern. *Theo* means "God" in Greek. The word "theology" is a combination of *theo* and *logos*: "God" and "word"; thus, "a word or discourse about God." A theotelepathy, then, is the experience of the love of God engendered by Him for another person at a distance. We can reach the needs of others by communication with God, who is more passionately concerned than we are.

Today's Thought: "We have the mind of Christ" (1 Corinthians 2:16).

We know that we have passed from death to life, because we love (1 John 3:14).

A.D. Living

A.D. love is empowered by the Lord Himself. It is vibrant with post-resurrection resiliency. Love before Christ was measured, qualified, limited. Christ called His disciples to love one another, people of all nations, and their enemies. His love combines words and action. The cross revealed the extent of His love, and the resurrection displayed its unconquerable power.

But Christ has given us more than a message and mandate about love. He has given Himself. A.D. love is allowing Him to motivate and mediate His own love through us. The dynamic of Christianity is dying to ourselves and being raised to be filled with the Lord and His Spirit of love.

The floodgate of loving is the will. The reservoir of our heart may be overflowing with good intentions to love, but the life-giving flow to others is dependent upon a decision of the will. Often we wait for the feeling of love. When we will to do and say what love demands, we will have the power for what love requires. We can ask, "If I loved God with all my heart, what would I do?" Get this clearly portrayed in your imagination. Then will to do it.

Jesus focused a good deal of His ministry on the will. He knew the convictions of the mind and the emotions of the heart require obedience of the will. The surrender of the will to Him provides Him with a ready instrument through which He can love. He asks us what He asked Rees Howells: "Are you willing to be made willing?"

Today's Thought: "One way of putting the question to ourselves is: are we being B.C. or A.D.? Are the standards of greatness which you accept those that for the most part pervaded before Christ came into the world with His insistence on a new measurement of service, or are you living in some year of our Lord?" —Helford Luccock.

September 27 Ephesians 6:21-24

Grace be with all those who love our Lord Jesus Christ in sincerity. Amen (Ephesians 6:24).

Eternally Yours!

The last word before "amen" at the conclusion of Ephesians gives us the basis for resurrection living. The word in the New King James Version is "sincerity." The meaning from this translation is that grace is to be with all who love the Lord Jesus with sincerity. The New English Bible has a somewhat better rendering: "unfailing love." William Barclay suggests "a love which defies death."

Our question is "What did Paul intend?" The word he uses is *aphtharsia* which actually means "in incorruption." A key to what the apostle meant is given us by considering his use of the word in 1 Corinthians 15:42. Speaking of the resurrection of the dead he says, "The body is sown in corruption, it is raised in incorruption." Here "incorruption" signifies the indestructibility of the resurrection body that lives forever in Christ—that is, our eternal soul. Now we wonder why Paul used this same word to describe the love of Christians for Christ. Then the rendering would be: "Grace be with all who love our Lord Jesus Christ with love undying...." But that still puts a qualification on grace—given only to those who have undying love. Yet, it is grace that enables us to love Christ in return.

My conclusion is that the verse means not just the quality of our love, but its eternal dimension. Grace has freed us to live fully now. Death holds no fear. We are alive forever. Not even death can cap our potential. We will go on loving our Lord for eternity.

Today's Thought: For us there is no cap on the grave or the length of eternity. Christ is our Lord forever. We can sign our commitment to His Lordship, "Eternally Yours!"

He who answers a matter before he hears it, it is folly. . . (Proverbs 18:13).

Hearing

It is not generally known that the great Cunard ship, *Queen Mary*, was originally to have been christened *Queen Victoria*. A Cunard official was dispatched to Buckingham Palace to inform George V of the choice of the name. The man nervously began to explain the decision to the king by saying that Cunard had chosen to name the new ship after "the greatest of all English queens."

King George was delighted. He exclaimed, "Oh, my wife will be *so* pleased!" His wife's name, you'll remember, was Mary. The befuddled Cunard executive did not have the courage to point out the king's mistake. Thus, the ship was renamed and christened the *Queen Mary*.

It's often said we hear what we want to hear. And there's often a difference between what we think we said and what people heard. Communication is a challenge in the best of relationships. Think of how often people have side, "You weren't listening!"

Since this is so, our calling as Christians is to take the initiative in being sure we heard what people wanted to say. We can do this by saying, "Let me be sure I understand. What you say is important to me, so let me respond by sharing what I heard."

It was said of a great leader that he listened so intently he tired the person talking. I doubt that. People are affirmed when we really listen, and when we make an effort not to hear only what we want to hear, but what people *mean*. Then we have communicated esteem and corrected 50 percent of misunderstandings before they happen.

Today's Thought: Today I will affirm others by really listening to them to hear what they are saying and not just what I want to hear!

September 29 Acts 4:32-37

With our beloved Barnabas (Acts 15:25).

The Liberating Power of Affirmation

The one need we never outgrow is for affirmation. We all long to be assured that we are cherished, of value, and loved just as we are. Most of us know about our failures and inadequacies. What we ache for is someone to say, "I believe in you!" Affirmation gives us courage to be the persons we were meant to be.

Who in your life needs your affirmation? What could you say or do that would communicate your belief in that individual? Make this an affirmation day. Make a list of people who need affirmation and what you will say or do. Then see or call these people. Don't wait until tomorrow!

Affirmation is expressed delight. What God said at Jesus' baptism, He says to each of us: "This is My beloved Son in whom I am well pleased." Put your own name in that statement. In Christ, God affirmed you and me. He came for us, lived for us, died for us, and was raised for us so that we might know how much He loves us. When we realize His affirmation, we can become affirmers.

"Barnabas" means "Son of Encouragement." Wherever Barnabas appears on the pages of Acts, he's encouraging people. He encouraged the church, was Paul's friend and fellow missionary, and cared for Mark after the young man was a missionary dropout, helping him to become a great leader. Barnabas was distinguished because of the greatness he made possible in others. What we need is an Order of St. Barnabas, a fellowship of people who build up rather than tear down, who infuse hope and not discouragement, who believe that people can change when affirmed. I want to be a charter member. What about you?

Today's Thought: Boosting others will send them and us soaring beyond the capabilities we thought we had.

But the Lord said to him, "Go, for he is a chosen vessel of Mine to bear My name before Gentiles, kings, and the children of Israel. . . ." And Ananias went (Acts 9:15-17).

A Miracle of Obedience

Ananias received a miracle before he performed one. The miracle of transformation of his fear and hatred of Saul of Tarsus had to happen before he could be used to lay hands on Saul for the restoration of the blinded apostle-elect. There was probably a lot more conversation between the Lord and Ananias than is recorded in the brief verses here in Acts.

Think of the people for whom you'd most abhor being the Lord's agent of love, reconciliation, and healing. It's difficult enough when people hurt or criticize us or become our "enemies." But when we have justified anger and rejection of them because of what they do to our Lord or in the ridicule of our faith, it's all the harder. When our enemies also happen to be people we know are out of line with the Lord, our indignation seems so justified. Then we are shocked to have the Lord command us to do the loving, forgiving, gracious thing to these very people.

But note carefully that as Ananias laid his hands on Saul who had been his feared enemy, *immediately* he received his sight. Note also that Saul arose and was baptized. How did he know to do this? There must have been conversation between him and Ananias, then some teaching, and finally baptism. And who baptized him? Ananias, of course. Two miracles were accomplished, and the Lord had arranged both. Ananias could have refused. The Lord could have found someone else. But what would have happened to Ananias then? What would that have done to his future spiritual growth? We know what might have happened if he had said "no" because we've been saying it in our lives about our brand of difficult or impossible people. We may still have a Saul waiting!

Today's Thought: Our ministry as Christians is to unbind and free people in Christ's name.

October 1 Acts 16:11-15

Now a certain woman named Lydia heard us. She was a seller of purple from the city of Thyatira, who worshiped God. The Lord opened her heart to heed the things spoken by Paul (Acts 16:14).

The Gift of an Open Heart

Lydia was a remarkable person. We are told much in the lines of our text, and much is implied between those lines. She was a businesswoman, a spiritual leader among a group that gathered to pray, and a worshiper of God (the Hebrew faith in a Roman province was not the most popular religion to practice!). When Paul preached Christ, her heart was opened to the gospel. We are told she had a house, but are left to wonder if she was married or had a family. Chances are she did and invited Paul and his companions to stay in her home. Also, parenthetically, we are given a somewhat different view of Paul's relationship to women than is implied in other places in his writings. Lydia was a woman, a professional, and a leader when Paul met her and introduced her to Christ.

Most important for our consideration of Lydia is that she became a person in Christ and a leader in the newly formed church that resulted from Paul's ministry in Philippi. This church became very dear to the apostle (Philippians 1:3-6).

Notice that it was the Lord who opened Lydia's heart. He gives the gift of faith so we can respond to the gospel. Conversion is His miracle—but so is daily living of the abundant life. The Lord opens our hearts each morning so we can glorify and enjoy Him and the wonder of life all through the day.

Today's Thought: I will accept the gift of an open heart today. The Lord has great plans for this day, and I'm ready!

The unity of the Spirit in the bond of peace (Ephesians 4:3).

The Joy of Being a Holy Catholic Saint

World Communion Sunday is celebrated on the first Sunday of October. The actual date is different each year, so I want to share a thought about the meaning of the celebration and ask you to apply it to whatever Sunday it falls on in the year you read this devotional.

When we repeat the Apostles' Creed, we affirm our oneness with Christians of many different denominations across the world. We say, "I believe in the holy catholic Church; the communion of saints. . . ."

I am a catholic Christian, who happens to belong to the Presbyterian segment of Christ's church, who loves Baptists, Methodists, Episcopalians, charismatics, Congregationalists, Roman Catholics, and all the Lord's people throughout the world. This is no flip remark. The word "catholic" means universal and is not just an exclusive term applying to Roman Catholics. Because we belong to Christ, we are equally united with Christians of many denominational affiliations.

We all are "holy" not because we are perfect, but because we have been elected and called to belong first and foremost to God. The word for "holy" is *hagios*, meaning "different, set apart, belonging to God." We have "communion," *koinonia*, with one another because we are all a part of the *ekklesia*—those who are called out and have responded to the call of God in Christ. "Communion of saints" is a magnificent phrase that describes the mutual love, unity, care, and mission we share.

Today's Thought: In essentials, unity; in nonessentials, tolerance.

October 3 Colossians 4:10-18

And say to Archippus, "Take heed to the ministry which you have received in the Lord, that you may fulfill it" (Colossians 4:17).

An Original

When the Quakers decided to publish George Fox's journal, they asked William Penn if he would write the preface. Fox was a genius and mystic of great spiritual depth. Penn wrote, "Fox was an original and no man's copy."

George Fox was no man's copy because he sought to be Christ's person. The more he concentrated on the Master, the more he became the unique, never to be repeated miracle he was meant to be.

We all have heroes and heroines we would like to emulate. This is fine if we don't miss our own uniqueness. Sometimes we get bogged down by the "if onlys"—if I only had his talents or her leadership skills or their opportunities.

God created each of us to be part of His plan for our time of history. He has an individualized destiny for each of us—given to us and to no one else. We can get insight and inspiration from others, but only the Lord can guide us in living His special plan for us. This requires daily prayer and obedience to follow through on His guidance.

At the end of Colossians, Paul has a word for Archippus, a champion of the gospel and an officer in the church. He must have needed an extra boost to get on with his own appointed calling. Paul's words to him are the formula for discovering and expressing the Lord's individual plan for us. We must take heed of the ministry we have been appointed to do and fulfill it.

This means faithfulness to Christ in doing the particular work He's given us to do, caring for the people He has put on our agendas, and bringing His justice and mercy to suffering places. Our uniqueness and originality are discovered in this way.

Today's Thought: By the Lord's grace, I am an original and no one's copy!

God is the strength of my heart and my portion forever (Psalm 73:26).

The Strength of My Heart

The other night I was awakened by concern over four major problems I had been wrestling with for days. One related to my work, another to a concern over a member of my family, another over a friend, and still another over a broken relationship. In the long hours of tossing and turning, I finally prayed.

The Lord showed me how I was trying to solve these problems on my own and revealed how I actually contributed to a couple of them with my own attitudes. He helped me see in my mind's eye some uncreative attitudes and revealed a picture of how He wanted me to act and react the next day. Again self-sufficiency was broken. Another strand of the bond of willfulness was severed. Once more, a fresh infilling of the Lord's Spirit resulted.

I slept the rest of the night and arose refreshed, aware of the power of His Spirit. That day, equipped with the fruit of His implanted character and His gifts of wisdom and faith, I became a partner in the solution of many of the concerns that had awakened me in distress.

As I went through the day, I was a different person. More of me was open to the Spirit and, having greater access to me, He did through me what I could not have done alone. I was broken open to be built up another step in becoming a free person.

Christ has promised to guide our thinking and give us His perspective on our problems. What are your concerns today? Have you asked the Lord for His thought control? Right now, put your hands before you. In one, place your needs; in the other, your deepest convictions about Christ's power. Then bring your hands together and lift them up as your commitment to trust the Lord today.

Today's Thought: I confidently face today knowing Christ will give me insight, wisdom, and guidance for my problems.

October 5 Ephesians 1:15-23

The eyes of your understanding being enlightened; that you may know what is the hope of His calling, what are the riches of the glory of His inheritance in the saints (Ephesians 1:18).

How Are You Thinking?

True spiritual freedom is rooted in Christ's unassailable truth which controls our thinking and pervades our emotions. When we do not feel free, it is usually because of emotions which are not under control of our thinking. An emotion of fear, anxiety, worry, or insecurity is rooted to some distorted thought about who we are in our relationship to the Lord.

Often when we meet another person we ask, "How are you feeling today?" or "How are you?" Instead, we should ask, "How are you thinking?" or "How's your thinking today?" How we feel is directly traceable to what we think about what has happened to us or around us. Much of our thinking is not controlled and conditioned by the Lord—what He has done for us, and His unconditional love for us. Becoming a truly free person requires battles for truth in the midst of the untruth of our irrational thinking which creates our incarcerated, unfree feelings.

Emotions follow thought. We cannot change how we feel until we change our thinking. Solomon was right: "For as he thinks in his heart, so is he" (Proverbs 23:7). Our perception of life will control how we feel about it in any one day. Circumstances do not control our feelings. What we think about those circumstances results in our feelings of joy or frustration. Often we feel victimized by our emotional responses to people. But in between the impact of what they say or do that distresses us is the split-second cognitive response that triggers our feelings. Often what we think is based on ideas and accumulated attitudes creased in our brain which are not consistent with Christ, the gospel, and His revealed truth. Start today by yielding your thinking to Christ.

Today's Thought: Today I will allow Christ to transform and control my thinking.

Even when we were dead in trespasses, [God] made us alive together with Christ (by grace you have been saved) (Ephesians 2:5).

Our Status

The truth of Christ establishes our status. He is the unmerited love of God incarnate. His love is given before we can earn or deserve it. We are forgiven in spite of what we say or do. Christ who said repeatedly, "Neither do I condemn you; go in peace," went to the cross to suffer and die for the forgiveness of our sins.

A Christ-centered, cross-oriented mind is one that is rooted in convictions of justification, forgiveness, and eternal acceptance. Christ sublimely changes our minds about self-justification, self-oblation, and self-condemnation. When we think contrary to Christ's atonement of our sins and His complete and eternal justification for us, we trigger emotions which eventually rob us of the freedom He died to give us.

And yet, think of all the days you have spent feeling unfree because of guilt and subsequent self-justification. Remember all those down times when your feelings were pervaded by self-condemnation because of mistakes in the past or fear of failure in the future? Or remember how often you have felt unfree when you based your perceptions of your value and worth on other people's opinions and were dragged into the prison of feeling their judgments or negative evaluations? Consider how much of life has been spent nursing feelings of hurt over the rejections and put-downs of people. You probably became cautious and reserved in the expression of your own unique personality.

In each time of emotional lack of freedom, liberation comes only through clear thinking about our status as the chosen, called, cherished, forgiven, and accepted loved ones of the Lord. We need to wake up to reality, see our irrationality, and ask the Lord to help us live His truth in totality.

Today's Thought: When we accept our status as His cherished, beloved children, we begin to grow in His likeness.

October 7 Luke 16:14-17

You are those who justify yourselves before men, but God knows your hearts (Luke 16:15).

Our Security

Recently, I spoke to a gathering of evangelical leaders. They are the spiritual giants of our time. Early in the morning as I did my final preparation, I was guided by the Lord to change my message. The clear instruction from the Lord was to preach on the theme of freedom in the Spirit through grace and justification by faith alone. I dealt with the problem of self-justification.

After the meeting, the leaders shared with me that the emphasis on justification by faith alone was just what they needed most to hear to set them free again to press on with their work, reaffirmed in their status as people who are loved unqualifiedly by God, saved by grace.

One of them shared an unsettling personal experience. He had been falsely criticized by a negative person. His integrity and behavior had been questioned severely. Though he knew the judgment was untrue, he was tempted to defend himself with elaborate, self-justifying explanations.

That morning during my talk on grace and freedom, he had prayed, "Lord, I'm in need of Your grace and assurance. This criticism has triggered an old pattern of defensiveness. I have no security other than Your love and the atonement of Calvary. Forgive me for muddling with this criticism, thinking I could handle it alone. I claim again the sure Rock on which I stand."

Later, the man said to me, "If I could make one wish for myself and my growth in grace, it would be that when I feel unfree, I would not wait so long before going back to the source of healing. What I preach to others, I need most of all myself."

Today's Thought: Security does not come from removing the outward causes of insecurity, but by consistently rediscovering our security in Christ and drawing on the inward reservoirs of His assurance.

That He would grant you, according to the riches of His glory, to be strengthened with might through His Spirit in the inner man (Ephesians 3:16).

Our Strength

A third basis of our freedom is Christ's strength. Not only the status of His possession and the security of His presence, but also the strength of His power transforms our thinking and subsequently our feelings of being free. We can be free to face the challenges of life only if we are sure that Christ Himself will be the power to give us exactly what we need in each situation. He promised that He would be with us and in us. This is the secret of thinking freedom. His indwelling Spirit is the Spirit of truth. This is the secret of silent strength we have stressed in this book.

Freedom comes as a result of habitually thinking His truth and claiming His power every day. He gives us power to think His thoughts and will to do His will. He floods our emotions with the fruit of His Spirit.

What would be a better description of a free person than someone who has the fruit of Christ's Spirit? Such a person is free to give love; experience and share joy; abide in peace; have patience with oneself and others; be kind in spite of people's weaknesses and failures; maintain a consistency of goodness in the changing circumstances of life; express faithfulness to Christ, oneself, and other people; be gentle in judgments and attitudes toward others; and be under control because of liberating commitment to Christ as an obedient bondservant.

Now we must face the question "If Christ offers us the status, security, and strength of true freedom, why are so few Christians free?" Look at it this way. Our minds are like a garden filled with flowers and weeds. We need to pull out the noxious weeds that are contrary to the life, death, and resurrection of Christ.

Today's Thought: A mind filled with Christ's truth is a place where freedom can flourish and emotional peace can grow.

For who makes you differ from another? And what do you have that you did not receive? Now if you did indeed receive it, why do you glory as if you had not received it? (1 Corinthians 4:7).

Vulnerable to Be Loved

There is no more frustrating challenge than to be told to love ourselves. How can we?

We know what we are. All the hidden memories known only to us mock us. How can we love the person inside us, knowing all we've said and done?

A lively self-esteem is a rare gift. This is why only Christ's love can break the bond of self-negation and justification. When we accept His unqualified love, we can dare to love the person inside us He loves so much. A new freedom to be loving begins in a healing experience of Christ's love, acceptance, and forgiveness.

A dynamic expression of caring is to be able to receive caring. Let people love you! But that means to be vulnerable. People cannot care about us if they do not know our needs. We give people a special gift when we become honest and open about what's happening to us. Independence and self-reliance block deep caring. A person who refuses to be cared for by others will usually end up caring little about the people around him.

Share your needs, ask for others' prayers, seek their insight and wisdom. Your openness will create an openness in the people you want to help. It takes a lot of energy to keep the facade of adequacy. People feel put down and guilty in the presence of a person who pretends to "have it all together."

Today's Thought: We begin to become caring persons when we let God care for us. Then our hearts are set on fire with care for others. Being open to their care for you is often the first step in preparing an openness for you to care for them.

He shall also bring him to the door, or to the doorpost, and his master shall pierce his ear with an awl; and he shall serve him forever (Exodus 21:6).

Real Freedom

The servant's response was filled with passion: "Master, I love you. I love my wife and children. How can I leave you all behind? My duty, my joy, is here. It is not freedom if I go, but a slavery!"

The ceremony of the piercing of the servant's ear with an awl must have been a jubilant celebration. The pain in the lobe of the ear lasted only for a moment, but the scar was a constant reminder that he had chosen to be free to serve his master, love and enjoy his wife, and raise his children.

Our commitment to the Lord must pass through the same turbulent sea of ultimate choice. We are free to leave our Master, but would that be freedom? We are released to throw off the responsibilities of being a bondservant of righteousness, but would that bring us freedom? No, but given the choice, we are introduced to the real person inside us and to what we really want. And we exclaim, "Master, there is no real freedom without You. Serving You and doing Your will is all I want!"

Truly free people are confronted with this choice and have made a commitment to serve Christ forever. They are free because of a controlling passion for an ultimate purpose which is grand and demanding enough to call forth all they are. Then all competing, secondary loyalties are marshaled into place to march to the orders of the Lord's commands. Because we've put Him first in our lives, we are ready to serve Him more creatively.

Today's Thought: "Prone to wonder Lord I feel it
Prone to leave the God I love
Here's my heart, O take and seal it
Seal it for Thy courts above."

(Taken from the hymn "Come, Thou Fount of Every Blessing" by Robert Robinson.)

October 11 — Romans 6:15-23

Having been set free from sin, you became slaves of righteousness (Romans 6:18).

Captivated Freedom

When we were born, we inherited a fallen nature. We were not inherently inclined to love God or seek His will. It was by His choice that we were privileged to hear about His love in Christ and what He had done for us in the cross. Our will was not free. It was in bondage to the confused thinking for our mind. Then by sheer grace He came to us. Through the preaching and teaching of the gospel, or the gracious explanation of a friend whose life in Christ attracted us, we heard the liberating truth of love and forgiveness. Our response was also a gift. We were incapable of accepting Christ as our Lord and Savior until the gift of faith was given to us. The same Lord who made us a little lower than Himself broke the bonds of self-will and gave us the power to believe and the will to commit our lives to Him. We were born again!

Today's Thought: George Matheson discovered the only way the will is liberated from the bondage of willfulness and wrote the secret in a poem:

Make me a captive, Lord,
And then I shall be free;
Force me to render up my sword,
And I shall conqueror be.
I sink in life's alarms
When by myself I stand;
Imprison me within Thine arms,
And strong shall be my hand.

My will is not my own
Till Thou hast made it Thine;
If it would reach a monarch's throne
It must its crown resign;
It only stands unbent
Amid the clashing strife
When on Thy bosom it has leant
And found in Thee its life.

For though I am free from all men, I have made myself a servant to all, that I might win the more (1 Corinthians 9:19).

Free to Serve

The Lord created us to need and love Him and then to love people. He is the only Person we have to please. And when we know His pleasure in us is freely offered not because of anything we do but out of sheer grace, we are free to become so secure in Him that we don't have to please anyone else. Thus liberated, we can focus on loving people out of the artesian flow of the Lord's love. Our deepest concern becomes how to communicate His grace rather than using people to fill our own emptiness.

Loving people instead of needing them is the sublime level of freedom expressed by Paul in chapter 9 of his first epistle to the Corinthians. He declares his profound love for his friends without needing anything from them. This leads to his remarkable declaration in verses 19 through 23 regarding his freedom *from* people to live *for* people.

Paul declares his liberation from all people and his commitment to be a servant of all people. Then he spells out the implication of what it means to be that kind of liberated servant. And finally, he states the purpose of his servanthood.

Let's think about this today so its truth can set us free. That leads us to pose and grapple with four questions prompted by Paul's startling statement of relational freedom. We can get to the core of what it means for us by asking:

- What does it mean to be free from people?
- What does it mean to be free for people?
- What is the purpose of this freedom?
- How can we measure the success of that quality of freedom?

Today's Thought: Christ sets us free from needing people and calls us to serve people who need Him.

October 13 (Matthew 10:39-42).

He who finds his life will lose it, and he who loses his life for My sake will find it (Matthew 10:39).

Out of the Dungeon of Self

Self-concern is a prison indeed! The more we think about ourselves, our needs, and our desires, the more incarcerated we become. The reason is that we were created to share. Happiness is in interdependence, not independence. When we contradict God's plan, we get moody and down on ourselves, others, and life in general.

The door to the prison of our own making must be thrown open to the world filled with people who need us. A bad mood is dispelled when we get involved in listening to others and helping them to solve the problems they are facing. We can feel badly about our own situations until we are confronted with what others are enduring.

When we are in the dungeon of self-pity, we need a fresh flow of grace from God. But He usually does not come to us in our prison of self. He calls us to join Him in what He is doing. If we want God, we must go where He is—to people in need, those who suffer, the lonely, the frustrated.

Think of three people who need you today. Call, write a letter, or go see them. You need them more than they need you. They are the door out of your self-imposed prison. Two things will always occur: You will bring joy to them and you will receive joy from the Lord for them. You, most of all, will be blessed!

Today's Thought: "The love of our neighbor is the only door out of the dungeon of self" —George MacDonald.

I thank my God always concerning you for the grace of God which was given to you by Christ Jesus (1 Corinthians 1:4).

In Good Repair

Life is dynamic, not static. The only consistent thing is change. We are constantly changing, facing new problems and opportunities. As we change, so do our relationships. None of us is the person he or she was and—thank God—will be as the future unfolds.

A great friendship is one that gives people the freedom to grow and keeps up with their progress. It is no compliment to say to a friend, "You haven't changed a bit!" We know this is meant to be an affirmation of a person's consistency in personal attributes. But are we also aware of the advancements our friends have made as they have turned life's struggles into steppingstones?

A friendship that's kept in repair is one in which we are in touch with what a person is learning on all levels of life. When we say, "How are you, friend?" we should be ready to share the excitement of discoveries battled for and won. It is so easy to lose contact with friends even when they are not separated by distance or time.

The apostle Paul's letters to his friends were filled with his delight over their growth. He kept his friendships in good repair. The passage we read today expresses profound love and encouragement. Paul knew about the strengths and weaknesses of the Corinthians. He confirmed their progress and challenged them to continue to grow. He kept in touch with their problems and communicated that he was standing with them claiming the Lord's best for them—all because his friendship with Christ was in good repair.

Today's Thought: "A man, sir, should keep his friendships in constant repair" —Samuel Johnson.

October 15 Ephesians 4:17-29

Put on the new man (Ephesians 4:24).

Is Your True Self Out This Morning?

I received a letter recently from a friend whom I had met at a conference where I spoke on the will of the Lord. I had focused on becoming a new creature in Christ as the purpose of His will. As is often my custom, I ended my last message with "Why not?"

Why not live life in Christ without reservation? Why not allow Him to transform our will? Why not accept the character transplant He wants to perform so we can think, will, and act as His liberated persons? Why not, indeed?

My new friend decided to ask himself "Why not?" and dared to answer. It led him to Paul's challenge to put on the new man and be renewed in his mind. This led to a commitment to do some things he was putting off in his discipleship, as well as to do some new things the Lord was putting on his agenda. He wrote me to communicate his gratitude. He used a way that he knew I would appreciate. He knows of my love for Scotland and chose to relate an account from his life to express his new joy in the will of the Lord.

An old Scots woman by the name of Mrs. Ferguson used to greet him in the mornings with the expression, "Ah, Jim, is it yourself that's out this morning?" The man related that the woman now has gone on to the next phase of her eternal life in heaven. "But if she were here now to ask me that question again," he wrote, "I would say to her in sure confidence, 'Ah, Mrs. Ferguson, it's my true self that's out this morning. Indeed it is!' "

And the man who's out is a person integrated around the will of God—a newly transformed man because of the renewing of his mind. Is your true self out this morning?

Today's Thought: The self is a container. It can be filled with egotism or Christ, grimness or His grace, pride or praise, fear or faith. Daily surrender of the self to Christ is the secret to being our true and new self.

A broken and contrite heart—these, O God, Yo[u will]
not despise (Psalm 51:17).

A Contrite Heart

Does the Lord ever give up on us? No, He persists. He will never leave us or forsake us, as He promised in Hebrews 13:5. We need not pray as King David did: "Do not cast me away from Your presence, and do not take Your Holy Spirit from me" (Psalm 51:11). David's plea from his abyss of sin and self-condemnation was a projection of human attitudes onto God. By all human evaluation, God had every right to turn away from David and depart. David's panic was probably based on what he had observed happen to his predecessor, Saul. First Samuel 16:14 says, "The Spirit of the Lord departed from Saul." But close study of Saul reveals that Saul departed from the Spirit and persistently resisted being broken of his willfulness. To the very end, Saul was in charge of Saul. He blamed his problems on everyone else, including David. His final act of imperious self-determination was to commit suicide. The Lord saved David from that fate. David's brokenness was the prelude to a deeper oneness with his Lord. The same Lord wants nothing less for you and me.

Brokenness seems like a cruel word. We use it to describe someone who is deeply dejected by life's tragedies. Or it is used to describe the domesticating of a young colt. But neither type of brokenness is devoid of positive benefit. I do not know of any Christians who have grown in freedom without passing through a time of realizing the futility of putting ultimate trust in their own strength, people's reliability, or dependence on circumstances. Eventually the chains to those false gods must be broken.

Today's Thought: "When I vacillated about my decision to serve the Lord my God, it was I who willed and I who willed not, and nobody else. I was fighting against myself. . . . All You asked was that I cease to will what I willed and begin to want what You willed" —Augustine.

You have a mighty arm; strong is Your hand (Psalm 89:13).

The Master's Touch

During a difficult time in his life, Arthur John Gossip, a great Scots preacher a century ago, expressed a concern we all have at times: "I cannot keep the thought of Christ in my mind. I rise and say my prayers, and pass on, as I must, into the press and throng of daily duty, and waken up at night to find that for the whole day, I have lived without Christ."

Has this ever happened to you? We appreciate Gossip's honesty expressed at a time when he needed and subsequently received a fresh touch from the Master's hand. Perhaps that's your need at this moment. The hand of the Lord is synonymous with His power, presence, guidance, and healing.

Gossip discovered that it was he, not the Master, who was resisting moment-by-moment communion. "He haunts me," Gossip wrote, "keeps following me about. And when I peevishly push past Him, and twitch my shoulder from underneath His hand, and bury myself again in this or that, He waits; He, the Lord, stands waiting patiently, until there comes a lull in my busyness, and, with that, He breaks in on me again with renewed offers of divine kindness."

The touch of the Master's hand! He will be there with us all through the day—be sure of that. When we feel that the Lord is distant, it is because we have closed Him out, not that He has left us. Willfulness, busyness, unconfessed sin, resistance—these are usually the cause. Start the day by asking the Lord to give you a fresh touch of His love and expect Him—count on Him—all through the day.

Today's Thought: In all the uncertainties of life, I can be certain of one thing: the Master will never forget me.

He will baptize you with the Holy Spirit and with fire (Luke 3:16).

On-Fire Christians

In one of the most challenging of His hard sayings, Jesus said, "I came to send fire on the earth, and how I wish it were already kindled! But I have a baptism to be baptized with, and how distressed I am till it is accomplished!" (Luke 12:49,50). This hard saying presses us to enter Jesus' inner thoughts about His ultimate mission.

Some think Jesus was speaking about the fire of judgment. While He did talk about the fires of hell, here He speaks about sending fire *on the earth*. We grasp what He meant when we recall John the Baptist's prophecy that the Messiah would baptize "with fire." After His suffering on the cross and the victory of the resurrection, Christ returned to live in the disciples. He set the disciples on fire with love, power, and a passion to serve.

Christ Himself living in us is the fire we are promised today. When He takes up residence in us, we are set on fire. He is our intellectual fire as He thinks His thoughts through us; He is our emotional fire as He loves through us; He is our volitional fire as He gives us courage to do what servanthood demands.

Would you describe yourself as an "on-fire" Christian? If you don't feel the fire within, what has extinguished it? What happened to the inner glow of joy, excitement, enthusiasm? The desire to be a fire-filled person is to live fully and completely for Christ. This desire prompts us to pray for the baptism of new fire every day. All we do is provide the kindling of our dry hearts longing to be aflame again.

Today's Thought: Lord, our own resources often are burned out. Set us aflame with the fire of Your Spirit, and make us radiant with Your love today. Amen.

October 19 Luke 24:13-32

Did not our heart burn within us . . . ? (Luke 24:32).

Fuel for the Flame of God

Amy Carmichael's poem "Make Me Thy Fuel" is a daring daily prayer for our life of sharing. When we truly believe that the joy of life is sharing, this prayer of commitment is the charter for our caring.

From prayer that asks that I may be
Sheltered from winds that beat on Thee,
From fearing when I should aspire,
From faltering when I should climb higher,
From silken self, O Captain, free
Thy soldier who would follow Thee.
From subtle love of softening things,
From easy choices, weakenings,
Not thus are spirits fortified,
Not this way went the Crucified,
From all that dims Thy Calvary,
O Lamb of God, deliver me.
Give me the love that leads the way,
The faith that nothing can dismay,
The hope no disappointments tire,
The passion that will burn like fire,
Let me not sink to be a clod:
Make me Thy fuel, Flame of God.

Another favorite poem, whose author is unknown to me, expresses a fervent plea for forgiveness of the cowardice and fears that diminish the fire of love within us. The last line reads, "Fire of love, burn in us, burn evermore till we burn out for Thee." However, with Christ aflame in us, we will not burn out.

Today's Thought: I want to suggest a different line to close the poem mentioned above: "Fire of love, burn in us, burn evermore now and for eternity."

I have this against you, that you have left your first love (Revelation 2:4).

Time to Fall in Love Again

Remember the joy you felt when you first knew Christ loved you and you loved Christ with all your heart? Recapture in your mind the excitement of that time when you gave Him your life and committed yourself to be His disciple. You were captivated and motivated by a liberating love.

Christianity is a love relationship—for the individual and for the church. Our love relationship with Him begins when we are gripped by His grace, power, and joy. We are like a person who has fallen in love. All of our intellectual, emotional, and spiritual faculties are focused on our unreserved desire to live for Him as an expression of our love.

But then this relationship becomes routine and can lose its fire. Prayer becomes less exciting, reading the Bible an obligation, and serving a chore. The love we felt is pushed aside by obligations. Expectation of blessings is supplanted by blandness.

This is what happened to the church at Ephesus. The first of seven letters of Revelation is addressed to this crucial problem. The Lord who holds the church in the center of His love, first gives Christians commendation for their faithfulness and efforts to keep the faith. He affirms their works, labor, and patience. And yet, something was missing. They had lost the zest of their first love. They lacked the vibrancy, vitality, warmth, and enthusiasm of their beginning relationship with Christ.

Can you say your experiences of Christ's love and your love for Him is stronger today than it was when you became a Christian? Or has your relationship with Him become increasingly routine and dutifully dull? The danger is that we can become so preoccupied with a busy life working for the Lord that our personal relationship with Him becomes perfunctory rather than primary. It's time to fall in love again!

Today's Thought: Gracious Lord, today we want to receive and express more of Your love than ever before. Amen.

October 21 Proverbs 16:6-9

A man's heart plans his way, but the Lord directs his steps (Proverbs 16:9).

"Let Me Fill It In"

Dr. James Dobson in his helpful book *God's Will* tells a penetrating story of the Rev. Everett Howard, a veteran missionary to the Cape Verde Islands for 26 years. His call to the mission field has implications for all of us.

After finishing college and dental school, Howard was still uncertain about God's will for his life. One night he went into the sanctuary of the church where his father was serving as pastor. He knelt down at the altar and took a piece of paper on which he wrote all the things he was ready to do for God. He signed his name at the bottom and waited for some sign of God's affirmation and presence, but nothing happened. He took his paper again, thinking he might have left something out—still no response from the Lord. He waited and waited. Then it happened. He felt the Lord speaking within him. The Lord told him to tear up the sheet.

"You're going about it all wrong," He said gently. "Son, I want you to take a blank piece of paper, sign it on the bottom, and let Me fill it in."

Howard responded, and God guided a spectacular missionary career from that day forward.

God is not as interested in our commitment to what we decide to do for Him as He is in what we will allow Him to do through us. Our task is not to list our accomplishments or our plans for service, but to give Him a blank sheet and let Him fill it in.

Today's Thought: God will reveal His will if we offer a signed blank page on which He can write the agenda.

Stand fast therefore in the liberty by which Christ has made us free, and do not be entangled again with a yoke of bondage (Galatians 5:1).

A Gaol or a Goal

Two little letters: an "a" and an "o." It makes all the difference which comes first when preceded by a "g" and followed by an "l." Put the "a" before the "o" and you have a prison—a gaol. But when you reverse the letters, you have a purpose instead of a prison—a goal.

The Liberator releases us from the gaol of sins which have already been forgiven, even though we often try to repay these debts that are paid in full.

Recently, I had a disagreement with a department store computer. I tried to pay a bill I thought I still owed. Finally, the account manager wrote me a letter stating, "Sir, you are trying to pay a bill that has already been paid."

I thought about how often I try to atone for my own failures. Christ has paid the full debt on Calvary. It's foolish and self-defeating to try to pay a bill that has been erased.

Still, the memory of past failures makes life a gaol. Charles Wesley affirmed what Christ can do about this: "He breaks the power of *canceled* sin, He sets the prisoner free; His blood can make the foulest clean, His blood avails for me."

It is for a life of freedom that Christ has set us free. Nothing hinders this goal more than the gaols of the past. "One thing I do," said Paul, "forgetting those things which are behind and reaching forward to those things which are ahead, I press toward the goal for the prize of the upward call of God in Christ Jesus" (Philippians 3:13,14).

The prison door is open. Why not leave the gaol and get on with the goal of loving, glorifying, enjoying, serving, and obeying the Lord?

Today's Thought: Lord, forgive me for clutching my past failures. I commit myself to leave my self-incriminating gaol and dedicate myself to Your goal for my life. Amen.

October 23 — Luke 15:11-24

I will arise and go to my father, and will say to him, "Father, I have sinned against heaven and before you (Luke 15:18).

Come Home

Ian Maclaren was distinguished for his great Scottish stories. He told a delightful tale of Lackland Campbell and his daughter Dora.

Dora left home and fell into the wrong kind of relationships. She began to misuse the gifts of life. Soon she did not respond to her father's letters because of guilt and shame.

Maggie, Dora's aunt, wrote her a letter that finally melted her heart. "Dora, your Daddy is grievin' ye. Come home for your own sake. Come home for your dear Daddy's sake. But, Dora, come home most of all for the dear Lord's sake!"

Christ gives us the same invitation every day. Come home! He is grieved when we wander from Him. We need to come home to receive forgiveness, acceptance, grace. Often we wake up to a new day with a feeling of estrangement between us and God our Father. The mistakes and failures of the past days may have contributed to a sense of unworthiness. We live in a sort of quasi-exile we impose on ourselves.

The parable of the prodigal son moves us deeply. We identify with the anguish of the son's separation from his father. Our sins my not be as blatant, but the anxiety of estrangement is no less painful. Then the parable stirs our desire to come home to our Father God. He's not only waiting for us, but He comes running to meet us. Don't miss this vivid picture of God that Jesus paints for us. All we have to do is admit that we don't want to stay in the far country, that we long to come home to God and that we need to have things right between Him and us again.

Today's Thought: "Softly and tenderly Jesus is calling. Calling for you and for me. Come home . . . come home . . . come home" (taken from the hymn "Softly and Tenderly").

And he said to him, "Son, you are always with me, and all that I have is yours" (Luke 15:31).

A Far Country in the Heart

We can live in a far country without ever leaving home. The younger son left home to go to a far country; the elder brother stayed home with a far country in his heart. He really was as estranged from his father as his brother was.

According to the Deuteronomic law, when an inheritance was divided, the firstborn was given a double measure (Deuteronomy 21:17). This means the elder brother was given two-thirds of the father's inheritance. All the land, stock, and other assets were his to use as a gift from his father. And yet, he was enraged when a welcome-home party was given for his prodigal brother. In a sense, he had his party when the greater portion of the inheritance was given to him. How quickly he forgot his father's generosity, and how little did he share his father's love for his brother who had been lost!

The parable of the elder brother is a look in the mirror for many of us. We see our own pride, judgmentalism, and self-righteousness. Our far country is thinking that we have earned God's acceptance with our impeccable characters and good behavior. Our false sense of superiority makes us very intolerant of the failures of others.

Think of what might have happened if the prodigal had met his older brother before he reached home! He might never have made it to the father's embrace of love and acceptance. This makes us wonder about our attitudes toward people who have failed. Do we stiff-arm them with indignation or take them by the hand and lead them home to the Father?

Today's Thought: "A darkened heart is a far country, for it is not by our feet but by our affections that we leave Thee or return to Thee" —Augustine.

October 25 1 John 3:1-3

See how very much our heavenly Father loves us, for He allows us to be called His children—think of it—and we really are (1 John 3:1 TLB).

A Special Friend

A friend is someone who makes us feel special. We all need the self-esteem that comes when a person helps us to know that we are unique, never-to-be-repeated miracles of God.

What can we do and say to our friends that communicates this dynamic inner assurance? The key is in the word "affirmation." Most of us know all about our inadequacies and failures. What we need are friends who believe in us and help us imagine and realize our full potential. It is easy to get down on ourselves and devaluate the special person we were created to be. A friend is a lift, not a load; a boost, not a burden.

The liberating power of affirmation flows from a person who feels of value himself. When we experience the Lord's delight in us and the lengths He was willing to go to show us how special we are, we become people with whom others feel the excitement of their specialness. People who have the gift of self-esteem are able to make their friends feel good about themselves.

If we're not excited about being ourselves, we can be sure no one around us will be excited about himself. The scales of our lives are heavily weighted with the self-negation of years of conditioning. We are to be friends who tip the scales with the precious gift of affirmation.

Today's Thought: "The deepest principle in human nature is the craving to be appreciated" —William James.

The grace of God which was given to me for you (Ephesians 3:2).

Given to Me for You

The secret of life is that all we have and are is a gift of grace to be shared. Everything that happens to us prepares us to develop deep, sharing relationships. We have been called, chosen, and elected to receive grace—unmerited favor. Christ has loved us to the uttermost. In our experience, His forgiving love is sheer grace. We have not earned it, nor have we deserved it. Life in fellowship with Him has given us wisdom and insight. The challenge to love Him with our minds has provided us with knowledge. Daily we discover new truth about who He is and what life was meant to be.

But grace is kept only if it is given away. Everything grace has given us is for others. What a lovely way to live! When we go through the valleys of trials or stand on the mountaintops of victory, we are being prepared to enter into the difficulties and victories of others. We go through all of this so that we will be able to say those empowering words of empathy, "I know what you are going through—I've been there!"

Life is the school of grace equipping us for a ministry of sharing, developing confidence so we can say, "Thank You, Lord, for what has happened. I can't wait to see how You are going to use what You have taught me in sharing with someone who will need just what I've discovered!"

The apostle Paul teaches us how to live that prayer. In today's Scripture, he tells us his purpose and passion in living. Paul thought of himself as a steward of grace. The grace he received from Christ was for the purpose of communicating grace to others.

Today's Thought: "A state of mind that sees God in everything is evidence of growth in grace and a thankful heart" —Charles Q. Finney.

October 27 2 Corinthians 5:16,17

So stop evaluating Christians by what the world thinks about them or by what they seem to be like on the outside (2 Corinthians 5:16, TLB).

See Through Me

A friend of mine has a new working postulate—a scientific assumption—which developed as a result of this idea of prayer: "Act as if Jesus Christ were present in other personalities for His redemptive purpose, not on the basis of my own very human precepts and predictions of where their weakness will take them."

This man's long dealings with people in his ministry as a trial lawyer has sharpened his human skill at diagnosing people. He often sees them at their worst. In the past he had formed judgments, and people reacted within the confines of those judgments. He allowed negative reactions to block the divine inflow. Then he began reading the Gospel of Mark to study how Jesus dealt with people. He tried to see what Jesus might have seen in the harlots, the lepers, the publicans, and the blind before these people were healed. My friend realized that he himself would have seen so many horrible, negative facts and prognoses that healing would have been impossible through him. The fact that Jesus got rid of the negative thinkers around Jairus' daughter before he could heal her impressed him. He realized the power of his negative pictures of people that frustrated them in becoming what God desired.

Then, in a dream, this man had a conversation with Christ. He awakened and, as the conversation continued, Christ seemed to be saying, "See through Me, through My mind filter."

In that time of deep prayer, this man learned that ministering to people meant trying to see things through Christ's eyes. He was refocused in a positive image. People who came to him for help were seen in the light of Jesus' potential in them, not as categories of weakness.

Today's Thought: Today I will see people through the eyes of Christ.

Putting on the breastplate of faith and love, and as a helmet the hope of salvation (1 Thessalonians 5:8).

Hopeful Thinking

The helmet of salvation is a crucial part of the whole armor of God described by Paul in Ephesians 6. In 1 Thessalonians 5:8, the apostle calls the helmet the *hope* of salvation.

The purpose of the helmet was to protect the soldier's head. Paul draws our attention to the need for protection of the brain in the spiritual battle with evil. It's in our thinking that we become tempted to discouragement and disappointment. Satan seeks to pollute our thinking with negative thoughts about ourselves, others, and the world. We tend to get weary in the battle against the negative thinking around us. This is why we need our minds to be protected by hope in the cynicism of our time.

We often hear the expression, "That's only wishful thinking." It is used to describe unrealistic thoughts about life or the future. A hope-filled, hope-dominated mind looks at the future with complete assurance that the Lord who saved us once and for all on Calvary will defend our minds against discouragement all through our lives.

The world urgently needs Christians with hopeful thinking. We are meant to be among them. This requires the consistent renewing of our minds (Romans 12:1,2) with hope.

The American Express Company cautions us never to leave home without our card. I say: Don't get out of bed without your helmet of hope firmly in place. Christ is our hope. Invite Him to take charge of your thinking the moment you wake up. This is a sure way not to be grouchy at breakfast and discouraged all through the day.

Today's Thought: Life is a battle against Satan's discouragement and people's negative attitudes. Get fitted up for the battle with hope!

October 29 — Proverbs 12:25

A good word makes it [the heart of man] glad (Proverbs 12:25).

Don't Expect the Worst—Expect God

Carlyle built a soundproof chamber in his house in Chelsea. All sound was excluded so he could have silence to write—except the crow of a cock owned by a neighbor, once at night and once in the morning. The author complained, but the neighbor said the cock crowed so seldom. "But," Carlyle said to him, "if you only knew what I suffer waiting for that cock to crow!"

There are lots of people who would say the same thing about trouble. They spend a great deal of time waiting for something that might go wrong. Life becomes a tedious anticipation of the worst happening. We all know what this is like. And yet, we also know that many of the things we worried about never happened.

Today's verse should be memorized. It's one of those one-line zingers from Proverbs. What is the good word to make us glad today? I can think of several, and they are all names for God used in the Old Testament. Think of them while you are waiting for the cock to crow or the other shoe to drop.

Our God is *Jehovah-jireh*, "The Lord-Will-Provide" (Genesis 22:13,14); *Jehovah-rapha*, "I am the Lord who heals you" (Exodus 15:26); *Jehovah-shalom*, "The Lord our peace" (Judges 6:24); *Jehovah-tsidkeno*, "The Lord our Righteousness" (Jeremiah 23:6); *Jehovah-shammah*, "The Lord is there" (Ezekiel 48:35); and *Jehovah-ra-ah*, "The Lord is my shepherd" (Psalm 23:1).

These names of God incorporate His promises of the quality of care He will give us today. They change our expectation from the worst that might happen to expectancy for the interventions of God to bring good out of whatever happens.

Today's Thought: I am determined to spend more time waiting for God than waiting for trouble.

Will a man rob God? Yet you have robbed Me! (Malachi 3:8).

Embezzling God

Those who live in the flow of God's silent strength do things His way and He blesses them. He is the Lord of all life. All that we have and are belong to Him. From Abraham on, the people of God tabulated their stewardship of all life by tithing. The first tenth of the proceeds of the harvest or their earnings was not theirs to use for themselves. To keep back the tithe was to embezzle God.

This is what the people were doing around 432 BC. God called Malachi to declare His incisive word: The people were robbing Him! Just as His nature does not change, so too His demands of righteousness are unchanging. The passage we read today from Malachi is one of the most forceful statements in the Bible about the requirement and the rewards of tithing. It's still in force today. Jesus assumed the tithe. Through His death and resurrection and our new life in Him, we have the liberating motivation to fulfill the irrevocable requirements of God, including the tithe.

We often hear the demand, but too seldom the delights, of tithing. Those who tithe with an attitude of gratitude find that God meets their needs and gives them more to give. Note the emphasis on tithes *and* offerings in today's passage. After the tithes were paid, the offering of special gifts was to be given. God has chosen us to be channels of His blessing in the world. The first step in solving our money problems is to tithe. Then watch how God will bless. The windows of heaven are open—now open yours!

Today's Thought: We can't outgive God. Nor can we rob Him and get away with it. Stewardship begins with the tithe, and the blessings never end!

October 31 2 Corinthians 9:1-15

And God is able to make all grace abound toward you, that you, always having all sufficiency in all things, have an abundance for every good work (2 Corinthians 9:8).

Don't Miss the Blessing!

Money talks! We often hear that when a person of means tries to use financial manipulation to get his or her way. But everyone's money talks. It tells the world what we believe. How we give communicates the extent of our gratitude for Christ, our redemption, and His indwelling strength.

Money is concealed personality—an extension of what we are. Today we underline the fact that money is concealed power. It can be used to glorify Christ or it can stunt our growth in Him. Eventually every Christian must face the danger of money mania. It keeps many from the silent strength the Lord wants to give us.

Gratitude is the stethoscope that monitors the strength of our spiritual heart. We are not to give as a grudging obligation but as a joyous cooperation with the Lord. He delights in cheerful givers. They emulate His own heart. To enable our giving, He has all the power to provide abounding blessings so we will have an abundance for good works. These good works include introducing people to Christ, feeding the hungry, caring for the poor, and participating in projects to expand the kingdom in the world. We give our tithes to churches and ministries involved in these good works. And the exciting thing is that the Lord provides beyond this for giving to special challenges to meet the needs of people.

Indeed, money talks. Sometimes its message is about the false security we've placed in it. But it can also say that we've decided not to miss the blessing of blessing others.

Today's Thought: Money talks, but what does yours say about you and your faith?

Thus also faith by itself, if it does not have works, is dead (James 2:17).

Faith and Works

More than 100 years ago, one of the greatest philanthropists of history was George Moore. He was transformed from a traditional religious man into a dynamic Christian when he heard and claimed Christ's promise, "Most assuredly, I say to you, he who hears My word and believes in Him who sent Me has everlasting life, and shall not come into judgement, but has passed from death into life" (John 5:24).

From that point on he delighted in giving away his money. Every New Year's Day as he started a new calendar, he inscribed on the flyleaf these lines:

What I spent, I had;
What I saved, I lost;
What I gave, I have.

Moore would begin the year by sending gifts to support Christ's work around the world. Many of the missions he had started himself. "If the world only knew half the happiness that a man has in doing good" he said, "it would do a great deal more." That conviction led the philanthropist into the slums of London to give personal caring as well as money.

On the wall of Moore's study was an illuminated plaque with the words of 1 Corinthians 13. In very large type at the top were the words *Love Never Fails* and at the bottom, *Now Abides Faith.* The wedding of love and faith was the secret of Moore's life.

We may not have George Moore's resources, but we can live that wonderful inscription he put on his calendar. It's a good motto for the giving of our time, energy, and ourselves *as* we put our faith to work.

Today's Thought: "I believe the gospel. I love the Lord Jesus. I want to give all that I have and am to help the suffering" —George Moore.

November 2 **Matthew 6:19-24**

Do not lay up for yourselves treasures on earth, where moth and rust destroy and where thieves break in and steal; but lay up for yourselves treasures in heaven, where neither moth nor rust destroys and where thieves do not break in and steal. For where your treasure is, there your heart will be also (Matthew 6:19-21).

Getting Treasures into Heaven

How do you get a treasure into heaven? The answer is found in response to another question: Who is going to heaven? We are. In Greek, the word "treasure" is used not for the valued object but for the container. When Jesus challenges us to lay up treasures in heaven, He's really telling us to use money and the things we possess with it in a way that makes us, His treasure, ready for heaven. It's as if He said, "Your heart is the treasure. You are destined to live forever. Now prepare your treasure in a way that's fit for heaven." How we use money often determines who is lord on the throne of our hearts. Some of us will be very uncomfortable in heaven if our passion in this life has been money.

But let's press the point further. Who else goes to heaven? Other people. Therefore, the only other way to lay up treasure in heaven is to help others get there. This provides an excellent basis for determining the causes to which we should pay our tithes and give our gifts. People should be the focus.

Will the funds we give be used to introduce people to the Savior, help them to grow in Him, care for their physical needs, and heal aching sores in society? Often caring for people's temporal needs gives us an opportunity to meet their spiritual needs.

Imagine the joy of entering heaven and being greeted by the people who are there because you personally introduced them to Christ or were the Lord's channel of providing the resources for workers and programs which did. Your treasure will be those waiting for you.

Today's Thought: Imagine someone living forever because of you!

For the love of money is a root of all kinds of evil, for which some have strayed from the faith in their greediness, and pierced themselves through with many sorrows (1 Timothy 6:10).

Philarguria

Philarguria. Don't reach for your English dictionary for a definition. It isn't there. But if you check a biblical Greek dictionary, you'll find it's a compound word made up of two good Greek words. The combination of them, however, equals trouble. *Philia* means "love" and *arguria*, from *arguros*, means "silver," or "money."

There are some probing questions that will help us consider the extent our freedom in Christ may be jeopardized by *philarguria*.

- Do you ever worry over money—having enough and keeping what you have?
- Is bill-paying time a stressful time for you?
- What about income-tax time? Ever disturbed by reading your autobiography in the cancelled checks of a year?
- Has money ever been a source of argument or misunderstanding between you and another person?
- Do you sometimes experience twinges of competition or even envy over what others earn, have inherited, or have been able to do because of money they have and you don't?
- Have you ever equated your value as a person with what you earn?
- Can you remember a time when you bought clothing or things to "solve" hurt feelings, setbacks, or disappointments?
- Do you ever get anxious about what inflation has done to depreciate your savings and preparation for retirement?
- Do you spend more time thinking about money in any one day than you do in prayer?

Today's Thought: If you said "yes" to several of these questions, you may be having an affair with money.

Render therefore to Caesar the things that are Caesar's, and to God the things that are God's (Luke 20:25).

Both Sides of the Coin

The chief priests and scribes tried to trap Jesus. After a fulsome compliment, they asked Him, "Is it lawful for us to pay taxes to Caesar or not?" They thought they had impaled Him on the sharp horns of a dilemma. If He spoke out against paying taxes to Rome, He would be in trouble with the Roman authorities. If He affirmed paying taxes, He would raise the indignation of the strong anti-Rome movement among the Jews.

At first glance, Jesus' answer seems like He sidestepped the issue. Not so when we understand the full impact of what He meant. There must have been a long pause between the first and last portions of His saying. We wonder what was the look on His face when He said firmly, "And to God the things that are God's."

The implication is that Caesar and his realm belonged to God as much as any religious possession or responsibility. Actually, Jesus' answer exposes the false division between the sacred and the secular. He claimed all of life as sacred. Everything we have and are belongs to God. He cannot be excluded from any realm of life. We are responsible for everything we say, do, spend, and save. The secret of dynamic discipleship is using all things, all of life, as a sacred trust from the Lord.

This passage is an excellent basis for a fresh approach to claiming the Lord's ownership of all life, our responsibility to use all things to His glory, and our accountability in our tithing and giving. It changes everything when we render to God what is God's—and that includes everything! Then stewardship is a privilege.

Today's Thought: Once our true calling as stewards of God's grace is understood, then tithing and support of the mission of the church and other causes follows naturally and creatively.

Let everyone give as his heart tells him, neither grudgingly nor under compulsion, for God loves the man who gives cheerfully. God can give you more than you can ever need, so that you may always have sufficient for yourselves and enough left over to give to every good cause (2 Corinthians 9:7,8 PHILLIPS).

Hilarious Sharing

The Greek word for "cheerful" is *hilaros*, from which our word "hilarious" comes. Paul calls us to be hilariously free in giving what we have been given. That level of freedom comes about when we know that we have tapped into unlimited resources. God supplies all our needs so that we can become involved in sharing joyously.

There is a giving barrier which must be broken through, just as an aircraft breaks the sound barrier and then is free to soar. That barrier of "What's mine is mine" is broken only when we are overcome by God's love, His willingness to give us more than we need, and the fact that He has a strategy to meet people's needs through us. A truly joyous person has discovered that life and its resources are lent to be spent. To share the heart of God, we must join Him in what He's been doing since creation—sharing!

Love is the liberating motivation of giving. Paul concludes his message on giving with this motivation: "Thanks be to God for His indescribable gift." Jesus Christ is that amazing gift.

Robert Rodenmayer said, "There are three kinds of giving: grudge giving, duty giving and thanksgiving. When Christ is the motive of our giving it is thanksgiving. Our giving for the physical and spiritual needs of people is a telling measurement of what Christ means to us. We are writing our autobiographies every day—in our checkbooks!

Today's Thought: "God has given us two hands—one for receiving and the other for giving" —Billy Graham.

November 6 1 Corinthians 4:6-8

What do you have that you did not receive? (1 Corinthians 4:7).

Rebuilding Your Life

In Edwin Markham's *Parable of the Builders* there was a very rich man who owned great expanses of land. One day he walked over the hillsides and surveyed all that he owned. He saw a lovely sun-drenched hilltop beyond the hovel cottage of his carpenter. He went to the carpenter and said, "I have plans for a lovely home on the sunny hill. I want you to build a house there. I want you to build it good and strong. Employ the best workmen, use the best materials, for I want it to be a good house."

Then the rich man went away. The carpenter began to build the house. But as he proceeded, he decided to cut costs and pocket the difference. He built the house of inferior materials and poor workmanship. He thought he had outsmarted the owner.

When the rich man returned, the carpenter told him that he had finished the house with the best he could find and do.

"Good," said the owner. "I am glad that it is a good house. I have intended all along to give it to you. The house is yours!"

The carpenter was shocked: "Oh, if I had only known that I was building the house for myself."

The attitude of the builder is not unlike our own when we put less than our best into our relationship with our Lord. But He has not left us to build the house of our life without His help. If we invest time in prayer, He guides our thinking and reshapes our attitudes. Daily Bible study shows us His blueprints and specifications.

Today's Thought: The Lord wants to surprise the world with what He can do with a life totally surrendered to Him. And He's building a life in which He can live with us.

Blessed is the man (Psalm 1:1).

The Cancer of Cynicism

The Hebrew word for "blessed" means more than "happy" or "joyous." A deeper penetration into the root meaning of *'ashrê* reveals that it comes from a verb meaning "to go forth, to advance," or even "to lead the way." A blessed person presses on to clearly defined goals with his eyes on the Lord. Psalm 1 tells us what the blessed person does *not* do and what the Lord does do for him.

The blessed person does not take the three steps that result in cynicism. Cynicism begins when we take our eyes off the Lord and the goal of running with Him. It begins when we slow up and walk in the counsel of the ungodly, *rāsha'*. These are people who live life on the horizontal level with a white-knuckled grip on life. Taking the advice of these negative people is disastrous. We get infected by their "If we can't do it, it can't be done" limited view of what is possible.

The next step to cynicism is to stand in the path of sinners. The Hebrew word *ḥaṭṭā'*—translated "sinners"—denotes those who are living by the wrong values and goals. Standing with them is to move away from God. The ungodly live without dependence on God; the sinner excludes Him entirely. Standing among them is dangerous because we are tempted to think trusting the Lord doesn't really work.

The final step is to sit down among the scornful. The Hebrew word is *lētsîm*, "scoffers," those who mock God. They ridicule what they call the simplistic idea that God knows, cares, and can help us. When we sit among the scornful, it isn't long before a permanent place is reserved for us. Skepticism becomes a way of life. Pessimism soon follows.

We become like the people with whom we associate and whose thinking influences our attitudes. Don't slow down to walk, stand, and eventually sit among the cynics.

Today's Thought: I will keep my eyes on God and intentionally avoid the infection of cynicism and the influence of the skeptic.

He shall be like a tree planted by the rivers of water (Psalm 1:3).

Overcoming Cynicism

Cynicism is catching. It's difficult to live around cynical people without having their skeptical thinking invade our outlook. Psalm 1 goes on to tell us how to live in a cynical world without becoming cynical. Verses 2 and 3 give us the antidote to cynicism.

The first step out of cynicism is to submit to God's authority. To delight in the law is to do things God's way. For the psalmist, the law meant the Ten Commandments and all the promises of God encompassed in the Pentateuch—the first five books of the Bible. For the Christian, the implication is to follow the whole Bible. A cynic is a spoiled child who resists authority. Because he can't get things his way, he has a jaundiced look at life. It is not that he has tried God's way and found it lacking; he never tried God's way.

The second step away from cynicism is to meditate day and night. This means to pray without ceasing. People will disappoint us and situations will frustrate us if we don't seek God's wisdom and patience. Cynicism is life without trusting in God's management of things. The alternative is to ask for His will for what we are to do and say.

The third step out of cynicism is to begin to draw on the presence of God. The blessed are "like a tree planted by the rivers of water" (verse 3). What is implied is that the tree of our life is transplanted from the desert and rooted by the river. The simile is of a palm tree beside a river with its roots running into the river. It draws from an unlimited supply. It becomes stable, strong, and stands with strength. The river is symbolic of the Spirit of God. A constant supply of the Spirit gives us a positive view of what can happen and the power to attempt it.

Today's Thought: The only way to overcome cynicism is to replace it with God's authority, guidance, and strength.

But [the ungodly] are like the chaff which the wind drives away (Psalm 1:4).

Sour Perfectionism

The word "cynicism" comes from a Greek philosophical school in the fourth and fifth centuries BC called the Cynics. The philosophers held that virtue, rather than intellectual or sensual pleasure, was the goal of life. Eventually this perfectionism went sour. The Cynics became judgmental of others who did not live up to their standards. The real problem was that they were no better than the people they criticized. They got down on life, people, and any divine power to make things right according to their specifications.

The same self-righteousness was the proclivity of many of the Jews. They took pride in their traditions and religion. Legalism resulted. Superiority and aggrandizement led to cynicism. Their self-generated righteousness also turned sour when they set themselves up as critics of everyone else.

The blessed person knows he cannot live without God's grace. With a fresh daily supply, he can seek forgiveness and forgive others. He can live in the incongruities of a messed-up world without despair because he knows that, in spite of human sin, God is in charge and is working out His purposes.

The problem with cynicism is that it sets us up to be our own gods. Soon we don't need or want the Lord God. The psalmist states the destiny of the cynic: He is like chaff that is driven away by the wind.

Break the addiction of cynicism by claiming the grace of God in Christ. You are a blessed person. The cynics around you need to see that hope in God really works in your life.

Today's Thought: Lord, give me a hopeful attitude based on Your grace. May that grace radiate from me with contagious joy!

November 10 1 Corinthians 15:9-11

Not I, but the grace of God . . . (1 Corinthians 15:10).

That's Grace

I called to wish a good friend "Happy Birthday! Have a wonderful day—you deserve it!"

"I don't deserve it, but that's grace," my friend responded.

What a wonderful attitude! My friend is one of America's most able communicators of God's grace. He knows that the abundant life is more than we deserve. God's unmerited, unqualified love is not measured by whether or not we deserve it.

It's a great delight to get off the kick of trying to earn God's love. We can never do enough to qualify. If we could measure up by our own strength, the cross would not have been necessary. The wonder of it all is that God reconciled us to Himself when we least deserved it. When we accept His love, He keeps pouring out His blessings even when we fail. The assurance of this grace gives us the power to fail less and less.

Too often our days are lived in a graceless grimness. We withhold our approval and affirmation from others because of what they have said or done. Silence or cool aloofness expresses our displeasure. We give people what we think they deserve. We wake up feeling that we don't deserve to be loved by God. Our own way of dealing with others is projected onto God.

This bond is broken only when we are shocked back into reality by the question, "What if God gave me what I really deserve?" Instead, He offers us forgiveness and a fresh start—thousands of times.

Have a grace-filled day. You may not deserve it by your standards, but that's grace!

Today's Thought: Here's a new rendition of "Amazing Grace" to sing today: "Amazing grace how sweet the sound. I often get lost, but always am found."

Therefore, whatever you want men to do to you, you also do to them (Matthew 7:12).

The Everest of Ethics

"Here lie I, Martin Elginbrodde.
Hae mercy o' my soul, Lord God;
As I wad do, were I Lord God
An' Ye were Martin Elginbrodde."

This epitaph quoted by George MacDonald in the book *David Elginbrodde* humorously gets us to the heart of the motive of sharing. The truth, however, is that God is gracious to us far beyond our desserts. He loves us in spite of what we've done or been.

The question is, Can we do the same for others? Jesus' golden rule, often called "the Everest of ethics," is possible only through what God has done to and for us beyond what we have been able to do in return. We can do for others the things that we wish they would do for us only when we are motivated by His amazing grace.

The secret is that we are to do for others what God has done for us, not just what we would like them to do for us. The more we receive from our Lord, the more we will want to do for others. When we get in touch with our own needs, we become aware of the needs which lurk beneath the highly polished surfaces of others. Everyone has the same longing for love and understanding.

Today's Thought: We are friends of Christ by His choice. That should give our self-esteem a boost. But also, we are called to be to others the kind of friend He is to us. This must be by our choice.

November 12 Romans 12:14-21

Do not be overcome by evil, but overcome evil with good (Romans 12:21).

Manipulations with Fear

In our relationships, fear is a manipulative method of getting what we want. Threats of reprisal, the withholding of love, or coercing others with the possible withdrawal of acceptance are all methods of manipulation by fear. The difficulty is that these methods boomerang—they increase our own fears. And with the manipulation of fear, we perpetuate the epidemic of fear all around us. The "If you don't, I won't" of life coerces people to do right things for the wrong reasons. In the end, we are the ones who suffer. Our life becomes one of judgment and criticism. We become filled with fussy anxieties and sour bemoanings. Manipulation by fear can be so subtle that we don't realize we're doing it. The cry of "wolf" can be dripping with sweet-and-sour sauce, but it's still seasoned with fear.

There's a deeper problem. When we keep people agitated by fear of us, we distract them from dealing with either their authentic fear of God that can lead them to faith, or from their fearfulness which needs to be dealt with by the Lord. We get in the Lord's way. People respond to us rather than to Him.

The whole point is that, knowing what fearfulness has done to us, we do not want to pass on the virus that's already spreading with epidemic proportions in the world around us.

The alternative to manipulating with fear is to motivate with love. This means taking time with the people who concern us. It requires listening to them to discover what is causing their problems. Then with probing questions we can help these individuals discern what the Lord may be saying to them. Our task is not to tell them what to do but to help them discover what God wants them to do. Then when they launch out in obedience to Him and not in fear of us, we are to be cheerleaders.

Today's Thought: Today I will motivate others by pointing toward the silent strength of God's love.

Truly my soul silently waits for God (Psalm 62:1).

Keep the Communication Lines Open

We are told that the reason the *Titanic* hit an iceberg was because the ship's radios were completely jammed for hours with silly "ship to shore" conversations of the passengers with friends and families in Britain and America. Other ships in the area were not able to get through with a warning signal.

Sometimes the communication lines between us and the Lord can get so jammed by constant talk that we have no time to listen to Him. Our prayers can become one-way conversations.

I have a friend who calls me to share problems. He goes on endlessly explaining his needs. Just about the time I have a word of insight to share, he says, "Well, thanks for listening—bye!" and hangs up.

Often we say "Amen" and hang up on the Lord. After we have told the Lord about our problems, silence in His presence gives Him an opportunity to show us a chart to avoid the floating icebergs that could sink us. When the lines of communication are open, He will give us creative insight about how to solve our problems and guidance for how we can help the people who concern us.

The psalmist was determined to wait silently for God. He reminds himself that God is his *only* rock and salvation. He will wait silently for Him alone. Advice from people can be helpful, but constantly casting about for human direction can jam the communication lines with God. We can have so many opinions from people causing "static" in our minds that we can't hear God when He speaks to us.

Before you press on with the demands of today, take time to be quiet. Share with the Lord what's on your mind and heart. Then clear the communication lines by telling the Lord you want to know and do His will. Then listen!

Today's Thought: Daily silence in the Lord's presence provides silent strength.

November 14 **Psalm 63**

I meditate on You in the night watches (Psalm 63:6).

In the Night Watches

When we fall asleep before we have finished our prayers, sometimes we are awakened in the middle of the night with worries and unresolved problems. Often we toss and turn, going over the "what might have beens" and "if onlys" of relationships and situations that are troubling us.

David obviously had times like these. In his case, it was concern over his enemies that awakened him. He tells us his formula for dealing with sleepless nights. He intentionally drew his mind from his fears to the Lord. He meditated on the Lord and remembered His faithfulness in the past. David pictured the presence of the Lord as the shadow of a protective wing. Then, having reviewed the worries troubling him, he made a new commitment to follow the Lord and claimed the strength of His right hand, His power.

When a troubled mind and a restless heart wake us, often we are worried not only by the troubles we are facing but by concern over losing sleep. We are concerned we will not be rested the next day to face the battles ahead of us. Now our anxiety is multiplied.

When this happens, try David's strategy. Rather than fretting about being awake, spend a brief time facing the worries. Remember the times the Lord has helped you in the past and meditate on His glory and goodness. Ask Him for creative solutions and action steps to take the next day and make a commitment to do them. Claim the presence of the Lord right there with you. Hear His assurance that because He never sleeps He will be at work on people and situations while you go back to sleep.

Today's Thought: When worries awaken me, I will thank the Lord for time alone with Him, remember His grace, ask for guidance, and listen to Him as He gives me fresh insight and wisdom.

And cause His face to shine upon us (Psalm 67:1).

The Face of God

In the Scriptures "the face of God" means His presence. The Lord said to Moses, "My Presence will go with you, and I will give you rest" (Exodus 33:14). The Hebrew word for "presence" is really "face." We are told, "The Lord spoke to Moses face to face, as a man speaks to his friend" (Exodus 33:11). Moses didn't actually see God's face, for the Lord said, "You cannot see My face; for no man shall see Me, and live" (Exodus 33:20). What Moses did see was the glory of God's presence.

When Christ came, the face of God was revealed. "For it is the God who commanded light to shine out of darkness who has shone in our hearts to give the light of the knowledge of the glory of God in the face of Jesus Christ" (2 Corinthians 4:6). He is God's presence with you and me today. The simile of "face" is not just poetic. It implies the powerful expression of the Lord's presence. We can feel the impact of what is on His face as He goes with us through the day. The Lord's face has compassion and forgiveness when we fail, bracing assurance when we're fearful, confident affirmation when we're under pressure, a look of caution when we are tempted to make the wrong move, and an uplifting expression of hope when we stumble and fall. Our Lord's face is clouded with judgment only when we habitually refuse His love and guidance. And when we repent, His face shines again with delight.

This background on "the face of the Lord" helps us join with the psalmist in his prayer that "God be merciful to us and bless us and cause His face to shine upon us." He has and He will—today.

Today's Thought: I will live today in the presence of the Lord and will be inspired and instructed by what I sense is on His face.

Then I understood their end (Psalm 73:17).

The Failure of Success Without God

Psalm 73 sets us free of comparisons, fills us with compassion, and gives us a commission.

The psalmist had almost lost the footing of his faith. He looked around and saw the prosperity of those who did not believe in God. His question wasn't "Why do bad things happen to good people?" but "How can God allow good things to happen to bad people?"

We've all shared this question. We observe people who make no pretense of trusting in God. Some of them get ahead, live successful lives, and acquire an abundance of things. On the other hand, we see that some who trust in God face struggles and difficulties. We are forced to question our assumption that faith in God is a ticket to an easy ride through life. Believing in God is not an assurance of material prosperity. Nor should we think that temporal success is a sign that we are a "darling of the Lord."

When the psalmist began to see things in the perspective of eternity, he moved from comparisons to compassion. It was in the sanctuary, in God's presence, that he realized the real issue. He understood the end of those who do not know God. For them, death will be an irrevocable separation from God for eternity.

This startling realization brings the psalmist to put new trust in the Lord and to accept the commission to declare the good works of the Lord. This psalm helps us to take no one for granted. People who have everything except God have nothing when the end comes. Instead of envying them, our calling is to pray for opportunities to share true success: to know Christ and live with the assurance of eternal life.

Today's Thought: Three resolves: no more comparisons with unbelievers who have material abundance, greater compassion for the plight of their eternal lives, and unqualified love and prayer for a chance to share the true abundant life in Christ.

Mercy and truth have met together; righteousness and peace have kissed each other (Psalm 85:10).

A Needed Embrace and Kiss

Everyone wants it, so few have it, and only Christ can provide it: peace... the lasting peace of righteousness... the profound peace of forgiveness, reconciliation, and obedience... deep inner peace because we have decided to do things the Lord's way.

Psalm 85 was written after the exile. The people have returned from captivity. Prior to the demise of the nations of Israel and Judah, the people had separated what God had put together. They took their status as God's people for granted and fell into apostasy. Lack of social righteousness eventually brought God's judgment, and they lost the precious gift of His *shalom*, His peace.

Now that the exile was past, the psalmist calls for a needed embrace of mercy and truth, and a kiss of righteousness and peace. The lovely image is of the coming together of what the people had wrought asunder.

So many Christians do not have an abiding peace. Some want the assurance of salvation without obedience to righteousness. We think that faith in Christ has made us right with God and now we can get on with our own priorities. There will be no lasting peace until we submit to Christ's daily guidance and follow through on what He commands.

A friend of mine hung a sign in the window of a store he had run for years: "Under New Management." His renewed commitment to Christ had motivated a desire to glorify Him in all his business dealings. I'm not suggesting you have a sign like that to hang around your neck. When righteousness and peace have kissed in your heart, it will show.

Today's Thought: As a person made righteous through faith in Christ, I will live under His management in my relationships and responsibilities.

November 18 Psalm 86

Oh, turn to me, and have mercy on me! Give Your strength to Your servant (Psalm 86:16).

Here for the Helpless

Throughout this year we have been searching the Scriptures for the secrets of silent strength. The psalm we read today has a gem for us in verse 16. Renewed inner strength is the result of fresh experiences of God's mercy.

There are times when we don't feel worthy of God's mercy. "How can the Lord continue to be merciful when I constantly fail Him?" we ask. It's in those times that we need to remember that the Hebrew word for "mercy" is rooted in the image of compassionate love for a helpless unborn child. The Lord is merciful like that to us when we need a new lease on life.

A feeling of helplessness comes over us when life's burdens become too great or when we become discouraged with our performance. There is nothing we can do to make things right in our own strength. All we can say is, "Lord, I'm helpless! Have mercy!"

This is one prayer the Lord always honors. Christ is merciful with us. He has the power to forgive us and infuse the strength of His Spirit into our depleted hearts. When life "de-powers" us, He empowers us.

It's amazing how each new experience of mercy produces reinvigorated strength. The assurance that He has lifted the burden liberates us from the anguish of worry. The sheer wonder of the Lord's grace changes our attitude and releases energy in our bodies. We are ready to make a fresh start. Now our challenge is not to forget what the Lord has done for us. In fact, every day has its moments when we need to claim with the psalmist, "You, O Lord, are a God full of compassion, and gracious, longsuffering and abundant in mercy and truth."

Today's Thought: The merciful Lord is still the same to all who will call on His powerful name. He brings help to the helpless.

Lord, You have been our dwelling place in all generations (Psalm 90:1).

Where Do You Live?

The other evening, I went to a party at which most of the people did not know each other. As we got acquainted, a frequent question was "Where do you live?" People's answers identified where their houses were, and this launched conversations about how long they had lived there, mutual friends who were neighbors, and shared concerns about property values. I was struck by how important our houses become to us.

If Moses had been at that party, his response to the question of where he lived would have been, "The Lord is my dwelling place." Psalm 90 is attributed to Moses. It expressed the hoped-for permanence of God's place for Israel in the promised land. The word "place" in Hebrew is *mā'ôn*, meaning "the abode of refuge, protection, and sustenance."

In the instability and brevity of life, God alone is our security and protection. Moses' conviction that "the eternal God is your refuge" (Deuteronomy 33:27) is sounded throughout this psalm in which God's eternity is compared to life's brevity.

Psalm 90 often is read at funerals. We are reminded of the length of eternity and the shortness of our time on earth. A corollary reading is Paul's words, "For we know that if our earthly house, this tent, is destroyed, we have a building from God, a house not made with hands, eternal in the heavens" (2 Corinthians 5:1). He was speaking of our temporal body in which we live. Neither the body in which our eternal soul lives nor the house in which we live physically is to be so crucial to us that we forget our true address in heaven.

Moses' psalm seems to be saying, "Fear God and get right with Him, for this life is all you have to live in His dwelling place." But the whole truth is, "Dwell in God's house now, and you can be sure where you will live for eternity!"

Today's Thought: This life is but a short phase in the span of our eternal life. Where do you live?

Today, if you will hear His voice: Do not harden your hearts (Psalm 95:7,8).

How to Get Up When Your Friends Get You Down

I woke up with a heavy heart. The day before I was deeply hurt by a trusted friend. I ached inside. As I dressed for the new day, I felt angry and thought of ways to retaliate. Resentment surged. For a brief time I wanted to give the man what I felt he deserved.

By the time I got to my morning devotions, I really needed the Lord. It so happened that my morning quiet time was focused on reading a psalm a day. Psalm 95 was next up for that morning. The words "Oh come, let us worship and bow down; let us kneel before the Lord our Maker" left me cold. I didn't feel like worshiping. But years of living with the Lord had taught me that feelings follow thought, and I knew I needed my thinking changed. So I read the rest of the psalm on my knees. From the position and perspective of humility and submission, I read verse 8: "Do not harden your hearts."

My ability to hear the Lord's voice the rest of the day was in jeopardy. So I said, "Lord, speak; I'm ready to listen. I don't want to allow this hurt to harden into a settled attitude." In the quiet, the Lord captured my thinking and seemed to be saying, "Lloyd, this disappointment can make you bitter or better, and it all depends on whether you will express the forgiveness I have given to you all through the years. Now go and forgive this man and act as if he had not hurt you." I followed orders, and a new surge of the Lord's love and strength flooded my mind and heart.

You, too, may have mornings like I experienced. Every day, hour by hour, we have a choice: hardness of heart or humble openness to the Lord. We can become bitter or better people.

Today's Thought: Honesty with the Lord about how we are really feeling and willingness to be different is the first step to a new attitude and creative action.

For in that He Himself has suffered, being tempted, He is able to aid those who are tempted (Hebrews 2:18).

The Power to Make You Strong

Many people ask about how Christ aids us in times of temptation: "Does the Lord ever lead us into temptation? If not, why is that petition in the Lord's Prayer?"

The greatest temptation is to be our own gods and try to run our lives. We constantly break the First Commandment. There are other gods we are tempted to worship but they all are related to the worship of self. All other temptations flow from this. When we take charge of our own lives and try to be the director of the drama of our lives, we become vulnerable to doing and saying those things which distort our relationship with the Lord and throw our lives into confusion. The Lord does not lead us into temptation. He doesn't have to; there's enough temptation around for all of us. In the phrase in the Lord's Prayer, "Lead us not into temptation, but deliver us from evil," the word for temptation means test. "Lord, do not put us to the test; instead deliver us from the evil one," would be a way of praying it.

The Lord is with us. His presence not only gives us an example, but an encouragement. There are things we would never consider doing with the Lord there with us. If we could not do or say a thing with Him with us, it is surely wrong. Also, when we are tempted to weaken under the pressure of temptation, He actually takes charge and gives us the courage to resist. He knows what we are going through; He's faced it all. There's nothing we must endure that He has not confronted and won over during His incarnate ministry. Think of it!

Today's Thought: We can win over temptation—Christ is on our side!

November 22 Psalm 20

May He grant you according to your heart's desire, and fulfill all your purpose (Psalm 20:4).

How to Pray in Trouble

In times of trouble, good friends often say, "I'm praying for you." Sometimes we would like to respond, "Thanks, but tell me: What are you praying?" Often, people's prayers for us are very general because they don't know how to pray for others when life becomes difficult.

David gives us a magnificent prayer in Psalm 20 to guide our prayers for others and for ourselves in times of trouble.

In verses 1 and 2, David boldly asks the Lord to provide strength for the people who belong to the Lord and who have asked for His power. The "name of God" is the power and authority of His Spirit. Our greatest need in difficulty is for God Himself. The one prayer He delights to answer is for an intimate communion with Him.

David simply asks in verses 3-5 that God would give a person his heart's desire and provide him courage to press on with his purpose. Our purpose is to glorify God and enjoy Him forever. When this is our heart's desire, problems can be put into perspective. Our prayer is that God will help us find a solution within keeping of our ultimate goal. God grants us our heart's desire when our purpose is His maximum purpose for us.

We can be sure of the Lord's strength because He "saves His anointed." Our Lord has called and commissioned us to live for Him and to accomplish the particular work He has given each of us to do. When troubles arise in accomplishing the Lord's commission, we can boldly ask for His intervention.

Psalm 20 concludes with a resolve to trust the Lord—not human might or clever solutions. No scheme will work. The Lord must get us through the trouble. He has in the past, and He will now.

Today's Thought: Lord, mold my heart's desire to be in keeping with Your purpose for me. Then give me courage to trust You to give me strength when trouble comes. All I want for myself and others is that we may know You, love You, and serve You. Amen.

Make a joyful shout to the Lord, all you lands! Serve the Lord with gladness; come before His presence with singing (Psalm 100:1).

Gladness

Focus your attention on all of the aspects of God's goodness that should make us glad. They are enumerated with excitement in Psalm 100.

What would it mean to serve and live with gladness? There is much we allow to get us down. Serving God often is done with dutiful drabness. The word "serve" in the Hebrew means "performing as servants or subjects of a king." Gladness is the mark of this service. It means "jubilant joy." Note that the King James Version's word "noise" is changed correctly to "shout" in the New King James translation. Our whole life of service should be a joyous shout for the Lord. The English word "glad" means "experiencing pleasure, joy, and delight." It expresses being pleased, willing, and delighted.

We are all called to be servants of Christ. Is gladness the distinguishing characteristic of our service? Often we feel "put upon," our privacy invaded, or our schedules disrupted when we are asked to help people or lend our time and influence to a crucial cause. Church work can make us less than glad when we forget whom we are serving. In our relationships in marriage, the family, among our friends, at work, in the church, and in the community, are we glad servants of the Lord? The secret is doing it "as unto the Lord." What we do for others is an expression of thanksgiving to the Lord. The psalmist is gladdened in his joyful shout by three great aspects of God: His goodness, mercy, and truth. The more we contemplate in an inventory of thanksgiving the impact of these on our lives, the more they will be incentives for invigorated service of God—with gladness.

Today's Thought: "Do everything for the glory of God" (1 Corinthians 10:31, TLB).

For "Who has known the mind of the Lord that he may instruct Him?" But we have the mind of Christ (1 Corinthians 2:16).

A Channel, Not a Reservoir

We are dependent upon God for everything. We could not breathe a breath, think a thought, move a muscle, work a day, or develop our lives without His moment-by-moment provision. Put your finger on your pulse; thank God for your life. Breathe in, saying, "Bless the Lord, O my soul"; breathe out, saying, "And all that is within me, bless His holy name."

List what is yours from God's loving provision. Praise Him for food, your body, the people in your life, the opportunities and the challenges of today. Daily bread is more than food to eat. Through the Bread of Life, Jesus Christ, all things we have and are become an evidence of unmerited favor from a Lord who knows our needs. Make this a day for "flash prayers" in which you repeatedly say, "Thank You, Lord," for the abundant mercies in every moment of life.

To have the mind of Christ is to have His attitude and disposition. The word for "mind" in Greek also means attitude and disposition. When we reflect upon His attitude and His consistent disposition toward others, we begin to catch the vision of what He wants to manifest through us.

A new creature in Christ is one who can love, forgive, care, and empathize with His indwelling Spirit as the motivating, engendering power. The Christian life is life as He lives it through us. Our task is to be a channel, not a reservoir. Inflow and outflow of love are perfectly measured.

Today's Thought: "A thankful heart is not only the greatest virtue, but the parent of all other virtues" —Cicero.

"Every virtue divorced from thankfulness is maimed and limps along the spiritual road" —John Henry Jowett.

November 25

In everything give thanks; for this is the will of God in Christ Jesus for you (1 Thessalonians 5:18).

Nonstop Thanksgiving

Thanks and praise in everything? "Paul, you've got to be kidding!" is our natural response. We recoil at the admonition that we should praise God in all difficult and painful circumstances of our life. Ask God for strength to endure, surely, but praise Him in our complexities? In sickness and hurting relationships? In failure and frustration? Paul's word does not budge. There it stands, mocking us at first, and then intriguing us with an invitation to a totally different way of finding out what God may be saying to us in our difficulties and hard choices. We pause for a moment and stop ramming our wills against this immovable challenge; some very important things begin to dawn on us.

The first is that praise is both a response to God's greatness and goodness and the ultimate level of relinquished trust. If we can praise God for what has happened to or around us, we are acknowledging that He can use everything. Praising God is affirming for ourselves His sovereignty and providence. The word "rejoice" is found more than 20 times in Paul's epistles. In his letter to the Thessalonians, the word "always" is used four other times in addition to the admonition to "rejoice always." It means "all the time, on every occasion, in every set of circumstances."

But does this really work? From years of experience trying it, I can say an enthusiastic "Yes!" Whenever I say in prayer, "Lord, I don't understand what You are doing in this, but I praise You for it," a tenseness inside me relaxes.

Today's Thought: Thanksgiving and praise open the floodgate of the power of God.

November 26 **Psalm 136**

Oh, give thanks to the Lord, for He is good! For His mercy endures forever (Psalm 136:1).

Say Thanks!

The other day at a community gathering, I sat next to an admiral in the Coast Guard. He is stationed in Los Angeles and is responsible for the West Coast operations of the Guard. I asked him how things were going. This brought forth the story of a distressing experience he had that morning. He had gone up the coast to decorate a sailor for an act of valor. The seaman had risked his life in a storm to save a man whose boat had capsized. He had pulled the man out of the sea, given him mouth-to-mouth resuscitation, and under perilous conditions had gotten him back to port and to a hospital. When the young Coast Guardsman went to visit the survivor later in the day, the sailor was astounded by the patient's attitude. The man could not say thanks. Even though he was alive because of the sailor's courage in danger, he treated him with an alarming lack of appreciation. The sailor said, "Sir, I'm the man who pulled you out of the sea!" The man's only response was to talk about how bad the storm was—no thanks, no praise for the heroism. Was he embarrassed? Or did he feel the sailor had simply done his duty and needed no thanks?

The admiral went on to say that when he decorated the sailor with a medal of honor, he gave him an opportunity to respond. "Thank you, admiral, for the honor," he said, and then blurted out, "but the man never said thanks!" The admiral shared the sailor's amazement and was still mulling it over when we visited later that day.

I am reminded of how much we have received from the Lord and how often we neglect or resist giving thanks. This cripples our ability to receive more of what the Lord wants to give. He delights to bless a thankful person.

Today's Thought: All of life is one continuous thanksgiving.

Oh, give thanks to the Lord, for He is good! (Psalm 107:1).

Thanksgiving Eve

When the pilgrims celebrated the first Thanksgiving, the children were given plates with five kernels of corn to remind them of the difficult year they had endured. It was only after prayers of gratitude for the Lord's providence that the full meal was served.

This might not be a bad custom for the first course of our Thanksgiving meal tomorrow. What about asking each person around the table to talk about the five things for which he or she is most thankful? What would you say?

I'd begin with God Himself. Joyce Kilmer said, "Thank God for His many blessings but thank God for God!" He is the source of all. Then I'd thank Him for salvation in Christ—the second birth and the power of His indwelling Spirit. The next kernel would represent prayer and the daily strength we receive. Fourth, I'd thank God for the problems in which I've grown in His grace and have experienced timely interventions. And fifth, I'd look each person in the eye and say, "I thank God for you!" But as you can see, five kernels of corn are not enough to cover all our gratitude. Conversation about the other blessings will more than cover all the courses of the Thanksgiving dinner and all through the afternoon as well!

Today's Thought: "No duty is more urgent than returning thanks" —Ambrose of Milan.

November 28 **Psalm 95:1-7**

Let us come before His presence with thanksgiving (Psalm 95:2).

Love-Motivated Thanksgiving

Thanksgiving Day falls on the last Thursday of November. This will be a different date in various years, so I will ask you to use today's meditation on the day set for Thanksgiving in the year you are reading this book.

There are three things I suggest we consider about the quality of thanksgiving: God desires it; we require it; others never tire of it.

God desires our thanksgiving because He created us for a love relationship with Him. Thanksgiving is a way of saying, "Lord, I love You, not just for all Your blessings, but for who You are." The most daring choice God ever made was to create us with free will. He knew we could misuse the gift and choose not to love Him. And when humankind made that tragic choice, He did not give up on us. He came in Christ to love and forgive us and make us new creatures who could respond to His love and allow Him to love them to the uttermost. Thank God for His love!

We require thanksgiving. It is a profound confession of faith. Thanksgiving breaks the illusion that we can run our own lives and be sufficient by ourselves. Today we humble ourselves before God and praise Him for all we have and are.

Other people never tire of our expression of thanks. Just as thanksgiving is the secret of a true relationship with God, so too expressing gratitude to the people of our lives communicates how much they mean to us. And best of all is the expression, "Thanks for being you!"

Today is a special day to love the Lord, to renew our commitment to Him, and to allow our gratitude to spill over in deep appreciation for the people of our lives.

Today's Thought: Thanksgiving is the overflowing of a heart filled with love.

I will bless the Lord at all times; His praise shall continually be in my mouth. My soul shall make its boast in the Lord (Psalm 34:1,2).

The Gratitude Attitude

I can remember it as if it were yesterday. Years ago, I sat spellbound, listening to the profound teaching of the great scholar, the late John Baillie, in a classroom at New College, University of Edinburgh. Dr. Baillie was talking about the attitude of gratitude as the motivation of Christian service.

What he said was seared into my memory: "Gratitude is not only the dominant note in Christian piety, but equally the dominant motive of Christian action in the world. Such gratitude is for the grace that has been shown us by God. A true Christian is a person who never for a moment forgets what God has done for him in Christ, and whose whole comportment and whole activity have their root in the sentiment of gratitude."

The words warmed my heart. I knew then that I must spend my life sharing gratefully what God had done for me. Whenever I get tired or momentarily discouraged by the slowness of progress in working with people, I reread those words. They have become a mandate to give myself away. Returning thanks to God is sharing with others.

Today's Thought: "O Lord, that lends me life, lend me a heart replete with thankfulness" —Duke of Suffolk in Shakespeare's *King Henry the Sixth*, Part II, Act I, Scene i.

November 30 Luke 17:11-19

Were there not ten cleansed? But where are the nine? (Luke 17:17).

Where Are the Nine?

As you read today's Scripture, watch Jesus carefully. Note His reactions thoughtfully. In Christ we behold the face of God. Listen to God—hear and sense His responses to us.

Jesus is on His way to Jerusalem. As He passed through Samaria, He was met by a band of ten miserable people: Samaritans, half-breeds—abhorred by the Jews and untouchable because of their leprosy.

But these lepers knew something about Jesus. He had broken down the boundaries of prejudice between Samaritans and Jews. *And* He had touched untouchable lepers and healed them. They had to bring their suffering to Jesus! "Jesus, Master, have mercy on us!" They were amazed by His response: "Go show yourselves to the priests." Hope! Only the priests could pronounce a leper well and give him a certificate of cleanness. Did Jesus mean that they were going to be healed? They had to trust Him as they started off to the priest. On the road they were healed.

Only one returned to Jesus to express gratitude. "Where are the other nine?" We feel the pathos of the heart of God over human ingratitude. Perhaps the nine thought they deserved their healing. Others may have thought they had earned it through the years of suffering.

We watch Jesus as He eyes the one leper who returned to thank Him. This was the response He wanted from everyone. He met ingratitude everywhere, with pride at the core.

The old hymn "Count Your Many Blessings" reminds us to count our many blessings and name them one by one. This helps us to never take God for granted. Begin today with a time of actually listing your blessings, and then thank the Lord for them—one by one.

Today's Thought: "To be thankful for what I have received and for what the Lord has prepared is the surest way to receive more" —Andrew Murray.

For this [is the] commandment which I command you today . . . choose life (Deuteronomy 30:11,19).

One Day at a Time

A great life is the accumulation of grace-filled days. We can't do much with our yesterdays, and worry over our tomorrows is futile. Today is what's crucial.

Throughout this book we have tried to live in day-tight compartments—to be faithful and obedient to our Lord in each new day He gives us. Anything's possible if we take it in day-sized bites. The recovering alcoholic makes a daily commitment to be sober for the day ahead of him or her—one day at a time! The same is true for all of us. The new person we want to be, the things we want to start doing, and others we want to stop can be accomplished today by God's grace. More than 100 years ago, Bishop Samuel Wilberforce gave us a prayer poem for living one day at a time:

Lord for tomorrow and its needs I do not pray
Keep me, my God, from stain of sin just for today.
Let me both diligently work and duly pray,
Let me be kind in word and deed just for today.
Let me be slow to do my will, prompt me to obey,
Help me to mortify my flesh just for today
Let me no wrong or idle word unthinking say;
Set Thou a seal upon my lips just for today.

So for tomorrow and its needs I do not pray
But keep me, guide me, love me, Lord, just for today.

Today's Thought: "Yesterday is already a dream and tomorrow is only a vision. But today, well-lived makes every yesterday a dream of happiness and every tomorrow a vision of hope."

—Author Unknown

December 2 **Titus 3:3-11**

Those who have believed in God should be careful to maintain good works (Titus 3:8).

Have You Done Good?

One day in London in 1885, a most unusual funeral cortege moved up Parliament Street to Westminster Abbey. All of London was amazed. Crowds lined the streets in the rain and watched the procession. Behind the casket, family, and dignitaries, hundreds of people walked carrying banners on which were emblazoned the words of Christ, "I was hungry and you gave Me food; I was thirsty and you gave Me drink; I was a stranger and you took Me in; I was naked and you clothed Me; I was sick and you visited Me; I was in prison and you came to Me." The banners were carried by people who had received love and care through the missions, schools for deprived children, homes for the homeless, asylums, and charities started and supported by the gifts of the man in whose honor and memory the service at Westminster Abbey was to be held.

The man's name was Lord Anthony Shaftesbury, statesman and champion of the poor and disadvantaged. His life's verse from which he gained the goal and generosity of his life was, "Assuredly, I say to you, inasmuch as you did it to one of the least of these My brethren, you did it to Me" (Matthew 25:40).

An entry in the crusader and philanthropist's journal on October 11, 1857, explains his commitment: "Read this afternoon Matthew 25. What a revelation of the future judgment on the human race . . . not for open blasphemy, not for sins committed, but for duties they have omitted. Men say, 'I have done no harm'; I am not worse than my neighbors; and so on. But the Lord takes another view. 'Have you done good?' He asks."

Gladstone wrote the inscription for Shaftesbury's gravestone: "He devoted the influence of his station, the strong sympathies of his heart, and the great powers of his mind to honoring God and serving his fellow men."

Today's Thought: Any Christian who is not involved in some ministry to people's needs has missed his or her calling. Have you done good?

As an eagle stirs up its nest, hovers over its young, spreading out its wings, taking them up, carrying them on its wings, so the Lord alone led him (Deuteronomy 32:11,12).

Out of the Comfortable Nest

Moses had never forgotten the metaphor of the eagle that the Lord had given him at Mount Sinai. "You have seen what I did to the Egyptians, and how I bore you on eagles' wings and brought you to Myself" (Exodus 19:4). Subsequently, during the wilderness wanderings, we suspect that every time Moses watched soaring eagles or observed how they cared for their eaglets, he thought of the Lord and how He was training His people.

In his final message to the people, Moses draws on his observations of the training of the eaglets to fly to remind the Israelites of the Lord's methods with them.

After an eaglet is born, it is totally dependent on the parent eagle for food. Like the eagle, the Lord had cared for His people. But eaglets will stay in the nest unless the eagle stirs up the nest and forces them to fly. If in their first efforts to fly they are in need of rescue, the eagle catches the eaglets on its wings.

The thrust of the metaphor is that the Lord stirs up our safe nests and pushes us out of our comfortable conformities. The Lord is constantly disturbing us, pressing us on to new challenges He has prepared for us.

This gives us a different perspective on change. Whenever new opportunities are given us, or problems and difficulties make new demands on us, or people around us trouble us, or even when our carefully constructed little world falls apart, we can be confident of this: The Lord will use the disturbance to help us on to a new stage of growth and new discoveries of His delivering power.

Today's Thought: "What is life for? To teach us to fly, to teach us to exercise our half-fledged wings in short flight that may prepare us for and make possible for us to take longer flights until we are able to graduate to being mature eagles" —G. Campbell Morgan.

December 4 Hebrews 7:25-28

Therefore He is also able to save to the uttermost those who come to God through Him (Hebrews 7:25).

An Up-to-Date Question

One Sunday a new member of our church brought her parents to the morning service. They sat in the sanctuary waiting for the service to begin. An usher looking for places to seat people noticed there was still room in their pew for two more people.

"Are those saved?" the usher asked, referring to the two seats.

"They sure are! They've been saved for years!" the young woman responded.

When the usher realized she misunderstood his question, they all had a good laugh. They were still laughing when they told me after the service what happened. Then the parents told me about their love for Christ and their assurance of salvation through Him. Their smiling parting shot was, "Good to be in a church where they don't take your salvation for granted!"

That same Sunday several people responded to the invitation at the end of the service to accept Christ as Lord and Savior. One man who had been attending for months received the gift of faith and made an unreserved commitment of his life to Christ. He, too, had come early to save himself a seat, and instead his life was saved.

It may sound a bit old-fashioned to speak of a person being "saved." Street-corner evangelists with their piercing question "Are you saved?" may jar some people. Perhaps we have lost something by our lofty, sophisticated presentations of the gospel. Paul didn't equivocate: "Christ came into the world to save sinners, of whom I am the chief" (1 Timothy 1:15).

During Advent, don't miss why Christ came: He saves us from separation from the Father, He forgives us our failures, He liberates us from self-centeredness, He makes us new people, He fills us with His Spirit, He gives us abundant and eternal life. This is the reason for our exuberant joy!

Today's Thought: The source of our Christmas joy is that out of sheer love Christ saved us. Rejoice! Think of what Christ has saved you from and saved you for!

Grace and peace be multiplied to you in the knowledge of God and of Jesus our Lord (2 Peter 1:2).

You're Not on Your Own

Some time ago, I was startled by an advertisement in *Fortune* magazine. It featured an infant in diapers looking you straight in the eye with childlike directness. The line above the picture was an attention-getter: "We're all created equal. After that, baby, you're on your own."

The ad expresses an attitude we have about the Christian life. After becoming Christians, we think we are on our own. It's all up to us to try to please the Lord, live good lives, and be strong. The result is either self-righteousness or defeatedness. Here's a prayer to claim Christ's power today:

"I praise You, Lord. You are the same yesterday, today, and forever! Your love is constant and never changes. You have promised to never leave or forsake me. My confidence is in You and not myself. I waver, fall, and need Your help. I come to You not trusting in my goodness, but solely in Your grace. You are my joy when I get down, my strength when I am weak, my courage when I vacillate. You are my security in a world of change and turmoil.

"Thank You for reminding me that I'm not left to live on my own. Even when I forget You in the rush of life, You never forget me. When I feel distant from You, it was I who moved not You. O Love that will not let me go, I claim your silent strength.

"Filled with wonder, love, and gratitude, I commit this day to live for You and by Your indwelling power. Control my mind and give me Your wisdom, fill me with Your sensitivity to people and their needs, help me be a servant to the troubled and lonely people around me, and give me boldness to take a stand for Your mandates of righteousness and justice.

"Thank You for the privilege of living this day to the fullest! In Your all-powerful name, Amen."

Today's Thought: After this prayer, I'm not on my own!

December 6 — 1 John 2:1-6

He who says he abides in Him ought himself also to walk just as He walked (1 John 2:6).

Christ Makes Up the Deficit

We talk a lot about the bottom line. This accounting term for tabulating the results of expenses, income, and profit has found its way into our everyday expressions. We say, "Well, the bottom line of the whole matter is..."

There's another kind of bottom line. It is calculated at the end of each day. Unlike our personal and business daily ledger, it should always show a surplus! Income of spiritual strength consistently puts us in the black. The line item of Christ's Spirit more than balances our relational books. The cross is the plus sign. Christ's love is our reserve account.

Think of it this way. We begin a day with our spiritual accounts showing a surplus. During the day we spend ourselves for others—solving problems, facing soul-sized issues, and dealing with the pressures of life. At the end of the day we rest and pray. We check our spiritual bottom line. We expect it to show a deficit; instead, there's still a surplus. The reason is that Christ has replenished our spiritual account.

We simply cannot outgive Christ. When we walk as He walked—loving, forgiving, serving—we can be sure of His power. Just when we think we've reached red on the bottom line, He makes a fresh deposit. With the Lord we have an automatic transfer account that's tied into the limitless supplies of His Spirit.

Recently, when I figured my personal monthly finances, I completely forgot to add the automatic deposit of salary. I scrimped and scraped to make ends meet. I sighed with a great relief when I discovered my foolish mistake. Sometimes I make the same mistake in my spiritual accounts by thinking I've come to the point of red at the bottom line. In our ministry to others, Christ makes up the deficit with His silent strength.

Today's Thought: "Give, and it will be given to you: good measure, pressed down, shaken together, and running over" (Luke 6:38).

If you love only those who love you, what good is that? Even scoundrels do that much (Matthew 5:46, TLB).

Isn't That What Friends Are For?

A friend had done me a great favor. I called him to express my gratitude. "Isn't that what friends are for?" he asked. We talked about how drab and difficult life would be without friends to step in to help with impossible situations, open doors for us, and use their influence for our advantage.

The danger is that we may begin to think of friends for what they have done or can do for us. If the only time we call on them is when we need something, the friendship disintegrates into a quid pro quo of bartered assistance. "I'll help you if you help me" is the unspoken message. I overheard an executive's comment when he was told that a "friend" had called. "Wonder what he wants now?" was his guarded response.

Another man responds in a very different way. When he answers the phone, he says his name and immediately asks, "What can I do for you?" And he means it. I know because I've been on the receiving end of his generosity and caring for years.

Do we care about our friends—not for what we can get, but for what we can give? What if there were absolutely nothing a friend could accomplish for us? Would we still cherish the relationship? "Friendship for friendship's sake" has become a good corrective for me. It spurs me on to spend time and energy to encourage friends when there is nothing I need. Then opportunities of mutual need are a delight and not a drag.

Today's Thought: "We make a living by what we get, but we make a life by what we give" —Winston S. Churchill.

December 8 Luke 1:34-38

Let it be to me according to your word (Luke 1:38).

The Fullness of Christ

Many years ago I set out on a pilgrimage to discover the fullness of Christ. I pondered Paul's words to the Colossians about "Christ in you, the hope of glory" (Colossians 1:27). I vaguely understood these words, but they were not real to me. Christ in me? The fullness of Christ in my mind, emotions, will, and body? Although I had often preached about this, the power of the words had not gripped me personally.

Then one day on my pilgrimage I stumbled onto Paul's yearning desire for the Galatians: "My little children, for whom I labor in birth again until Christ is formed in you" (Galatians 4:19). These words became the key. The whole process of realizing the fullness of Christ is like conception, natal formation, birth, growth, and maturity.

Just as Christ was conceived in the Virgin Mary, so too the first step in receiving fullness is for Christ to be conceived and born in us. This means yielding our total self to be the residence of His Spirit. All we can do is say with Mary, "Let it happen, Lord. Be born in me!"

Each Christmas we sing Philip Brook's carol "O Little Town of Bethlehem," often in thoughtless sentimentality. "O holy Child of Bethlehem, descend to us we pray; cast out our sin and enter in, be born in us today." I've often wondered if we realize what a radical prayer this is. We can pray, "O Christ, in all Your fullness, descend to us we pray, cast out our sin and enter in, be born in us today."

Thus begins a dynamic process which goes on throughout our lives. This process prompts me to pray a prayer every morning and often throughout the day: "Christ, be formed in me!"

Is this too much for us to ask or expect? Not if we take seriously Christ's promise to abide in us. He can be born in us, formed in us, and grow in us as we live each hour.

Today's Thought: "Oh, come to us, abide with us, our Lord Emmanuel!" (taken from "O Little Town of Bethlehem").

The stature of the fullness of Christ (Ephesians 4:13).

The Essence of Christmas

Once we yield our inner lives to the formation of Christ in us, we can face the struggles of our lives. In particular, we are relieved of three troublesome struggles. The first is our struggle with our human nature. It is a long, weary, grim battle to try to change ourselves. Resolutions, improvement programs, and efforts at self-discipline yield little change in our basic nature. But when we honestly confess our defeat in trying to get better and ask for the fullness of Christ, He enters in and performs a continuing miracle of making us like Himself.

Second, we are freed from the struggle to be adequate. I know I am insufficient for the demands of life, but I also know that Christ is all-sufficient. I cannot imagine any problem that He cannot solve, any person He could not love, and any challenge He would not be able to tackle. And so, from within me, Christ is at work giving me what I could never produce without Him.

Third, we don't have to struggle with worries over what the future holds. What the Lord allows to happen will be used for the greater growth of His fullness in us. We can relax. Whatever we face will be an occasion for new dimensions of His character to be formed in us.

Think for a moment: What could happen if we made the fullness of Christ our quest! So much of our limited vision, lack of love and forgiveness, and unwillingness to serve others and the world would be transformed.

Paul challenged the Christians in Ephesus to press on to the "unity of the faith and the knowledge of the Son of God, to a perfect man, to the measure of the stature of the fullness of Christ" (Ephesians 4:13). That commitment is the essence of Christmas.

Today's Thought: "Born that man no more may die; born to raise the sons of earth; born to give them second birth."

—Charles Wesley

December 10 Luke 4:18,19

He has sent me to heal the brokenhearted (Luke 4:18).

Give Him Your Struggles

Under all our outer layers is who we really are—sometimes lonely, often troubled, constantly battling for security and peace. Christ wants to penetrate those layers to find us right now. He wants to know us as we are and have us love Him as He is: present, powerful, the Lord who makes things happen. He can move us beyond the cycle of strain, stress, and struggle.

When we make up our Christmas list of people to whom we want to give gifts, don't forget the One who made it all possible. Put the Lord on the top of your list! And what is an acceptable gift for the Lord who cared enough to come? Nothing but ourselves! We wonder what that means. Perhaps it's *nothing less* than giving Him our struggles and then accepting His gift of a rebirth of hope.

Identify the struggle that is your deepest need. Imagine how Christ would have dealt with people who struggled in His earthly ministry. The words "He had compassion" are repeated 14 times in the gospels. What would He have said if you were that person? What would you tell Him about your need, and what would you ask Him to do? Now affirm the fact that He knows and cares. Tell Him all about your struggle. Next, expectantly anticipate that He will make the struggle a stepping-stone. Instead of asking, "How can I get out of this?" ask, "What can I get out of this?" Lastly, praise Him that He has resources, people, and unanticipated potential to unleash to help you which you could never have imagined possible. That's the excitement of knowing Immanuel, "God with us." When we least expect it, Christ breaks through with blessing—perfectly timed, magnificently meeting our needs.

Suddenly, we are filled with vibrant hope. Christmas is alive with hopefulness, and it will last all through the year.

Today's Thought: Whatever my need, Christ is able!

The life was manifested, and we have seen, and bear witness, and declare to you that eternal life which was with the Father and was manifested to us (1 John 1:2).

Alive in the Alive

E. Stanley Jones in *A Song of Ascents* wrote, "I'm afraid of nothing. What can death do to me? I've already died. You cannot defeat defeat. You cannot break brokenness. I've come back from my own funeral. I'm alive in the Alive."

Those who knew Dr. Jones can attest to the authenticity of his statement. I vividly remember the last time I saw him. I took the missionary preacher to catch a flight after a retreat where he spoke. Just before he entered the plane, he turned and gave me his customary gesture—his right hand with three fingers pointed up for the three words of the motto of his life: "Jesus is Lord!"

Jones really believed that his surrender of his life to Christ was the funeral to self-centeredness. The throne of the kingdom of self was yielded to Christ. Pride was defeated and willfulness broken. He was alive in the Alive—Christ, the Life. Throughout his life, he lived with the assurance and conviction the apostle John wrote in the passage we read today.

The apostle had witnessed the Christ, the Word of Life, in the flesh as His disciple. And yet, he knew Christ more intimately three hours after Pentecost than he had known Him during three years of His incarnate ministry. It was only after Christ took up residence in the apostle that he was converted and made a new man. This is the reason he could boldly invite others to know Christ with the same intensity that he knew Him.

As John Henry Jowett put it, "Our self-importance shrinks, and we grow in grace and in the knowledge of the Lord. It is when we are full of self, self-opinionated, self-centered, self-seeking, that Christ is crowded out."

Christ who came comes to take His place on the throne of the kingdom of our selves and reign so we can be alive in the Alive.

Today's Thought: Christ came so that we might be included in the fellowship He has had with the Father from the beginning.

December 12 Isaiah 9:6,7

And His name will be called Wonderful (Isaiah 9:6).

Oh, the Wonder of It All!

By far the greatest problem of our contemporary celebration of Christmas is the lost sense of wonder. Faithless familiarity with the Christmas story, the rote repetition of the carols, and the pressures of the holiday season keep many from breathless wonder over Christ's birth.

Recently while reading John's gospel, I came to five words that riveted my attention and filled me with wonder: "If I had not come" (John 15:22). What if Christ had not come? I made a list of all that we have received because He came, revealed the kingdom of God, died for our sins, rose victorious over death, and returned as indwelling Lord. The wonder of our wonderful Savior!

My mother was not an educated woman. She knew hardship and difficulty. The joy of her life was Jesus. She did not have the gift of words to express the depth of her love. Often when she was overcome with a realization of His power, majesty, and grace, she would exclaim, "Oh, the wonder of it all!" At Christmastime she could not contain her amazement, and repeatedly expressed her humble praise with these words.

The accounts of the birth of Christ are filled with wonder: Mary's awe in being chosen to be the mother of the Savior, the shepherd's wonder at beholding Him in a manger, the three kings bearing gifts. Wonder surrounded the Savior's ministry. He did wonders and signs of the power of God incarnate. And wonder and praise distinguished the church He founded.

Humility precedes wonder, and adoration follows close after. That's what we should mean when we say, "Have a wonderful Christmas!"

Today's Thought: Today I will let myself go in a full experience of the wonder of Christ's birth and all that He means to me.

If in this life only we have hope in Christ, we are of all men the most pitiable (1 Corinthians 15:19).

What If?

Yesterday we were startled into new wonder over all that Christ means to us by His words, "If I had not come." Today we focus on some other "ifs" that deepen our praise for what Christ has done for us.

Paul challenges the Corinthians to think about what life would be like if Christ had not been raised from the dead. Reading this passage heightens our Christmas joy with Good Friday gratitude for Christ's forgiveness of our sins and lasting Easter hope in our victorious Lord.

If Christ has not been raised, we are still in our sins! Only a vindicated, risen Lord has the authority to forgive us. Recapture those times of confession when you asked for forgiveness and thought you were set free. Reflect on all that you have thought was washed away. Consider what it would be like to live again with all those incriminating mistakes and failures. Take them all back if Christ who was born did not die for your sins and was not raised up!

Also, if Christ has not risen, death has not been vanquished. Think of what it would be like to face the physical death of loved ones if we did not have the assurance of their eternal life. Linger for a moment with the thought of what our own lives would be like if the grave spelled the ending. But thanks to our risen Lord, we are forgiven, fear of death is behind us, and we can celebrate His birth with unreserved praise!

The final "if" the apostle uses to jar our thinking is that if Christ is no more than one more teacher who gave us platitudes for this life, "we are of all men the most pitiable." Who needs another dead leader to remember? We need a living Savior to know, love, and serve. And so Christmas is a celebration of all that is ours because Christ lived, died, rose, and lives today as our victorious, all-powerful Lord.

Today's Thought: For us every day is Christmas, Good Friday, Easter, and Pentecost. Let's celebrate!

December 14 Luke 1:26-38

Behold what manner of love the Father has bestowed on us, that we should be called children of God! (1 John 3:1).

Eleven Days for the Transfer of Power

Some time ago, I was leafing through old copies of *Life* magazine and came across a picture of Lord Mountbatten, then viceroy of India. The photograph in the August 18, 1947, edition pictured the leader in front of a large wall calendar. The words on the tear-off calendar were clearly distinguishable in the photograph: "4 August 1947, 11 days left to prepare for the transfer of power." Mountbatten and his aides were directing Great Britain's withdrawal from India. He had ordered calendars to be displayed in the office of every British official in India. They provided stark reminders of the urgency of action needed to complete their tasks and transfer power at the appointed time.

Today our calendars should read: "11 Days till Christmas and the Transfer of Power!" instead of "Only 11 Shopping Days till Christmas!" We have 11 days to prepare for the transfer of power. King Jesus is coming. Christmas is our time to welcome Him as Sovereign and Lord of our lives. He comes as Prince of Peace to our turbulent hearts and troubled world. "Peace I leave with you, My peace I give to you; not as the world gives do I give to you." And His peace is ours only when we transfer our power over ourselves and our destiny to His power to reign in us and through us.

Christ is the only one who can give us the power we need: power to forgive the past, power to meet the needs of the present, power to love people with something more than an armed truce. He alone can give us power to forgive. Only Christ can satisfy our lust for dominance and control over others. And added to that, He provides for our needs with sublime sufficiency. He denies any wants that will hurt us and supplies our needs to help us. He gives us insight when we are confused, direction when we are undecided, assurance when we are worried. Make this Christmastime a real transfer of power.

Today's Thought: Christ is King. There's no real celebration of Christmas unless He reigns in us.

That fiftieth year shall be a Jubilee to you (Leviticus 25:11).

Sound the Ram's Horn

During the Christmas season, if you heard the blast of a ram's horn in a church, you'd not only be surprised, you'd wonder what that has to do with the preparation for Christmas. I think it would be both appropriate and profoundly significant. In Hebrew the word for a ram's horn is *jobel*, the word from which "jubilee" is derived. In ancient Israel the Jubilee year came every fiftieth year. Debts, hurts, and grievances were canceled. Prisoners were released and property was returned to those who had lost it through poverty or misfortune.

Christmastime should be a Jubilee celebration each year. Sound the ram's horn! It's time to forgive and be forgiven. Now is the season to make restitution for things we have done to people and to cancel our grudges. Get rid of the pout on your face that makes people feel they are suspended between heaven's joys and hell's fury. Set the captives free!

The birth of Christ was a declaration from God that all of life was now to be a Jubilee time of reconciliation. Christ came to die on the cross for our sins. The debt of our sin has been canceled. The sure sign that we have accepted Christ's Jubilee grace is that we declare a season of Jubilee caring, forgiveness, and liberation. Sound the ram's horn!

Today's Thought: "Add one more beatitude: 'Blessed are those who give us back our self-respect' " —Mark Rutherford.

December 16 Isaiah 40:1-5

Prepare the way of the Lord (Isaiah 40:3).

Bah Humbug!

A few years ago a friend gave me a very special Christmas tie. It has some words woven into the silk that express my desire to celebrate an authentic Christmas. I'm reminded by those words that I'm constantly in danger of missing the true meaning of Christmas in the busy season. You may be surprised when I tell you that the words are "Bah Humbug!"

Now, I'm no Scrooge. He used those words to deprecate the joyous celebration of Christmas. I'm just the opposite. I'm happily addicted to Christmas. I love every part of the celebration of Christ's birth: the worship services, the majestic and tender music, the children's excitement, the recovery of the child in us, the giving and receiving of gifts in affirmation of the gift of Christ.

So why the "bah humbug" tie? The word "humbug" means "anything calculated to deceive, the spirit or practice of deception, a sham." The tie opens lots of conversations about the deception we play on ourselves and others when we miss Christ in the celebration of Christmas.

So now, before the season gets too far along, stop and think about what would make this one of the best Christmases of your life. Take time alone each day for meditation and prayer about what Christ means to you. Take time to express deep love to family and friends. Include the poor and hungry on your Christmas list. And, filled with Christ's love, ask Him to give you at least one person each day with whom to share what He means to you. Anything less than this may very well be humbug!

Today's Thought: Each of us has the responsibility to prepare the way for the coming of the Lord to our hearts, and to family, people who don't know Him, and those for whom Christmas is humbug.

December 17

You received me as an angel of God (Galatians 4:14).

You're an Angel

A fifth-grader complained to her parents about having to be in a Christmas pageant. "I don't like being an angel. I've never seen one, and I don't know how to act."

At Christmastime we hear a lot about angels. They play a prominent part in the nativity accounts, they appear on our Christmas cards, and we sing about them in our carols. Then for the rest of the year there's little or no reference to angels. And yet, every day we need angels and need to claim our calling to be angels.

The word "angel" means "messenger." God has a limitless host of heavenly messengers who watch out for us, help us, and inspire us. The New Testament is filled with references to angels. They announced Jesus' birth, ministered to Him after the temptation, were referred to in His message, and were present at the tomb on Easter morning. Angels mediated strength and hope to the apostles and played an active part in the growth of the early church. And they are active in our lives today. Billy Graham wrote an excellent book on the work of spiritual angels in combating the forces of evil and giving us strength.

The word "angel" was also used for the leaders of the early church. Paul spoke of himself as an angel, a messenger of God (Galatians 4:14). The letters to the churches of Asia Minor in Revelation greet the angel of each church.

You and I are meant to be angels. We are to be messengers of the Good News, hope, and encouragement. During the holidays is a good time to begin our ministry as angels. Unlike the little girl who didn't know how to act like an angel, we know how much people need love, affirmation, and practical help. So the title of today's devotional is not a sentimental endearment; it's a challenge. You're an angel, and there will be lots of opportunity to serve today.

Today's Thought: Expect your angel and expect to be one!

December 18 Hebrews 13:15,16

But do not forget to do good and to share (Hebrews 13:16).

A Christmas Hug

One Christmas Eve, after all the worship services were completed and the happy crowds leaving the sanctuary were greeted, one lovely elderly lady remained.

"Would you give me a Christmas hug?" she asked winsomely. "Before I go home to my apartment, I need a family kind of hug."

This woman lives alone. Her family could not visit her that Christmas, and she could not afford to go visit them. She had been to several Christmas parties during the holidays, but she missed the closeness of loved ones. Leafing through the *Los Angeles Times* on Christmas Eve afternoon, she saw the announcement of my church's services. During the service she attended, she had felt the warmth of the fellowship, but her heart ached for her family. Acting as a surrogate son, I gave her a Christmas hug. Subsequently she began to worship regularly, and in the last year of her life became a Christian.

Think of people you know who need a special expression of love from you this week. Make a list of the lonely people who need the love of Christ. Think of what would mean the most to them during Christmas week. What could you do to communicate that Christ loves them and you love them? What gift could you bring them? Chances are, the time you spend with them will be the most memorable gift.

Christ came to a lonely world on the first Christmas, and He continues to come to comfort the lonely. Now He visits them through you and me—Christmas people in whom He lives. The glow of Christmas love is to be given away. Do something for at least three lonely people. Do it for them, do it because of Christ, and do it for yourself—you'll be blessed as you share the blessing of Christ.

Today's Thought: If there's no time to care for the lonely this week, we're too busy!

Now may the Lord of peace Himself give you peace always in every way (2 Thessalonians 3:16).

Enter into Peace

A conversation between two Highland Scotsmen suddenly became serious as they talked about peace.

Robin said, "Weel Jamie, how lang since is it that ye made yer peace wi God?"

"Jamie," Robin continued, "ye kin what I mean, how lang since ye sought and found God?"

Jamie smiled, "Oh Robin, Robin, I niver saught and found God. He saught and found me. And I niver made peace with Him, I entered into the peace He gave me two thousand years ago!"

Christmas is the time we enter into the peace of Christ. Our verse for today gives us the secret. Christ is the Lord of peace. Peace is knowing we have been forgiven, that we are alive forever, and that we will receive abundant strength for every challenge. Peace is the ambience of heaven that becomes the attitude of our hearts.

Peace is like a time-release capsule. Christ Himself dwells in us and releases His peace for every moment. He is the source of lasting peace. Can you say what Jamie said?

Today's Thought: "A great many people are trying to make peace, but that has already been done. God has not left it for us to do; all we have to do is enter into it" —Dwight L. Moody.

December 20 Matthew 2:1-12

When they saw the star, they rejoiced with exceedingly great joy (Matthew 2:10).

Bursting with Joy

A friend called me on Christmas morning. He said, "Lloyd, I'm bursting with joy. It happened to me about three this morning. The family had gone to bed. All the presents were wrapped and under the tree. I sat there all alone. Then it hit me. Christmas hadn't happened to me. I'd become too busy. And there had been some problems and pressures that made me feel that I had no right to joy this year. But there in the quiet, I reread the story of the adoration of the wise men. The words 'they rejoiced with exceedingly great joy' leapt off the page. 'Did I have that kind of joy?' I asked myself. I prayed for the gift of joy in spite of my troubles. And there in the quiet, I thought about the wonder of Christ and His love, forgiveness, and power. Suddenly I felt a surge of sheer joy. It was more than just a happy feeling. It came from outside me. And it's lasted. I just had to tell you. I'm bursting—literally exploding with joy!"

Joy pulsates from the accounts of Christ's birth. The wise men "rejoiced exceedingly with great joy." Phillips translates it, "They were filled with indescribable joy." The New English Bible says, "They were overjoyed." Matthew had to find superlatives to explain the expression of overflowing joy.

The message of Christmas is love, but the sure evidence that we have received a fresh touch of love is that we feel the uncontainable flow of joy.

Today's Thought: I will not miss the joy this Christmas. Joy is the outward expression of grace.

Glory to God in the highest, and on earth peace, good will toward men! (Luke 2:14).

God's Good Pleasure

The words of the angelic chorus really should be translated "Glory to God in the highest, and on earth peace among men with whom He is pleased." Let that soak into the love-parched place in your heart. In spite of all that we have done or been, God is pleased with us. We are His beloved; we belong to Him; nothing we can do or say will make Him stop loving us.

This is your special moment. God has something to say. Listen! Put the personal pronoun in the familiar words, "God so loved me that He gave His only begotten Son, that believing in Him, I should not perish but have everlasting life. For God did not send His Son into the world to condemn me, but that I through Him might be saved." Our hearts leap. God is for us and not against us. His love is unconditional. The deepest, most exciting discovery I've ever made is that life really begins when we let God love us!

But we are not only loved just as we are; we're also forgiven for all that we've done, said, and been. We know more than those shepherds knew. We can see the shadow of a cross over the creche. We know why He came and what it cost Him. The Babe in the manger is also the crucified Lord. "You shall call His name Jesus, for He will save His people from their sins" (Matthew 1:21).

He comes to us when we won't go to Him. Christ came into the world when we least deserved or wanted Him. There's nothing we can do to earn His forgiveness or make Him stop loving us. From the creche to the cross, from an open tomb to His impelling presence with each of us, we hear His imploring love: "You belong to Me. You are loved and forgiven. I came for you, lived for you, died for you, defeated death for you and am here now for you."

That's God's Christmas gift to us. Don't leave it unwrapped! Open it and enjoy the healing, liberating, motivating power.

Today's Thought: "If God is for us, who can be against us?" (Romans 8:31).

December 22 Exodus 28:1-30

So Aaron shall bear the names of the sons of Israel on the breastplate of judgment over his heart, when he goes into the holy place (Exodus 28:29).

Upon His Shoulders

At Christmastime often the repetition of words said and sung rob us of the experience of the deeper meaning of Christmas. From Thanksgiving on, carols are played on the music systems of department stores to put shoppers in the mood of the season. Handel's "Messiah" is presented in churches and concert halls repeatedly. A kind of faithless familiarity sets in and we may miss the radical—that is, "to the roots"—quality of Christmas.

For example, take the words, "And the government shall be upon His shoulders." A true celebration of Christmas is to place the government of our lives upon Christ's shoulders. The background of these words is fascinating. The ephod, or ornamental vest, worn by Aaron and the priests in the tabernacle in Exodus had six onyx stones on each shoulder. The name of one of the 12 tribes of Israel was engraved on each stone so all the tribes were represented. Aaron carried the concerns of all the tribes before the Lord in the services. Now, in Isaiah's words, the Messiah will take the burden of government of all of God's people upon His shoulders.

Have you placed the lordship of your life on Christ's shoulders? Have you done it for today? He can carry us and our problems. He came to lift the burden of sin, of running our own lives, of trying to control others, and of worrying over all our problems. Sin is trying to control what is not ours to control and refusing to take responsibility for what is ours to do. Get the management of your life where it belongs—on the shoulders of the reigning Christ. His shoulders are broad and strong. Trust Him! Your name is on one of the stones.

Today's Thought: If the celebration of Christmas doesn't start with putting the government of our lives on Christ's shoulders, it has no real beginning. But if it starts there, there will be no end to the joy and peace—all through the year, life, and eternity!

Thanks be to God for His indescribable gift (2 Corinthians 9:15).

The Unopened Gift

It was only because of his mother's pleading that the young man came home for Christmas. It was the last place he wanted to be because of a long-standing conflict he'd had with his dad over a valuable piece of property. The young man wanted it then and not as a part of his father's will. The disagreement had started mildly enough, but had grown through the years. It had become a wall between the father and his son. The father ached over it. He wanted things to be right between him and his son. If his son had only asked forgiveness, he would have deeded the property over to him immediately. The son just couldn't bring himself to that point.

The Christmas festivities were strained. When it came time to open presents, the son opened all of his except one—a tie-shaped box with a tag on it, "From Dad, with all my love." The son refused to open it, thinking it was one more tie.

After the family had gone to bed, the son sat staring at the box. He was haunted by the look on his dad's face when he had refused to open it. Suddenly he felt impelled to open the present. As he unwrapped it, he realized it was not a tie as he had expected. Inside was the deed to the property! He rushed into his dad's bedroom and woke him up. Tears streamed down his face. "Dad, you made the first move! When I couldn't seem to change the way I was acting, you broke the bind! Forgive me . . . I love you!"

Today's Thought: There's a gift of love God wants to give us this Christmas. Don't leave it unopened.

December 24 Luke 2:1-7

And she brought forth her firstborn Son, and wrapped Him in swaddling cloths, and laid Him in a manger, because there was no room for them in the inn (Luke 2:7).

The Soul'd Out Vacancy

There was room in the inn. One room left. I believe the innkeeper's own private room was still available in his overcrowded caravansary. Chamaan, the innkeeper, was not sold out—he was soul'd out. Though there were weary travelers occupying every available room and nook, surely his own quarters could have been available. When Mary and Joseph arrived weary from the arduous journey, why didn't he move out for the night? It was obvious that Mary was about to give birth, and Joseph probably had told him that the contractions had begun.

And what about all the people in the caravansary? Why didn't they give up their spaces and clear a place for Mary? Surely they saw the emergency. Why did no one object when Chamaan said, "There's a cattle cave down the path, use that if you like"? They too were soul'd out—there was no room in their hearts for sympathy or compassion.

And so Luke records the condition of the world in one telling statement: "There was no room for them in the inn." The Son of God was born in a cattle cave and a feeding trough became His creche. And the world was no more hospitable all through His life and ministry. The leaders rejected Him and many of His followers turned away when the cost of discipleship became clear.

Today most people are soul'd out. Their souls are occupied by the busy concerns of life. Worry, fear, and stress fills every waking and sleeping moment. And yet, the Son of God continues to come seeking to reign in our hearts. There is a room left. It's in your heart and mine. Christmas is the time for Him to be born in us and for us to be reborn.

Today's Thought: O come to my heart, Lord Jesus, there is room in my heart for You!

But you, Bethlehem Ephrathah, though you are little among the thousands of Judah, yet out of you shall come forth to Me the One to be ruler in Israel, whose goings forth have been from of old, from everlasting. . . . For now He shall be great to the ends of the earth; and this One shall be peace (Micah 5:2,4,5).

The Secret of a Sublime Christmas

One of the clearest and most undeniable prophecies of the Messiah's birth is given us in this passage from Micah. By divine inspiration 700 years before Christ's birth, Micah recorded these awesome words that declare the Son's preexistence with the Father, where and how He would be born in His incarnation, and what He would come to give the world. This passage was quoted by the priests and scribes when Herod inquired about the place of the Messiah's birth.

These verses give us a threefold motivation for uncontainable joy at Christmas. Meditation on the preexistence of Christ fills us with awe. He existed with the Father before the world was created. Note the capitalized pronouns in today's reading from Micah. God sent Christ because He loved the world and wanted to reconcile us to Himself. Four words express the meaning of Christmas: "You are loved now!"

Christ was born in time to be the Savior of all time. The specificity of Micah's prophecy of the place reminds us of Christ's incarnate life and all He revealed about God and did for us on the cross. Take time today to reflect on all that is yours because He lived among us.

And don't miss what God said in Micah about the purpose of the coming of the Messiah. "And this One shall be peace." Christ doesn't just give peace; He is peace. He is the peace of forgiveness and reconciliation, the confidence of eternal life. That's the secret of a sublime celebration of Christmas.

Today's Thought: Christ came from the Father to reconcile us to the Father so that we might know the Father and live in peace with Him and accept that we are loved *now*.

December 26 Colossians 1:13-20

For it pleased the Father that in Him all the fullness should dwell (Colossians 1:19).

The Touch that Takes

Harry Reasoner, the esteemed commentator, had an incisive word about the meaning of Christmas:

> So it goes beyond logic. It is either all falsehood or it's the truest thing in the world. It's the story of the great innocence of God the Baby—God in the form of man—and was such a dramatic shock toward the heart that if it is not true, for the Christian nothing is true. So, if a Christian is touched only once a year, the touching is still worth it, and maybe on some given Christmas, some final quiet morning, the touch will take.

The touch that takes! It requires innocence to match God's innocence in the Christ Child. We become calloused with familiarity and lose the sense of awe and worship. Christ entered the world as a helpless child. The Word of God, through whom humankind was created, was born from Mary's virgin womb. No wonder we sing, "Joy to the world, the Lord is come." Say the meaning of the word "Immanuel" with three emphases mounting to a crescendo: *God* with us; God *with* us; God with *us*!

And don't stop at Christ's birth. Behold Him, the God-man in His ministry, on the cross suffering for your sins and mine, risen from the tomb, victorious over death, present with us as Savior and Lord. The touch that lasts is His Spirit, and it lasts because He will never let us go. We belong to Him now and for eternity. Sing your way through today thinking about that!

Today's Thought: A little girl was asked, "Did you get everything you wanted for Christmas?" To which she replied with wisdom beyond her years, "No, but then it's not my birthday!"

The one who breaks open will come up before them; they will break out (Micah 2:13).

The Breaker

Micah prophesies the release of the captives from the Babylonian exile. But a far greater deliverance is intimated. Christ is our Breaker. He enables us to break out of our jail.

Think about the many ways Christ is the Breaker. When He suffered and died for the sins of the world, the veil in the temple was broken. He broke the separation between a holy God and estranged, sinful humankind. His shed blood breaks the chains of haunting memories He's already forgiven. "Why these rusty old chains?" the Breaker asks. Charles Wesley gives us words to respond with praise: "He breaks the power of canceled sin, He sets the prisoner free; His blood can make the foulest clean, His blood avails for me."

And Christ the Breaker breaks us out of old habits and self-defeating patterns. How would you like to change in the New Year? You can! Christ also is the One who breaks the trail toward what He wants for our future. The manacles of self-limitation can be broken. We can dare to attempt what we've always wanted to do but were afraid.

Thought for New Year's Week:

God divided our life into years
To set us free from our past fears
He gives us a New Year inning
To prepare for a new beginning
He opens His forgiving heart
And offers us a fresh start
He goes before us to show the way
And gives us courage for each new day
With freedom from the past
We have a hope that will last.

December 28 **Proverbs 2:1-9**

The Lord gives wisdom; from His mouth come knowledge and understanding (Proverbs 2:6).

The Norm for Now

There are three kinds of people. It's very important to know the kind we are, since we might want to change.

First, there is the antiquarian. He believes that the past should be the norm for the present. "Give me the good old days!" he says. The "good old days" were probably not that good, even though he thinks so. The repetition of the past often limits what God wants to do now.

Second, is the maintenance person. For him the present is the norm for the future. "If it ain't broke, don't fix it," he says. But he means, "What we have is the best that can be. Don't try to improve it!"

The third group is made up of visionaries. The visionary sees the future as the norm for what should be done in the present. "Now's the time to begin with what the future holds!" he says. People like that are not disturbed by change. In fact, they become change agents.

I think God wants us to be people who are thankful for the past but are not stuck in it. He wants us to live to the fullest in each moment of the present. But He is constantly looking for people who will spend time in prayer to discover His guidance and goals for the future so that we can press on.

Today, take some time to meditate about the future. Ask God what He wants you to be and to do. I have a friend who likes to ask, "If you were king for a year, what would you do?" What he means is "If you threw caution to the winds, what would you do?" But there's a deeper question: "What does God desire; what's His maximum plan not just for what you are to do but for the quality of life God wants you to live?" Let that be the norm for today!

Today's Thought: What is God saying to me about His desires for my future—in my personal life, my relationships, my service to others? What's keeping me from starting now?

I have fought the good fight, I have finished the race, I have kept the faith (2 Timothy 4:7).

Backsliding into the Future

It's possible to backslide into the future. We do that when we back away from the cost of discipleship when the going gets tough because we don't trust Christ to bring good out of difficulties. We experience what might be called the Demas drift.

Demas was a disciple of Christ and one of Paul's companions in ministry. We know little about him except three references in Paul's letters. From these we can chart his drift from discipleship.

During Paul's first imprisonment, he wrote to Philemon and referred to Demas in verse 24, "As do Mark, Aristarchus, Demas, Luke, my fellow laborers." Demas had a great start and was listed in very good company. In Colossians 4:14, Paul's enthusiasm has dampened. Demas is mentioned, but with no special accolade. Note the difference between the reference to Luke and to Demas: "Luke the beloved physician and Demas greet you." Not even faint praise. Then note in 2 Timothy 4:10, written during the apostle's second imprisonment, the plummet of Demas' discipleship curve: "For Demas has forsaken me, having loved this present world." The Demas drift!

What happened to Demas? He had a hold on the faith, but it never got a hold of him. Demas was enamored with the present age and could not trust Christ's plans for the future. Demas defected when Paul and the cause of Christ needed him the most.

What about us? Are we growing closer to Christ or drifting? Today is the day to stop backsliding into the future!

Today's Thought: Am I closer to Christ today than I was a year ago? Is my discipleship more dynamic, or is it drifting? Does the curve on my chart go up to Christ's call or down to equivocation? What resolution does that call for in the New Year?

December 30 — 1 John 4

We love Him because He first loved us (1 John 4:19).

Take the First Step

There's a delightful New Year's Eve custom in Scotland called "first footing it." The idea is to be the first person to step across a friend's threshold to wish him a "Happy New Year" and toast his health and happiness.

Building on that tradition, I'd like to suggest a New Year's resolution that would transform our relationships. It's to commit this year to be a "first-stepper," and become an initiative lover. What a great year it would be if instead of waiting to have people express love to us, we would take the first step. And in misunderstandings, what if we were the first to say that we were sorry? Or what if in strained or broken relationships we didn't wait for the other person to ask for our forgiveness, but we became the one to take the initiative to give or seek forgiveness?

God is the original first-stepper. He stepped into history in Christ to reconcile the world. The apostle John said, "We love Him because He first loved us" (1 John 4:19). Our love for God is but a response to His gracious acceptance and forgiveness. John goes on in verse 20 to tell us one of the ways we love God is by loving others. We do that by emulating how He has loved us. Before we earned or deserved love or forgiveness. Paul said, "Therefore be followers of God as dear children. And walk in love, as Christ also has loved us and given Himself for us" (Ephesians 5:1,2). The Greek word for "follower" is *mimetes*, meaning "imitator." We are to imitate His love as we seek to express to others the quality of initiative love He's given to us.

Today's Thought: Resolved: that in the New Year I will take the first step in expressing love and forgiveness.

Behold, I make all things new (Revelation 21:5).

Three Looks

God has graciously divided our life into years so that we can draw a demarcation line with an attitude of gratitude for the past and faith for the future. New Year's Eve is a time for four looks, and for each look there is a special gift from God.

First, take a backward look on the year that is past. That reflective gaze at what has happened is a combination of thanksgiving for all God has done and confession for the failures and sins that lurk in our memories. God offers the gift of absolution.

Next, we take an inward look. Get in touch with the person who lives in your skin. Are you more the person you long to be today than you were a year ago? What can you affirm? What would you like to change? For this look, God offers the gift of resolution.

Now we are ready for a forward look. Ask God to help you clarify His goals for you. If you threw caution to the wind, what would you dare to attempt for His glory in your relationships and responsibilities? God's third gift is inspiration.

Lastly, take an upward look. Think magnificently about the majesty of God. Meditate on His grace that has brought you to the threshold of a new year and a new beginning. Commit the future to Him. Listen to His promise and feel the surge of hope. Memorize this verse from Jeremiah 29:11 and make it the basis of your New Year's prayer of dedication: "For I know the thoughts that I think toward you . . . thoughts of peace and not of evil, to give you a future and a hope." Now accept God's greatest gift: the gift of the fresh infusion of His Spirit.

Joyous New Year!

Today's Thought: I am a new creature in Christ. Old things pass away; all things become new!

SCRIPTURE INDEX

OLD TESTAMENT

TOPICAL INDEX

Other Good Harvest House Reading

CONVERSATION WITH GOD

by *Dr. Lloyd John Ogilvie*

Offers ten vital steps to prayer that will revolutionize your devotional life and explains in simple language and inspirational style the many facets of prayer to encourage an ever-deepening personal walk with God.

GOD'S BEST FOR MY LIFE

by *Dr. Lloyd John Ogilvie*

Not since Oswald Chambers' *My Utmost for His Highest* has there been such an inspirational yet easy-to-read devotional. Provides guidelines for maximizing your prayer and meditation time.

NO GREATER SAVIOR

by *Richard Lee and Ed Hindson*

A collection of 60 powerful meditations that glorify the Lord Jesus Christ and lift readers' hearts to the throne room of God. An invitation to witness our wondrous Savior up close and walk intimately with Him.

BELOVED

by *Kay Arthur*

Take an intimate daily journey through Scripture toward a life of prayer, sensitivity to God's leading, and obedience to His Word. Discover rich aspects of God's character and answers to the deepest questions of the heart.

EVERYDAY WITH JESUS

by *Greg Laurie*

Make each day an adventure of spiritual discovery and growth. These brief, powerful meditations, rooted in God's Word and sprinkled with good humor, invite you to take an intimate walk with the Savior.